DEATH
THE FINAL MYSTERY

DEATH
THE FINAL MYSTERY

LIONEL & PATRICIA FANTHORPE

A HOUNSLOW BOOK
A MEMBER OF THE DUNDURN GROUP
TORONTO · OXFORD

Publisher: Anthony Hawke
Editor: Don McLeod
Design: Jennifer Scott
Printer: Webcom

Canadian Cataloguing in Publication Data

Fanthorpe, R. Lionel
  Death: the final mystery

ISBN 0-88882-221-9

1. Death. 2. Near-death experiences. 3. Astral projection. 4. Reincarnation. I. Fanthorpe, Patricia. II. Title.

BF1275.D2F36 2000   I33.9'0I3   C00-931771-6

1   2   3   4   5   04   03   02   01   00

ONTARIO ARTS
COUNCIL

THE CANADA COUNCIL | LE CONSEIL DES ARTS   Canada   CONSEIL DES ARTS
FOR THE ARTS | DU CANADA   DE L'ONTARIO
SINCE 1957 | DEPUIS 1957

We acknowledge the support of the **Canada Council for the Arts** and the **Ontario Arts Council** for our
publishing program. We also acknowledge the financial support of the **Government of Canada** through the
Book Publishing Industry Development Program, The **Association for the Export of Canadian Books**, and
the **Government of Ontario** through the **Ontario Book Publishers Tax Credit** program.

Care has been taken to trace the ownership of copyright material used in this book. The author and the
publisher welcome any information enabling them to rectify any references or credit in subsequent editions.

                                                                            J. Kirk Howard, President

Printed and bound in Canada.⊛
Printed on recycled paper.

www.dundurn.com

Dundurn Press	Dundurn Press	Dundurn Press
8 Market Street	73 Lime Walk	2250 Military Road
Suite 200	Headington, Oxford,	Tonawanda NY
Toronto, Ontario, Canada	England	U.S.A. 14150
M5E 1M6	OX3 7AD	

This book is dedicated to the memory of our parents, Robert and Greta Fanthorpe, Arthur and Rosa Tooke, and all those other friends and relatives who have solved the Final Mystery and gone on to God's Realm of Everlasting Light and Joy.

CONTENTS

FOREWORD

BY

Canon Stanley Mogford, MA

Over the last ten years or more, Lionel and Patricia Fanthorpe have written a series of books, all of which deal with some of the great mysteries that have continued to perplex people down the centuries. They have often followed their patient research with their own interpretation of some of these mysterious happenings and unusual people. I have read all of these books. I own copies of them. They have introduced me to that most unusual of priests, Father Bérenger Saunière of Rennes-le-Château, who spent money as if there were no end to it, but took to the grave the secret of where he got it. I first encountered from one of their books the strange tale of the Money Pit of Canada, and am grateful never to have been tempted to throw away any of my money in the search for the treasure that may or may not lie at the foot of that pit! The *Mary Celeste* and its missing crew and passengers remains one of the great unsolved mysteries of the sea but, if you chance on the Fanthorpes' account of it, you will be intrigued by their explanation for the abandonment of that ship. These are but a few of the mysteries that have haunted them all their working lives. The stranger they are, the greater the Fanthorpes' fascination. It may have started as a hobby for them but has now become a passion.

In this book Lionel and Patricia go a step further. They face up to the greatest mystery of all – the mystery we call death.

Death, which lays its icy hands on Kings . . .
And in the dust be equal made with the poor.
— James Shirley, seventeenth-century poet.

Some people fear death. Some long for it years before it comes. Others find its grip, on old and young alike, both unequal and unjust. Death for some is the end of everything. For others it is the means to a new and fuller life to come.

The humanist takes his stance and brooks no argument. Death is no mystery. It is just part and parcel of the natural order of things. Everything that lives dies. Nothing sets man apart from the other beasts of the field. Supreme in intelligence he may be, dominating the rest of the natural world as if it were created solely to serve his life, he will yet surrender, as all else must, to slow decay and ultimately death. From dust he came, to dust he will return. Shakespeare in *Macbeth* speaks for all who take this stand: "Life's but a walking shadow, a poor player that struts and frets his hour upon the stage, and then is heard no more: it is a tale told by an idiot, full of sound and fury signifying nothing."

Many other people, of course, think differently. Humanity dares to believe itself to be immortal. The mystery of death for them is not that it happens, or when it happens, or how it happens, but what comes afterwards. As St. John puts it in the first of his *Letters*: "Now are we the children of God but it doth not yet appear what we shall be." Some need no evidence, no proof of it. They have the Promise of Christ and their Faith holds firm. There is evidence of immortality, however, to be found, and many of us lesser mortals need all the reassurance we can find. In this book Lionel and Patricia are trying to help us.

The search for understanding begins within the Human Being. We are, surely, something greater than mere flesh and bone, fat, blood, and water. Our component parts don't make us what we are. We simply use those components. Personality is greater than the sum of all our natural endowments. If, as the authors put it, "personality or consciousness has a real and discrete existence apart from the physical self, both brain and body," then the question of its survival after death becomes much more convincing. The authors have written about "out-of-body experiences." People, near death, have found themselves detached from both body and brain and, out of the body, seem able to look down on their physical selves. If, in any sense, these experiences are valid, then consciousness seems capable of an existence apart from the natural self — and this reinforces the belief that the human spirit, soul, or personality can and does survive physical death.

Such belief is strengthened by the longing of the human personality or spirit for natural justice. The human being shows potential for goodness, some more than others it has to be admitted, but even with the finest their potential is seldom fully realised. Surely this incomplete longing for goodness, and regret at failure to achieve it, deserves not be swallowed up in a final act of dying. Such unfulfilled longings, allied to the injustice of early, undeserved death, seem to point not to death as a final end to the human struggle but as the gateway to new opportunities and life.

If, then, death is not an end of everything but leads to a new life in an eternal existence, surely there must be evidence to be gleaned from this new world. Where men and women have been united closely in life, and over long years have borne and raised children and, in love for each other, have shared both joys and pains, death cannot be allowed to break the bonds of such devotion. Can one life reveal itself to another? What evidence can be plucked from the eternal world? What is to be found and can it be trusted? How can truth and the fake be separated? The authors of this book have researched widely and carefully and what they have found they have set out clearly for us to accept or reject. They are not pleading a case. Nearly half a century of investigations has gone into this book. We are introduced to ghosts and haunted houses, automatic writing, trance experiences, hypnotic regressions, poltergeists, out-of-body experiences, and much else. Psychics plead their cases and mediums relay their spirit messages. The authors have questioned the false, exposed the bogus, and challenged the absurd. They have sifted the real from the unreal, and conclude in their own words: "There is enough strong evidence from genuine contact with departed human beings to make survival not only reasonable but probable."

When you have read this book what conclusions, I wonder, will you reach? I have, of course, read it in manuscript before it ever reached the printers. The authors are Christian believers, as I am. We need no one to prove to us the glorious fact of Eternal Life. It is the Promised Gift of God through Jesus Christ our Lord.

Many have not been so blessed. They need help towards such Faith. Death may still be for them the final enemy. Perhaps, those who read this book may have their fear of death diminished, and the hope of eternal life given new conviction.

Stanley Mogford
Cardiff
January 2000

(The authors are once again deeply indebted to Canon Stanley Mogford, MA, for his great kindness in writing this Foreword. Canon Mogford is widely acknowledged to be one of the finest academics in Wales, and we are very grateful indeed for his most valuable help and support.)

INTRODUCTION

The quest for life and the quest for truth run parallel through the labyrinth of the human mind. Imagination and creativity are great gifts — but they are no substitutes for reality. Gazing at the most beautiful Gainsborough portrait can never be as satisfying as the company of the real person. Constable's landscapes in a gallery cannot replace the open meadows themselves.

We want life to go on eternally. We also want it to go on getting better and better all the time. We want an unlimited panorama of good, exciting, and exquisitely interesting things to do and to enjoy in the company of those whom we love most. We want *"They lived happily ever after"* to be a fact, not a fable. The hopes and dreams of a hedonistic hereafter are not enough — the human mind wants the truth about reality, and it wants that truth to be backed up by strong, reliable evidence.

We've been investigators of paranormal and anomalous phenomena for almost half a century. What we've found during those long years of research has led us to believe that there is something out there, and that death is not the end.

Freedom to think, however, is just as important as life and truth. The discerning reader is always the judge and jury. The investigative authors' privilege is to locate the evidence, share it, and suggest an evaluation of it. We, ourselves, think that there is a strong case for human survival — but in the last analysis it's the individual reader's own verdict that counts for her or for him.

Lionel and Patricia Fanthorpe
Cardiff, Wales, 2000

PROLOGUE
THE CENTRAL IMPORTANCE OF EVIDENCE AND THE FALLIBILITY OF HUMAN MEMORY

When examining a subject as important as whether or not human beings survive physical death and progress to a richer, fuller, more abundant and eternal life, enjoying again the fellowship of those whom we have loved and lost, it is vital to look carefully at both sides of the argument.

Some cases that seem on first inspection to provide unanswerable evidence for survival may turn out to be mediocre disappointments.

For this reason, we begin our study of the evidence for survival with the cautionary tale of Sir Edmund Hornby. It is a valuable prototype. It is also especially germane in so far as Sir Edmund was himself a judge. His experience is, therefore, a poignant and ironic reminder of the need to take *extreme care* whenever we evaluate the evidence for survival.

The weird experience reported by Judge Hornby of Shanghai serves as a timely warning to all investigators of the paranormal — although that strange episode and its aftermath may well repay *further* close analysis and careful *re-investigation*. It happened like this. Sir Edmund Hornby was a nineteenth-century chief judge in Shanghai. The significant events allegedly took place during the night of 19 January 1875. Hornby said that he heard a tap on his bedroom door late that evening, and a local editor entered his room. Hornby protested that it was far too late to give an interview and asked the editor to leave. The man refused to go and sat down on the end of the bed. The judge looked at the bedroom clock and saw that it was 1:20 a.m. (It seems hard to believe that if the "visitor" were a normal human being, he would have dared to defy a chief judge. It also seems hard to believe that a man with Hornby's rank and authority would have put up with such an intrusion.) The editor said that he needed the judge's decision as given in court earlier that day, so that it could be included in the morning edition. Finally, after twice refusing, Hornby reluctantly gave the editor the information he wanted, as he was afraid that Lady Hornby would be awakened by their conversation. The judge then added angrily that this was the very last time he would ever allow a journalist into his house. The editor replied, "This is the last time that you will see me anywhere!" After the visitor had gone, the judge again checked the time. It was one-thirty a.m. At this point Lady Hornby awoke, and the judge told her what had happened. They discussed the matter again over breakfast, and Hornby left for court.

Here he was grimly surprised to learn that the unwelcome and persistent editor who had called on him had died during the early hours of the morning. It was alleged that the dead man's notebook contained the entry: "The chief judge gave judgement in this case to the following effect . . .," followed by a few lines of unreadable shorthand.

According to Hornby's account, the coroner reached a verdict of death by natural causes, and medical examination revealed that the journalist had died of a heart attack. The judge said that he had asked the doctor whether it was possible that the editor could have visited him before going home to die, and in the doctor's opinion he could not have done so.

The affair made such a deep impression on Sir Edmund that he talked it over again with his wife when he got home and made notes of what they both recalled of the event.

When Hornby told the story some ten years later, he was absolutely convinced that every detail was clear and accurate, and that he had not been dreaming. The famous Victorian psychic investigators Gurney and Myers recorded the judge's strange story.

Then came a *second* investigation, and some curiously contradictory "facts" appeared in *Nineteenth Century* magazine. It appeared that the editor who was supposed to have been involved in the late night visit to the judge's bedroom was the Reverend Hugh Lang Nivens, who was on the *Shanghai Courier* at the time. There was evidence that he had died at about nine a.m., rather than one a.m.

16   THE FINAL MYSTERY

PROLOGUE

Judge Hornby was not married then, so there was no Lady Hornby at that particular time. Sir Edmund's first wife had died two years before and he did not remarry until three months after the Lang Nivens episode.

There does not seem to have been an inquest on Lang Nivens's death, nor does there appear to be any record of the case that the dead editor had been so eager to report.

What conclusions can be drawn from the paradoxical and contradictory Judge Hornby episode? Sir Edmund was genuinely bewildered when the later investigations *appeared* to devalue his account. His response was far from the embarrassed, indignant bluster of a pompous liar who has just been caught out. What he actually said with quiet dignity was, "If I had not believed, as I still believe, that every word of it, the story, was accurate, and that my memory was to be relied on, I should not ever have told it as a personal experience."

The later allegations that Hornby's story was inaccurate are themselves open to question in one or two important areas. If, in bold contravention of the voluble humbug and hypocrisy that passed for sexual morality in Victorian times, Sir Edmund and the *second* Lady Hornby had been sleeping together *before* their marriage, that could easily have accounted for her presence in his bedroom during the crucial night of the weird visitation. Being a gallantly protective and chivalrous gentleman of the old school, Sir Edmund would far rather have allowed himself to be accused of memory failure, or worse, than to have had a breath of vicious, Victorian scandal directed towards the lady he loved.

Unless Lang Nivens had been obliging enough to drop dead surrounded by a crowd of witnesses with stop watches, a difference of only seven or eight hours is not a large one.

It is also tempting to ask how accurate and precise the records of inquests were in Shanghai at the end of the nineteenth century. Is it possible that the Lang Nivens inquest records were lost, or never entered, by an overworked and underpaid clerical officer in the Coroner's Department? Proof is a very unpredictable and whimsical creature — flighty as a moth in moonlight. Half a dozen equally rational and logical conclusions can be deduced from the same fragments of circumstantial evidence.

The question of the judge's memory — like the question of any fallible human memory — needs close examination. How reliable are our memories? They vary enormously, of course. There are men and women like Leslie Welsh with eidetic or photographic memories. They have the ability to refer to their mental records as most of us refer to an encyclopaedia in a reference library. At the other extreme are people who seem to have difficulty in recalling their own names, addresses, and telephone numbers without writing everything down. Most of us have memories that fall somewhere between the eidetic and the unreliable.

Psychologists who specialise in the study of memory and mnemonics regard memory as dependent upon three key factors: *recency*, *frequency*, and *intensity*. We can recall something we heard or saw just a minute or so ago; we can recall things that we hear and see frequently; we can recall things that made a deep impression on us, things that are highly significant and important to us. Memory specialists also advance the theory that we do not necessarily recall an event, but rather *our first retelling of that event*. This point may hold the key to the very puzzling Hornby episode.

Sir Edmund said that he *told* his wife (or uninhibited fiancée?) about it. In these retellings of a dramatic event, the industrious taxonomy of the human mind tends to amplify and exaggerate the most striking components of a story and abridges its less interesting elements. Sometimes they are suppressed altogether, or subtly altered to increase the humour or drama of an event, to make it more impressive, more interesting, or more entertaining. This is largely a subconscious or unconscious process, and does not imply the least trace of deliberate or conscious deceit or falsification on Hornby's part.

For example, we ourselves thought we recalled a scene from Disney's *Snow White* in which the Wicked Queen, in her hideous old hag form, went down some dungeon stairs and passed a skeleton with one dry, bony arm stretched out pathetically through the bars of its cell towards a cobweb-covered water jug. A cruel jailer had placed it there tantalisingly — just beyond the victim's reach — long ago.

As the Wicked Queen passed the skeleton she kicked the jug towards it and cackled, "Have a drink!" *When we saw the film again years later that scene wasn't there.* Had we imagined it? We questioned the validity of our own memories. It was some time later that we learned that the skeleton-and-jug scene *had* once been in the film, but had been edited out of later versions. This curious now-you-see-it-now-you-don't scenario can apply to situations like those in which Sir Edmund was involved: apparent contradictions are themselves vulnerable to later correction and amendment.

Survival of the personality is of major importance to us all. There is a great deal of interesting and persuasive evidence for it, but *because* it is of such high significance, that evidence — and our response to it — needs to be approached with the utmost caution.

CHAPTER ONE
WHAT IS PERSONALITY?

The problems of self-awareness and the existence of individual, personal consciousness are among the most significant questions in philosophy and theology.

There are deeply mystical people — often members of cultures that are less interested in technology than most typical Europeans and Americans — who seem to have a profound communal awareness, and are almost able to participate in the self-awareness and thought processes of a Group Mind. If such a Group Mind, or Hive Mind, exists, the investigator needs to consider whether it is something universal and ubiquitous throughout the entire biosphere, or whether it is exclusively human.

Is it possible that animals and plants contribute to it in their different and distinctive ways? The intelligence and self-awareness of whales and dolphins, anthropoid apes, dogs, cats, and horses, may well be greater than we are generally prepared to acknowledge.

Sagacious James Lovelock proposed the Gaia Hypothesis: the theory that all of us in the biosphere can best be understood as parts of one vast living organism — Gaia. This is of central importance to our examination of the allied phenomena of self-consciousness and the awareness of discrete individual identity.

Before there can be any serious investigation and analysis of the evidence for survival, it is important to understand the nature of what it is that is thought to survive.

Thought and language are often mutually reinforcing, and

The hive-mind of bees: does it exist?

The Gaia Hypothesis. Is the whole biosphere one great living organism?
Does it have a mind?

although some artistic geniuses seem able to think spatially and to conceptualise form and colour independently of words, for most of us ideas and meanings are inevitably clothed in words. When a creative, innovative mind moves off in a fresh direction, there is a vague feeling that an intriguing new idea is hovering just beyond our grasp — one that would be well worth encapsulating in words *if only the right words existed for it.*

In the field of social sciences this is particularly apparent: Keynesian economics, for example, attaches totally different, specific meanings to the terms *"multiplier"* and *"accelerator"* that are not the meanings implied when mathematicians or automobile engineers use those same terms.

There is also the ironic situation in which "good, old-fashioned common sense" lets us down like an elevator with a broken cable. We need to remember that common sense told our ancestors that the Earth was flat, that the Sun revolved around it, and that everything was made from earth, air, fire, and water mixed in different ratios.

The whole question of "Who and what am I?" seems, in common sense terms, to be superfluous simply because the questioner is capable of asking it. "Unless I exist," we persuade ourselves at basement level, "how am I able to question my existence?" Descartes worked along much the same lines in *cogito ergo sum* (I think, therefore I am), but there are philosophical minds at least as profound as his that would take issue with his conclusion.

The quest for artificial intelligence — or rather for non-biological intelligence — is strewn with major obstacles. If an interactive computer conversation programme can be devised that is so effective that the human respondent cannot distinguish between the computer and another human being, then, in logical, objective terms, *is there any significant difference?*

In the more sophisticated setting of a futuristic, science-fiction type of society, if an android, clone, or cyborg is constructed to appear identical in every way to a biological human character, and if that construction is fitted with an identical memory track plus a programmed conviction that it *is* the human being whom it resembles — then how are we to distinguish them? To what extent does the existence of personality depend upon the *belief* that personality exists?

We would suggest that in terms of objective, academic philosophy it may not be possible to produce the irrefutable proof that the human heart and mind would find reassuringly welcome. Unreliable as it may be, therefore, we have recourse once more to "introspective experience, instinct, a hunch, a gut reaction," or that same "common sense" that has already been queried. The best argument that any of us — including Descartes — can put forward for the reality of individual mental existence, expressed as feelings of self-awareness and sentience, is that we *think* we exist. We simply *believe* in our own conscious and discrete personalities.

If it is so difficult to *prove* something that is superficially so obvious, how much more difficult is it to prove that our individual personalities survive the dissolution of the physical body and brain, and go on to an unending life?

Dr. Skinner's pigeons and Pavlov's dogs were attempts to vindicate behaviourism: the idea that all human responses, decisions, and functional patterns can be explained in terms of stimuli and responses. In behaviourist theory, part of the internal or external environment produces a stimulus to which the human brain responds. Consciousness is then experienced as an illusion, a kind of mental "effluvium" that is generated from the behaviouristic functioning of the brain — in much the same way that hot stones in a sun-baked desert generate an insubstantial heat haze. To the materialistic behaviourist, consciousness and personality are the merest trivia that

Typical medium with the spirit of a military man and his dog.

can readily be discarded. But to those who accept the existence of their own individual, autonomous consciousness, nothing is more precious — except the continuation of the autonomous consciousness of the people whom they love more than their own lives.

If it may be agreed that consciousness has a real and discrete existence apart from the physical brain, then the question of its survival may be examined. If *something* survives death, is it in the form that is usually described as a "ghost"? For that matter, what exactly *is* a ghost? When a psychic claims to be in contact with a departed human spirit, the medium is usually able to describe that spirit in detail. The gender and age are often given first. A typical psychic commentary might include: "I have a rather distinguished looking military man here. He's above average height with bright grey eyes. There's a small dog with him. The gentleman's name is Captain Peter Winnington, and he's been over in spirit for several years. He has a message for John, someone christened John but often called Jack. Peter wants you to know that it's all right. He understands why you couldn't reach him. He says it's all in the past now. It doesn't matter. He doesn't want you to think of it ever again. He says if you want to respect his memory go to the local you used to go to together, the King's Arms in the old Market Square. Sit where you always sat together at that table by the window. Drink his health. He'll understand. He'll know. He'll be happy. The old bond will be restored as if it had never been broken."

Quite frequently the person for whom the message is *said* to be intended will respond to the medium with a comment such as: "I'm Jack. I know who Peter is. Please tell him I'll do what he asks, and that I understand exactly what he means."

What can be analysed from a mediumistic message of this kind? It certainly sounds as if someone who was once a living, human personality is continuing to exist in the spirit world. It also implies that the dead person (Captain Peter Winnington) wishes to communicate something to his old friend Jack. Those people hearing the message assume that Jack did something about which he feels guilty, or that he failed to keep an important rendezvous. The "conversation" between Jack and Peter suggests that this was a military situation. There are also detailed references that can be checked: references to a pub and a table near the window — a fact that could be confirmed by talking to regular customers, or a long-serving landlord of the King's Arms.

DEATH

In many cases of this type recorded in paranormal data, investigators have been able to confirm several significant details. The "Jack or John" character will frequently recall knowing the "Captain Peter" character and will often supply details of the event to which "Peter" has referred. The pub will exist and witnesses will come forward to confirm the story.

This all sounds very positive and factual, but it is vitally important to be careful, and to check and recheck the corroborative statements provided by those who sincerely believe themselves to have been witnesses.

Careful psychic investigators need to remind themselves of Judge Hornby as fervently as loyal Texans remember the Alamo.

CHAPTER TWO
WHAT IS A GHOST?

There are a number of major theories that set out to explain what the phenomenon popularly described as a "ghost" might really be.

In the first theory, the phenomenon is dismissed as a purely subjective mental experience. It's imagination; we only *thought* that we saw or heard it; a ghost is merely the product of a malfunctioning mind; materialistic prejudice assures us that ghosts do not and cannot exist — therefore those who *think* they see or hear them are suffering from some sort of mental abnormality. We may argue against this explanation in that so many sane, rational, normal, and sensible people have *reported* experiencing the phenomenon that if it *is* only a mental malfunction, the majority of people suffer from it. Dare we suggest that it is more likely the *inability* to experience psychic phenomena that is "abnormal"?

Using the analogy of full-colour vision, it is the colour-blind section of the population that is in a minority. What if they were in the majority and didn't believe that full-colour vision existed *except in the imaginations of those who proclaimed that roses were red and violets were blue?* If only those who have the necessary optical and neurological equipment to receive it experience the phenomenon of colour, how could they prove the existence of colour to those who do not have the appropriate biological equipment to share the experience with them?

The second group of explanations is the province of fundamentalist religious groups. They are either repelled by psychic phenomena, frightened of it, or both. They suggest that all supposed ghosts are demons, fallen angels, or evil spirits masquerading as departed human beings in order to mock and deceive the bereaved. This is a point of view that such groups are, of course, fully entitled to embrace, but it is not one that has any appeal to us as investigators of paranormal and anomalous phenomena.

If God is the loving, caring supra-parent that we believe the Deity to be, then like any other benign and caring parent, God's will for us is that we should all develop into happy, loving, and autonomous beings. With that basic concept in mind, it should be possible to entertain the idea that the whole universe — physical and spiritual, material and mental — is one vast adventure playground in which we are free to roam in order to learn. There's no part of it that we can't explore, and there's nothing we can't do. There *are*, of course, eternal laws and divine principles by which we must faithfully abide if we are to get the best out of ourselves and out of God's universe.

The first of these inalienable, sacred limits is that although freedom and autonomy are major virtues and highly desirable life targets, our individual, personal freedom ends at the point where it curtails someone else's. Our right to do what we like ends at the point where it prevents someone else from doing what he or she likes. Where resources are unlimited, we are free to take as much as we want. Where resources are limited, we are free to take our fair share — *but not a pennyweight more*. If a fearless psychic investigator or an intrepid anomalous phenomena researcher wants to explore strange, dark, mysterious places, he or she is at perfect liberty to do so. God *never* says, "I forbid you to carry out your research. This line of exploration is strictly forbidden for religious reasons." What we *are* duty bound to observe, however, is that we are not free to involve others in our investigations if they find psychic phenomena repellent or intimidating. Dauntless psychic explorers are free to enter the Caverns of Terror or not — just as they wish. They are *not* free to drive other people in, if those other people do not want to go there.

Nearly half a century of research into most aspects of the paranormal has led us to the conclusion that anomalous phenomena can be positive, negative, or neutral — rather like the human race itself. If ghosts are demons in disguise, many of them must be singularly good-natured demons, and the majority of the rest are so bland and ineffectual as to be practically innocuous.

WHAT IS A GHOST?

So, if ghosts are neither mental malfunctions nor evil spirits, what are they? A third theory suggests that they could be patterns or impressions left in the fabric of haunted sites and buildings. If audio and videotape can pick up the impressions that sound engineers and camera crews wish them to receive, why can't metal, stone, and wood pick up impressions naturally from events that are taking place in their vicinity? Then, when a sufficiently sensitive person comes within range of those recorded impressions, they are simply played back.

A fourth hypothesis uses the analogy of camera malfunction. It suggests that "seeing" and "hearing" are intellectual processes as well as physiological ones. Just very occasionally some elaborate automatic cameras are capable of a sort of "internalisation error" in which it is something inside the camera that is "seen" by the film, instead of the external object towards which the lens is pointing. Theory four suggests that the human eye and brain can occasionally make that same internalisation error. An internal impression is then registered as an external one: a memory, or creative thought, is seen as an external phenomenon or "ghost".

Theory number five involves telepathy and possibly an out-of-body experience. If a very sensitive and receptive subject picks up the powerfully transmitted thought forms of another person who is a strong telepathic sender, then the recipient might "see" either the sender or the image that the sender was transmitting.

After carefully examining and evaluating these five theories — interesting as some of them undoubtedly are — the authors' own conclusions (after half a century's research and evaluation) are that although some reports of ostensibly psychic phenomena *might* be explained in other ways, *there is enough strong evidence for genuine contact with departed human beings to make survival not only reasonable but probable*.

CHAPTER THREE
EXAMPLES OF HAUNTINGS

It would be possible to fill a vast library with first-hand, eyewitness accounts of hauntings. One or two, even a dozen or a score, might be dismissed as fanciful tales — but when the statistics rise into hundreds and then thousands of honest and reliable stories told by witnesses with integrity — then the evidence is not easy to dismiss.

Burke Hardison was driving from Raleigh, North Carolina, towards High Point where he lived. It was a rainy night during the spring of 1924. He had spent the evening with some friends, and as he drove through Jamestown the fog came in thickly. Through that swirling mist he saw the Highway 70 underpass. The fog cleared just for a moment, and, to his amazement in view of the time and the loneliness of the place, he saw a solitary girl. She was wearing a white evening gown and was signalling frantically for him to stop. He slowed down and halted the car beside her. When she spoke her voice was very soft, almost unnaturally quiet, and she had evidently been crying. *"Please,"* she begged, "please, could you take me to High Point?"

Burke Hardison was a pleasant, good-hearted, neighbourly man. He smiled reassuringly and helped her into the car. "I'm just on the way to High Point. I live there myself. It's no problem at all." In spite of the fog and darkness he could see the girl quite clearly. Her face was pale and her long, dark hair hung attractively all around it. Her full, white, evening dress billowed out on each side of her as she settled into the seat beside him. She gave him the address of a street that he knew in High Point and then they drove on. The girl didn't say much, and over the noise of the engine it was difficult for him to hear her because she spoke so quietly. Burke said later that there was a strange *distance* about her voice: it was almost as though she was speaking to him down a poor telephone line from a long way away. From the fragments that he could hear of what she said, he gathered that she was anxious because she knew her mother would be worried about her. Hardison also gleaned the information that she had just been to a dance in Raleigh, but he could not make out from what she said how she had ended up standing there alone in the fog by the side of the road close to the underpass. He was a thoughtful and sensitive man, and did not want to add to her distress by questioning her about something that she did not appear to want to discuss. She did, however, say something very strange: "Nothing matters now except going home."

He reached the address that she had given him, stopped outside her house, and walked around to open the car door for her. As he did so, he found himself looking into the dark, *empty* interior of his car. The girl had gone; the car was empty. He could not understand how she could have got out so quickly and so quietly without his even hearing the door open and shut. If she had slipped into the

The ghost of the hitchhiking girl waiting in the underpass.

house she must have moved almost unbelievably fast; and how could she have done it without his seeing her? For several minutes Burke could not make up his mind what to do, and then he took the bull by the horns and knocked on the door of the house. It was a long time before anyone answered. The woman who finally opened it bore a remarkable resemblance to the girl to whom Burke had given the lift, but she was much older. Hardison did not know what to say. At last, by way of explanation, he said, "I just gave your daughter a lift home, but when I opened the car door for her she wasn't there." The woman in the lighted doorway was unable to speak for several moments, and then Hardison saw tears running down her cheeks. When she brought her voice under control again she said, "I had an only daughter who was killed in a car crash near the underpass on Highway 70 in Jamestown — but that was over a year ago. She was on her way back from a dance in Raleigh." She drew a deep breath and looked at Hardison. "You're not the first good Samaritan who has tried to give her a lift home. *It's just that she never quite makes it.*"

Variations of the story of ghostly hitchhikers have passed into urban legend and some have been heavily embroidered. In some instances the girl who is hitchhiking borrows the driver's umbrella or coat because it's raining hard as he reaches her house and there is a long pathway or drive. When he returns a day or two later to collect the coat, he finds the house itself is no longer there. He asks in the village and is told that a young woman who once lived there was killed on that road. Out of curiosity he goes to look for her grave and finds that his coat, or umbrella, is resting against her headstone. Several interesting theories have been put forward to explain the spread and variations of these so-called urban legends.

Just as in the case of Judge Hornby's story, the tendency of the human subconscious to dramatise, embroider, and exaggerate a narrative must be taken into account. Nevertheless, a number of stories that have been dismissed as urban legends, in the way that the tale of the girl hitchhiker is often dismissed, can occasionally be traced back to a time, an event, and a witness whose name can be placed firmly on the story.

Just as a verifiable version of the urban legend of the hitchhiking girl is one that demands to find its way into any collection of hauntings, so it would be equally difficult not to mention Borley Rectory in Suffolk in the same context. Today there are barely 200 souls in the village, and in the days of its paranormal fame in the 1930s and 1940s, particularly, there were a great deal fewer. The name Borley comes from the Anglo-Saxon word *barlea*, which means literally "the pasture or field of the boar." It found its way into the record books a thousand years ago, during the reign of Edward the Confessor, when the owner of Borley Manor was recorded as a man named Lewin. After William the Conqueror took over, he gave it to his half-sister Adeliza, the Countess of Aumale. The village also managed to get a reference in the Domesday Book in 1086.

In the robust Victorian days of the Anglican Church militant, the squire's eldest son inherited the estate, the second son went into the army, and the third became a parson. The Reverend Henry Bull, known as Harry, built Borley Rectory. He put it up in 1863, allegedly on the site of a much older structure. A mixture of legend and tradition maintained that a Benedictine abbey had stood there earlier still, but evidence for the existence of that abbey is scarce.

Harry Bull lived up to his name: he was a characteristically productive Victorian parent. Four of his daughters were walking in the grounds of the old rectory in about 1900 when all of them together reported seeing the famous Borley Rectory ghost nun. This strange figure was seen by many other witnesses on numerous occasions, and the whole area became known as Nun's Walk.

A tragic story connected with a nun was told at a séance many years afterwards. In this narrative the girl had been brought over from France ostensibly to leave her religious order and marry a member of the Waldegrave family, who were wealthy local landowners in the Borley area at the time. She was murdered, however, and her remains were placed in the cellars. It may be possible that the Waldegrave who sent for her had ideas other than marriage, and she was murdered when she refused to become his mistress.

Whether the famous Borley investigator Harry Price, whose reputation was not unblemished, actually *imported* human remains from somewhere else and hid them in the cellars at Borley so that he could "discover" and unearth them later cannot now be decided either way. Certainly some human remains were produced from under one of the Borley cellars and Price arranged for a clergyman to give them decent burial.

Another of the Borley spectres seen at an upper window was alleged to have been the ghost of a young servant girl. A none-too-creditable tale attached to her sad little apparition suggests that she

34 THE FINAL MYSTERY

either fell from that attic window while cleaning it or she was attempting to escape the amorous clutches of the virile Reverend Bull and went backwards out of the window. Victorian "respectability" being what it was, and the Bulls' social position being pretty well unassailable in the district, the affair of the dead servant girl — especially if she was alone in the world, and had been hired from a parish orphanage or union workhouse — could have been quietly hushed up.

Another of the Borley hauntings concerned a coach with headless horses and headless passengers, driven by a headless horseman. If such an apparition was actually seen by reputable and reliable witnesses in the Borley area, then it seems likely to have been allied with the far older story of the Wild Hunt. A supposed explanation of the ghostly coach narrative is the romantic tale of a dashing young coachman endeavouring to elope with the nun who now supposedly haunts the Nun's Walk. He was captured and executed; she was bricked up alive in the wall of her convent.

Strange phenomena continued to be reported from Borley Rectory for many years after those sightings. When Harry Bull's son, also called Harry, died in 1927, his ghost was reported walking through the rectory corridors.

It was extremely difficult for the parish to find a successor to the Reverend Bull, Jr. There is the inevitable debate about whether it was the ghostly atmosphere of Borley Rectory or the simple inconvenience of trying to keep such a vast old ruin of a house lit and heated that discouraged all those who saw it from accepting the living. From 1928-29, the Reverend Eric Smith and his wife reported various psychic phenomena, strange knocking noises, showers of coins, and footsteps made by no human feet. The phantom coach is also alleged to have turned up on the drive again during those few months.

Unlike its counterpart in Norfolk, the Borley coach did not seem to presage any particular doom or disaster for those who saw it. The Norfolk phantom coach, by contrast, is alleged to gallop from Great Yarmouth to King's Lynn with its headless horses, headless passengers, and headless coachman. According to old Norfolk traditions, it is considered to bring very bad luck, if not necessarily fatally bad luck, to those who witness it. During the eighteenth century, a notorious poacher, general all-round hard-man, bully-boy, and petty criminal called George Mace, was the leader of a gang of thieves and troublemakers based in the little Norfolk town of Watton. The local constables and magistrates all forecast that George Mace would end his days on the gallows. He didn't. According to local tradition, George Mace was picked up by the phantom coach, driven away by its headless occupants, and dumped — stone dead — at Breccles Hall shortly before daybreak. It might be cynically suggested that the coach that picked up George Mace and disposed of him was a perfectly normal, solid, and material one, and that it was occupied not by headless ghosts but by hard-fisted gamekeepers who had had enough of George's trouble-making and had decided to take the law into their own hands — remaining blissfully anonymous in the shadow of the legend of the phantom coach. There were not very many mourners at George Mace's funeral. The general opinion in the Watton area was that it could not have happened to a nicer man, and that it was certainly not before time!

The headless coachman phenomenon.

After Eric Smith and his wife left Borley, the Reverend Lionel Foyster and his much younger wife, Marianne, moved into the rectory in 1929. Young and excitable Mrs. Foyster appeared to be the centre of some quite formidable poltergeist activity. Weird messages addressed to her were found on the walls.

A respectable justice of the peace named Guy L'Estrange paid a visit to Borley in the early 1930s and wrote an interesting account of poltergeist phenomena, including smashed crockery and bottles flying through the air like angry hornets. L'Estrange did not think that any human agencies were behind these phenomena, but Harry Price was rather suspicious of Marianne Foyster.

Price, himself, it must be remembered, was strongly suspected of fraud. He loved to be in the limelight and the alleged poltergeist activities at Borley did nothing to hinder the sales of his two books on the old house.

Hall, Goldney, and Dingwell undertook an evaluative investigation of Price's work on behalf of the Society for Psychical Research. Their report, published in 1956, accused him of being responsible for much of the Borley story. While it is true that he and a few like-minded characters may have amplified *some* of the Borley phenomena, there is more than enough evidence to indicate that a great many *genuine* hauntings took place there as well. Although the rectory itself burned down in rather questionable circumstances in 1939, strange phenomena have continued in the district.

Andrew Green, an experienced investigator, went to Borley in the early 1950s accompanied by members of the Ealing Psychical Research Society. At one point in their investigation a friend grabbed Green's arm and pointed to what he described as a woman wearing a long white gown who had appeared at the far end of the Nun's Walk. Green himself could not see the figure, but he heard sounds from the bushes and shrubs as though someone or something was walking through them.

This ability of some members of an investigating party to see psychic phenomena when other members cannot is reminiscent of the occasion at Bowden House in Totnes, Devon, when co-author Lionel, who was walking ahead of a small group of other psychic investigators, paused and sat down in a large armchair to await the rest of the party. Shirley Wallace, a very perceptive medium, was among those in the group. She looked towards the armchair in question and said that Lionel was actually sitting on the ghost of a Victorian lady wearing a voluminous brown crinoline dress. Shirley added that the ghost concerned appeared to be distressed because Lionel was in what Shirley described as the ghost's "living space"! It is therefore perfectly feasible that an experienced investigator like Andrew Green would have been unable to see the woman in the long white gown whereas he was able to hear the inexplicable rustling among the leaves.

Stephen Jenkins, who has made a special study of ley lines, has put forward the view that Borley church is at a point where four lines intersect. A photograph of Jenkins taken in the late 1970s beside the wall of Borley cemetery seemed to show strange faces visible in the trees. Another experience in which the Jenkins family was involved took place not far from Belchamp Walter Hall, which is less than three miles from Borley village. As the Jenkinses were driving their car, a group of men inexplicably appeared immediately in front of them. They wore black cloaks and carried a coffin of a pattern not used in the twentieth century. This sinister group disappeared through the hedge and, although they did not get a long look at them, the Jenkinses were convinced that one of the figures at least had a skull instead of a face.

The ghostly funeral procession that vanished into a hedge.

Borley church is as interesting as Harry Bull's rectory, and far older. There is evidence of a wooden building having been erected on the site in the middle of the eleventh century. Flint and rubble dating from a hundred years later were located in the south wall. Ethel Bull told Harry Price the story of a nineteenth-century incident when Waldegrave coffins in the vault below the church had apparently moved of their own volition. This ties in with the unexplained mystery of the coffins in the Chase-Elliot vault that we investigated for our BBC documentary. The vault is at Christchurch, near Oistins in Barbados. Similar moving coffin incidents were reported in connection with the Buxhoewden family vault in Osel in the Baltic

Co-author Patricia Fanthorpe with Emerson Clarke at the mysterious
Chase Vault in Christchurch, Barbados.

Co-author Patricia Fanthorpe at the weird
Chase Vault in Christchurch, Barbados.

Borley Church in Suffolk, England, near the site of the haunted rectory.

Borley, Suffolk, England, village signpost —
near the site of the haunted rectory.

region, from Gretford near Stamford, and from Stanton, Suffolk, in the United Kingdom.

Various groups of psychic investigators have studied Borley church, including Denny Densham the film director. Tapes made there for a very effective BBC documentary recorded inexplicable rappings, knockings, and a heavy crash against the door. Then a very strange human sigh was recorded.

Despite the disappearance of its famous haunted rectory, Borley is undoubtedly still well worth the serious psychic investigator's time.

Just as churches and rectories are frequently the sites of reported hauntings, so are ancient inns and taverns. If ever an old inn enjoyed the most beautiful possible setting it must surely be the Anchor Inn at Tintern. The inn stands on the banks of the beautiful River Wye, barely a stone's throw from the famous ruin of Tintern Abbey. Both are surrounded by scenic, forested hills. Although it is a perfect artist's dream-canvas of what a country inn should be like by day, in the depth of night it is a very different sight.

The main bar of the Anchor Inn is at least as old as the Abbey itself, and its restaurant was at one time the boathouse used by the monks. Walter de Clare built Tintern Abbey as his penance for the murder of his wife, and many psychic investigators have wondered whether it was the unhappy Lady de Clare who became the frequently sighted spectral Grey Lady of Tintern.

Co-author Patricia Fanthorpe in the haunted Anchor Inn at Tintern, England.

Co-author Lionel Fanthorpe outside
the haunted Anchor Inn at Tintern, England.

Like many of the most atmospheric old buildings of its kind the Anchor Inn has intriguing tunnels and passageways. History asserts that the monks of Tintern hid in the tunnels below the inn when Henry VIII's men were after their blood. The Abbey was sacked and most of the occupants slaughtered; a number of monks were almost certainly killed in the tunnels. What is now the Anchor's carvery restaurant witnessed several desperate launches when it was the monk's boathouse. Two arches that are today discretely curtained off from the main part of the restaurant mark the exact places where the monks boarded their boats.

It could well be argued that there are perfectly natural explanations for the feeling of *intense cold* that surrounds these curtained archways. Draughts of moist, cool air from the surface of the river on a winter's night could very well provide the logical, common sense answer to the problem of the coldness. Nevertheless, psychic investigators who have considered the area carefully wonder whether there is a paranormal reason for the anomalous cold.

On the other side of the river is a strange outcrop of rock. It stands high on the cliff and is known as the "Devil's Pulpit." According to medieval legends, Satan himself stood there doing his eloquent best to persuade the monks to change sides and work for him. The site offers an amazing aerial view of the Abbey far below it

EXAMPLES OF HAUNTINGS

The haunted slipway at Tintern, where the monks tried
to escape across the River Wye.

Co-author Lionel Fanthorpe at the haunted Anchor Inn in Tintern,
close to the haunted slipway.

Co-author Lionel Fanthorpe climbing the sinister "Devil's Pulpit" near Tintern Abbey, England.

Co-author Lionel Fanthorpe near the notorious "Devil's Pulpit" close to Tintern Abbey, England.

and across the river. There are some who sided with Henry VIII at the time of the Dissolution who would have argued that a number of the monks must have accepted the Devil's offer when he harangued them in legend from that strange stone "pulpit." Several inhabitants of Tintern, who know the area and its atmosphere well, wonder whether it is the troubled souls of these renegade monks that glide behind the inn when darkness falls.

Co-author Lionel Fanthorpe at Carlsbad Caverns,
near White's City, New Mexico, USA.

7,000-year-old mummified corpse in the haunted museum at
White's City, New Mexico, USA.

DEATH

When we visited White's City near the Carlsbad Caverns in New Mexico, we were shown around the haunted museum by the granddaughter of Charles White, the founder of White's City. In the lowest part of the White's City museum there are several strange and sinister exhibits, including a nineteenth-century hearse of the type that Yul Brynner drove in *The Magnificent Seven*. Not far from it is Charles White's old car, and many of the museum staff are convinced that from time to time his spirit returns and sits in it. His granddaughter always locks up that part of the museum herself. "I would never ask anyone who works for me to do a job I would be unwilling to do myself," she told us.

Alan Butt, landlord of Tintern's Anchor Inn, has the same kindly and considerate attitude towards his staff. It is said in the village that some are not too keen to go into the cellars or backrooms of the Anchor after night has fallen. Alan, a tough, rugby-playing sailor with common sense to match his physical strength, is not in the least nervous or imaginative. But he will tell in his typically quiet, sensible way of a dull winter afternoon when he saw the wraith of a woman in long, grey garments looking through the doorway of the inn. As Alan looked back at the strange spectral form of the woman, a picture fell from the wall with a loud crash. It seemed inevitable that the frame would be broken and the glass shattered, but when he picked it up the picture was, to his great surprise, *undamaged*. He checked the cord and the strong, secure hook from which the picture had been hanging. The cord was unbroken and the hook was still firmly embedded in the wall. Apparently, there was no logical, common sense reason why the picture should have come down so suddenly.

When Alan made a search for the Grey Lady in the gardens next to the inn there was no sign of her at all. She had vanished as suddenly and as inexplicably as Lydia the ghostly hitchhiker from Jamestown in North Carolina.

An Anchor employee named Chris James also spotted the Grey Lady in the same area where the landlord saw her. His attention was drawn to her by a young child whom he noticed running across the room while he was working in the tea shop. The child ran towards a lady in grey robes who was above average height. Chris had to attend to something else for a moment or two, and when he looked again in the direction that the young child had taken there was no sign of either the child or the Lady in Grey. The only exit was directly past the spot where Chris was working, and, although his attention was on his work, he had no doubt at all that no one had passed him.

The wife whom Walter de Clare had murdered was the mother of one small child. Was it the tragic Grey Lady of Tintern and her child whom Chris saw in the tea room that afternoon?

Another strange occurrence at the Anchor Inn concerned the landlord's daughter, his wife, and his daughter's fiancé. They were the only three people in the inn at the time; the young man was asleep upstairs while the two ladies were talking together in the kitchen. It was just after midnight when he came down sounding rather puzzled and asking why someone had come into his room and woken him!

Tintern Abbey, near the haunted Anchor Inn.

Strange, disturbing, poltergeist-type activities are also part of the recorded paranormal events from the old Anchor Inn at Tintern. Most frequently these take place in the carvery. Janet Hill, who has been a member of staff at the Anchor for a number of years, witnessed a very strange episode when a basket full of bread rose into the air for no apparent reason and emptied its contents all over the counter where Janet was working. Additionally, furniture has been seen to move, menu boards have vanished and reappeared, and episodes almost as dramatic as the Esther Cox poltergeist phenomena at Amherst, Nova Scotia, have been reported from time to time.

DEATH

In one ancient tradition, the grandfather of the legendary King Arthur was a good old king named Tewdric. In his day Tintern was known by the Welsh name Din Terwyn. After a lifetime of turbulence and battle good King Tewdric went into semi-retirement and moved to Tintern, where he hoped to live out his declining years in tranquillity. In this version of the Arthurian legend, Tewdric's son, Meurig got involved in a huge battle at Pontysaison ("Bridge of the Saxons"), not far from Din Terwyn. Being a good and protective father, old Tewdric came out of his semi-retirement and galloped to his son's aid, bringing with him his own loyal armed escort and his formidable royal bodyguard. A savage hand-to-hand fight ensued and father and son together defeated the Saxon invaders. Tewdric, however, was fatally wounded during the sharp engagement and was buried with royal honours at Mathern Church, less than ten miles from Tintern. There are some psychic investigators who wonder whether a few of the hauntings at the Anchor can be traced back to Tewdric's triumphant spirit coming home to celebrate that last great victory, in which he did his fatherly duty so well.

If it is the monks of Tintern whose psychic presence troubles the old Anchor Inn to this day, does it perhaps seem strange that men supposedly devoted to the cause of holiness during their earthly lives would be such negative and distressing spirits after death? The *original* Cistercians were generally regarded as being a severe and pious order who lived lives of the most rigorous religious discipline, giving away all their wealth and keeping strictly to vows of poverty, chastity, and obedience. In consequence, their lives were simple in the extreme: lives that the authors would personally regard as an infallible formula for chronic and abject misery — but there's no accounting for taste!

The Cistercians even wore robes that were woven from undyed wool and this, too, was in accordance with their principle of simplicity. Some investigators have put forward the theory that perhaps the strange figure in grey robes is not, after all, the unfortunate Lady de Clare, but a monk whose white robes have been glazed over with dirt until they look as though they are grey.

Although these original, sincere Cistercians seem to have followed the Order's rules of poverty, chastity, and obedience, poverty became an unwelcome stranger to Tintern Abbey as the years passed. Generous gifts and bequests of land made the monks

The ruins of haunted Tintern Abbey, England.

more and more wealthy. With wealth came power. Their original strictness and rigorous religious observations began to soften. They became "liberalised, progressive, and permissive," to use a kindly phrase. As their discipline faded and fell away, it was not only the King's propagandists and the monks' jealous enemies who talked about their gluttony and debauchery. It seemed that nothing and no-one could keep these rapacious ex-holy men under control, and there are historians who suggest that this was one of the reasons why Henry VIII felt that the safest plan would be to execute them all. If the souls of the Tintern monks haunt the old Anchor Inn by the River Wye, it is very unlikely the spirits of the first generation of benign and pious men are responsible for the uncanny events and strange phantom appearances there. There would, however, seem to be nothing to prevent the return of the restless souls of those *later* monks, seeking, perhaps, to find peace and tranquillity in the same location. Was this the spot where their vows of poverty, chastity, and obedience went up the same chimney as the smoke from the geese and swans that were roasting merrily for them and their raunchy young tavern wenches?

During the 1700s, builders working in the grounds at Tintern discovered a ponderous stone slab beneath which a number of skeletons lay as though huddled together in death. There was no trace of coffins under that great slab. Had some of the monks in conflict with Henry VIII been killed and buried there in a great hurry? Or had they been trying to hide from their pursuers under that stone — and ultimately died there? While having a well-earned meal in the inn that night, the workmen who found the skeletons were discussing who they might have been and how they might have met their deaths. It could, of course, merely have been coincidence, but as they discussed the skeletons the sky darkened like the worst point of an Arctic winter and a terrifying storm burst over the dining room of the inn. King-sized lightning bolts flashed all around them, and the thunder sounded like a legion of skeletons dancing on a corrugated iron roof immediately above their heads. The men began to wonder whether the vengeful spirits of those whose bones they had inadvertently disturbed were seeking vengeance on them.

Another prime candidate for the cause of the ghostly disturbances reported from time to time from the old Anchor Inn might be John Callice. A Tintern man, Callice made even the most debauched of the monks appear pious and mild mannered by contrast. Callice was a notorious Barbary Coast pirate and was not averse to a little lucrative white slaving on the side. Suitable girls aboard the ships he had captured were auctioned off as sex-slaves in North Africa. Like many similar boastful villains, Callice enjoyed shocking his listeners with stories — possibly wildly exaggerated — of the mayhem, rape, and murder he had committed at sea and along the notorious Barbary Coast. Is it possible that the savage, restless spirit of John Callice returns to trouble the bar where he once told his picaresque tales?

Yet another candidate for the cause of some of the Anchor Inn hauntings would be the fearless Sir Henry Wintour. During the English Civil War, Wintour, a bold — if reckless — Royalist, was galloping flat out to get away from a posse of parliamentary soldiers who were hot on his track. At the spot still known as Wintour's Leap, he urged his horse clean over the cliff top and down into the deep water of the Wye below.

Macaulay wrote a magnificent poem about Horatius holding the bridge in ancient Rome to keep the Etruscans at bay and defend the city he loved so much. At the end of the battle, when the bridge had fallen behind him and his delaying task was successfully accomplished, Horatius deliberately dived into the River Tiber rather than surrender to Lars Porsena and his Etruscan horde. For a long, long moment there was no sign of the gallant Roman hero, and in Macaulay's words:

EXAMPLES OF HAUNTINGS

No sound of joy or sorrow
Was heard from either bank,
But friends and foes in dumb surprise,
With parted lips and straining eyes,
Stood gazing where he sank.

Horatius, despite his wounds and the weight of his armour, made it safely back to Rome where he was appropriately rewarded for saving his city.

Much the same thing happened with Sir Henry Wintour. Like Horatius centuries before him, Wintour and his horse disappeared beneath the deep brown waters of the river. Unlike Horatius, however, from that day to this no one knows for certain what became of Wintour. Was he somehow trapped by his horse falling on him on the riverbed and drowned at the point where he had leapt in? No substantive evidence either of his body being found, or of his survival and reappearance after Charles II came to power, has ever been put forward. Did Wintour's wild leap generate such an explosion of emotion that it etched itself into the soil and stone of the riverbanks and bed? Is it Sir Henry's restless ghost that reportedly makes things leap about occasionally in the bar of the Anchor Inn, as he once leapt to his death not far away? A good inn would be an irresistible attraction to a good, hard-riding, hard-drinking cavalier hero.

Another candidate was a wonderful old character named Billy Budd, who lived in a cave in the woods less than a mile from the old Anchor Inn. The cave came to be known as Billy Budd's Hole. He earned a few coppers by playing his penny whistle in the yard outside the inn, and good-natured staff, as well as kind-hearted visitors, would throw a few coins into his cap from time to time. Billy became such a landmark in the 1950s that regular visitors who knew and loved Tintern and frequently returned to it would ask about him if he were not there. Old age and illness finally forced him into a nursing home. Could it be the restless ghost of Billy Budd that causes some of the paranormal disturbances in and around the inn?

There is one more strange event connected to the old Anchor Inn at Tintern. In 1996, Grantley James produced an outstanding guidebook to the area, which was launched on 6 June. All hell broke loose in the sky at around seven that evening in the form of a singularly violent and destructive storm. When the thunder, lightning, and rain were at their worst, the east wing of the Abbey was struck by lightning and two or three tonnes of stone were dislodged and hit the ground like a bomb. More lightning struck the Anchor Inn, knocking out the electronic tills, the telephones, and all the lights. If the spirits in and around the inn at Tintern are as evil and vindictive as some psychical researchers suggest, then that storm — remarkably similar to the one that frightened the workmen when they uncovered the skeletons centuries before — may possibly be regarded as a warning that the ghosts were angry because of the depth and accuracy of Grantley James's work.

A London inn known as the Guardsman during the reign of George IV, but now called the Grenadier, has also had its share of reported hauntings. An old story suggests that the Grenadier, which is in Wilton Row, was once part of the old Knightsbridge Barracks. Some of Wellington's officers were said to have been billeted there and the Duke himself, it was alleged, often attended for a game of cards. The legend of a tragic death is centred on the small, panelled card room that is preserved more or less in its original state. Reportedly, at the beginning of the nineteenth century, one of the officers billeted in the Guardsman was caught cheating at cards. The others decided that he deserved a sound thrashing for letting them down in this way, and during the course of it he died. No ghost has ever made its presence known visibly at the Grenadier, but there are so many records of unexplained minor poltergeist-type happenings that it certainly seems as if *something* preternatural is lurking in this old inn. Electric lights switch on and off for no apparent reason, small objects move — apparently of their own volition — from one room to another. Electric light bulbs have been observed to turn in their sockets and then float to the floor slowly and remain intact. Other Wilton Row residents whose homes are close to the Grenadier have also reported that electric lights and water taps have been turned on and off without any visible cause.

Tom Westward, who was at one time the head barman at the Grenadier, reported one of the strangest events in the whole history of anomalous phenomena associated with the inn. It was during lunch break and Tom was sitting with another staff member when he suddenly noticed what could only be described as a disembodied wisp of smoke. It was apparently emerging from beneath a shelf near the door. Tom's first conclusion was that a customer had left a burning cigarette end there, and he inspected the area carefully but found nothing. It was as if the wisp of smoke had no origin.

Some while after Tom first saw the disembodied wisp of smoke phenomenon, an inspector from the brewery visited the Grenadier. He was standing approximately where Tom had seen the smoke previously. Suddenly the inspector winced and withdrew his arm as though it had been stung. There was a small round burn on his skin about the size of a cigarette end. It might, of course, simply have been an insect bite, but at the very least it was an extraordinary coincidence.

A number of the famous stately homes of Britain have their fair share of reports of strange supernatural happenings. One well-known and well-authenticated example is Bisham Abbey, not far from Marlow in Buckinghamshire. It is actually a fine Tudor house built on the site of an old abbey. The building that is there today was originally a gift from Henry VIII to one of his queens, Anne of Cleves. When she died, the house became the property of Sir Thomas Hoby. During the reign of Queen Mary Tudor, Thomas Hoby was the official guardian to young Princess Elizabeth (later Queen Elizabeth I). Whether it was through enlightened self-interest or natural kindness, Sir Thomas was a caring, kindly, and thoughtful guardian. When turbulent Tudor politics performed one of their many dramatic somersaults and Elizabeth became queen, she made Sir Thomas her ambassador to France.

His old home at Bisham Abbey appears to be haunted by his wife, Lady Elizabeth Hoby. Like Shakespeare's Lady Macbeth, the spirit of Lady Hoby is reported to wander through the house and grounds washing blood from her hands in a bowl that floats mysteriously just ahead of her. Other witnesses have seen her in a boat on the Thames, which laps against the lawns of Bisham Abbey. Visitors staying at Bisham have been awoken in the early hours of the morning by the sound of feet moving along corridors that are no longer there. At other times, witnesses have reported hearing desperately sad weeping. Those who have seen the spectre of Bisham Abbey have had no difficulty at all in recognising her as Lady Elizabeth Hoby, as there is an old family portrait of her still hanging in the great hall. In the portrait her face and hands are significantly white and she wears the wimple, weeds, and coif traditionally associated with a knight's widow in Tudor times.

It is particularly odd that when Elizabeth Hoby's ghostly form appears it is almost as though she had become a photographic negative. (Could there be a clue here to the strange negative appearance of the Turin Shroud?) The face and hands of the Hoby apparition are dark, and her black dress comes out as a startling, almost luminous, white.

Admiral Vansittart owned Bisham Abbey as the nineteenth century drew to its close. The gritty old sea dog had never believed in anything supernatural until the night that he saw Lady Hoby. It appears that he had stayed up until the early hours of the morning in an intensely absorbing game of chess with his brother. They finally finished their game, and the Admiral's brother went off to his bedroom. Vansittart was alone beside Elizabeth Hoby's gaunt portrait in the great hall. He felt that someone was standing immediately behind him. Being a stalwart serviceman and prepared to tackle anything, Vansittart spun around defensively, thinking an attacker had crept into Bisham Abbey. It was no burglar that he saw. The strange phantom of Elizabeth Hoby was standing immediately behind him. With great presence of mind Vansittart looked up at her portrait as if to confirm that the weird female form that he could see was in fact Lady Hoby. Even his calm resilience and great presence of mind almost deserted him then: *the frame where her portrait should have been was empty.* A moment later everything was back to normal, but Vansittart was convinced beyond a shadow of doubt that he had seen someone, or something, which his thorough-going, pragmatic common sense was at a loss to explain.

During her life, Lady Hoby was a close companion of Queen Elizabeth I. Sir Thomas Hoby's widow had a formidable intellect. She could compose poetry in Latin as fluently as she could in English, and she was the author of several books on religion. Her great fault, tragically, was her driving ambition to make her children as scholarly as she was herself. No matter how bright they were or how much they achieved she wanted more from them. Sadly, her youngest son, William, was not in the same academic league as his over-ambitious mother. One version of the Hoby tragedy suggests that William died young because of brain disease, brought on by his mother's repeated blows to his head when she was dissatisfied with his work.

During the first half of the nineteenth century, workmen carrying out alterations and repairs at Bisham Abbey reportedly found some old Elizabethan schoolbooks that had been concealed underneath a Tudor window shutter. The books had been wedged between the joists and the skirting boards. A number of them were said to contain exercises written in a very untidy childish hand, and the name William Hoby was written on the front covers. Again, according to these reports, several of the pages were blotted with ink and tear stains.

This discovery may have been the stimulus for another version of little William Hoby's tragic death, and Lady Elizabeth's unending grief. According to this version, on an occasion when William's work was worse than usual, his mother lost her temper completely. She slapped him around the head viciously several times and locked him into a cupboard with his book and strict instructions to rewrite what she considered to be the hopelessly unsatisfactory work.

According to the story, an urgent message then arrived from Queen Elizabeth I, who wanted to see Lady Hoby at once. She left in a great rush and forgot to tell the servants that William was locked in the cupboard. When she finally returned from the palace, the boy was dead, slumped across the schoolbooks that had made his short life such hell. It is said that Elizabeth Hoby could never forgive herself for the way she had treated William, and his death was on her conscience until her own death at the end of the first decade of the seventeenth century. Her restless spirit has allegedly haunted Bisham Abbey ever since.

Gawsworth Hall is possibly connected with Shakespeare and the mystery of the Dark Lady of the *Sonnets*. Frank Harris, the notorious nineteenth-century editor and drama critic, wrote an interesting study entitled "Women of Shakespeare." Harris's main thesis was that Shakespeare's life was shaped by his mother, wife, mistress, and daughter. Harris claims to detect all four of them in Shakespeare's characters. According to Harris's theory, Mary Fitton was written in as Cleopatra. In act 3, scene 1, line 196 of *Love's Labour Lost* there is an intriguing reference to the "wanton with a velvet brow." According to Harris's theory this character is identical to the Dark Lady of the *Sonnets*, whom he also believes to have been Mary Fitton. The main theme of Harris's study is that it was his relationship with Mary Fitton that inspired Shakespeare to reach the heights of tragic genius that he achieved. Vivacious and sexually adventurous, Mary is not the only ghost of Gawsworth Hall, but she is one of the most spirited and lively supernatural characters associated with it.

The Hall itself stands about five miles from Macclesfield in Cheshire. The de Orrebby family lived there in the middle of the twelfth century. The Fighting Fittons, as they were known, occupied Gawsworth from 1316 to 1622, and Shakespeare's beloved Mary was one of these. Her father was very influential at Court and almost certainly this led to her appointment as one of Queen Elizabeth's maids of honour in 1596.

Sir Robert Cecil, who might well have earned a disreputable living as a treacherous underworld supergrass had he not been lucky enough to be a member of the aristocracy, took it upon himself to run bleating to Queen Elizabeth that the beautiful, and promiscuous, Mary was expecting a child by her then lover, the Earl of Pembroke. Queen Elizabeth practically blew a blood vessel and sent them both to the Tower. Fortunately Mary survived the ordeal and went on to be Shakespeare's inspiration — according to Frank Harris, at least. Mary's attractive and vivacious spirit, according to various witnesses, haunts not only Gawsworth Hall but also the ancient rectory nearby.

A number of earnest researchers once tried to find out whether Mary was really buried in the old church at Gawsworth. They managed to find a coffin from the right period secured with leather straps on which an intricate floral design could still be seen. It seems significant that this same floral design is featured in two or three portraits of the bright-eyed and nubile Mary. The attractive, life-like, dark-haired, female spectre reported on numerous occasions at Gawsworth is generally believed to be her. Interesting and prominent as she is among the Gawsworth Hall ghosts, Mary is by no means unique there.

At the beginning of the eighteenth century, the Duke of Hamilton fought a duel with Lord Mohun that proved fatal for both duellists. Their ghosts are said to haunt Gawsworth. And a certain Samuel Johnson — who had the unenviable nickname of "Maggotty" — arranged to be buried in a local wood that has borne his name ever since: Maggotty Johnson's Wood. The violin that he used to play, which dates from the late eighteenth century, still has a place of honour in the dining room at Gawsworth.

As recently as 1971, Mrs. Monica Richards, who lived at the Hall then, was often aware of the smell of incense percolating through the house. It was particularly noticeable in her bedroom, which was very close to an old "priest's hole." This particular priest's hole has an oratory with a cupboard and an escape route connecting them both to the cellars of Gawsworth Hall. Almost a century ago, a skeleton — believed to be that of a Catholic priest — was discovered behind the oratory cupboard. The skeleton was given decent burial in the adjacent churchyard, but its identity was never satisfactorily or definitively established.

A report from the village of Maisemore, which is less than five miles from Gloucester, concerns a very strange and apparently purposeful ghost — and a benign one. Up until the middle of the twentieth century, and a little after, the old vicarage of Maisemore was concealed from the road by a belt of tall trees. A large old kitchen, which was a kind of large basement to the rectory, had not been used since Victorian times. Curious sounds were said to emanate from it — sounds that gave the impression that people were walking about inside it. The incumbent went down to investigate and to his amazement observed the ghost of a monk standing in the centre of the old kitchen floor. The vicar was a kindly man as well as a courageous one; he asked the monk if there was anything he could do to help him, or if he had a spiritual problem of some kind. The figure looked extremely sad and woebegone but vanished without answering the priest's question. On a number of later occasions the vicar saw the curious spectral monk again. It never answered his questions, but always looked morose and melancholy. Archaeologists and historians reported that there were indications that a monastery might once have existed in Maisemore — but little or nothing remained of it. On one of his frequent visits to the old, disused basement kitchen the vicar noticed that the floor did not seem to be quite right. It was in fact bending to a significant degree.

The church architects arranged for builders to come in and examine the floor, which was duly taken up so that the area beneath it could be properly inspected with a view to putting things right. It then became clear that a huge water tank, which had perhaps been intended to supply the strangely designed old rectory, lay immediately below this basement kitchen. The kitchen was prevented from collapsing into it only by two sturdy beams that held up the entire floor. Probably because of the extremely damp conditions generated by the proximity of the old water tank both beams had practically rotted through. A few weeks more and the entire kitchen would have collapsed into the subterranean tank and might possibly have brought the rest of the house down with it! Those who were aware of the haunting, including the vicar, conjectured that the sad spectral monk had perhaps come to warn them.

DEATH

The collapse of supporting beams can be a major hazard in old buildings. At about the same time that the vicar of Maisemore was having problems with the beams holding up his basement kitchen, the authors were assisting their old friend Canon Noel Boston to do some renovation work on an ancient house that he had acquired (as an historian and antiquarian) at Buxton Lamas in Norfolk, England.

This wonderful old building had been converted in Victorian times into four or five terraced workmen's cottages. As a result, what had once been the Great Hall was split by a number of non-load-bearing partition walls — or so it seemed. Holding up the mighty roof of the old building was one huge beam that looked to those of us doing the renovations as if it ran the complete length. It was immensely strong, being some two or three feet square in cross-section. The renovating volunteers — including us — set about helping Canon Boston by knocking down the partition walls put up a century or more before to accommodate the Victorian estate workers. Unknown to any of us, at some period in the hall's Victorian history there had been a disastrous fire, which had burned its way *right through* the main supporting beam. Although most of the Victorian terrace cottage walls were non-load-bearing, serving merely as partitions, one was a vital piece of the support structure. It hid all trace of the point in the great ceiling beam where the fire had effectively cut it into two pieces. As long as that support wall held up the ends of the charred beam it was as structurally sound as it had been before the fire. When sledgehammers were applied to the wall that was holding up the charred, severed beam there was a creaking, grinding sound. We volunteer renovators looked up to see the two charred ends emerging from the wreckage of the support wall and moving slowly but relentlessly down towards the floor where we were standing — threatening to bring the roof in their train. It was indeed fortunate that among the equipment that the volunteers were using were a number of Acro-props. Two of these were thrust into place and wound upward with seconds to spare. The beam was safely supported again and the renovation work continued.

The emotional stresses and strains of war service may be partially responsible for generating the abnormal psychic energy that seems to be associated with some types of paranormal phenomena. RAF Bircham Newton, in Norfolk, holds particular memories for the authors. It is also the site of some strange and inexplicable events. In the early 1950s our friend Maurice Tooke was serving in the RAF at the Bircham Newton Base. He and co-author Lionel had been at school together at Swaffham in Norfolk and when Maurice had a weekend leave due, Lionel arranged to collect him on the pillion of his motorbike and take him home to Dereham, where they both lived.

It was a particularly foul day. At that time, long before the wearing of crash helmets became compulsory, most bikers of Lionel's generation wore ex-government flying helmets and goggles. There was no screen on the bike and the goggles were incapable of dealing with the heavy rain. Visibility was down to not more than five or ten yards. To get from Dereham to Bircham Newton it was necessary to go through Fakenham, which had heavy traffic and a busy marketplace. In order to save time Lionel detoured around Fakenham on a road he had not used before. Shoving the totally useless goggles up on his forehead out of the way, he shielded his eyes with his left hand and squinted between his gauntlet fingers in an effort to keep most of the rain out of his eyes. Through this restricted and obscured observation slit he suddenly saw the brick wall of a bridge looming up very close. There was a *very sharp* bend associated with that bridge. He made an instant decision that turned out to be the wrong one. It did not seem possible from his road angle that the bend could be quite as sharp as it actually was. He guessed that the wall he could see must be the *inside* one, or, from a biker's point of view travelling in that direction, the left hand kerb side wall of the bridge. It wasn't. It was the *outside wall!* Having sailed gracefully through the air for what seemed several yards, but was realistically only a few feet, Lionel's motorised aerial adventures ended with a resounding slap and squelch in the soft mud below the bridge. He was not hurt and the bike was still functional, but it was more that any one man — however powerful — could do to haul it out of the mud and water by himself.

After tugging and heaving in vain for several moments in the torrential rain, Lionel saw an Aldiss's furniture van making its way at a sensible speed over the quaint little humped-backed bridge situated on its vicious bend. The driver stopped and came down to the river to see what he could do to help. Between them they got the bike back onto the road. The rain was still pouring down as heavily as ever. As they parted company Lionel naturally thanked the driver profusely. He had a typical Norfolk man's sense of humour. "I nearly didn't stop," he said with a chuckle, "because I thought at first you'd taken it down there to wash it — and then as I looked out at the rain I thought to myself nobody would wash a bike on a day like this!"

But it is the Bircham Newton RAF camp, rather than the area of Fakenham known as Goggs's Mill, that is the centre of the paranormal activities. (The little humped-back bridge that led to the muddy motorcycle episode seemed once to have been part of an old watermill's river system that was no longer there, but the name Goggs's Mill still clung to it.) RAF Bircham Newton opened in 1916. It did excellent service until the end of World War I, and from 1919 onwards things slackened off considerably. During the 1930s, more up-to-date C-type hangars replaced the old World War I hangars. Under the control of Coastal Command, RAF Bircham Newton was equipped with Vildebeest torpedo-bombers, Wellingtons, Blenheims, and Avro Ansons. There were also some Hudsons there connected with 279 Air-Sea Rescue Squadron. The 415 Royal Canadian Air Force Squadron did arduous and gallant service from Bircham Newton and there were also a number of Hurricanes operating from there. Many fearless and carefree Canadian and Australian pilots flew from Bircham Newton alongside their British allies. When the war ended the station changed hands so that by October 1948 it was under the control of Technical Training Command. Servicemen and women frequently reported a spectral car full of celebrating airmen who were laughing and singing as it raced through the camp and crashed silently into the back of one of the huge hangars. A young woman serving with the WAAF allegedly committed suicide at the camp. Ghostly footsteps were frequently heard in the hut where it had happened. The steps approached one particular bed. Then came the sound of a body being pulled out and dragged out of the room and along the passage outside. One airforce woman reported that she had been awakened in the middle of the night by the touch of an icy hand. Two other off-duty airforce women were playing table tennis in a building at the Bircham Newton complex that was thoroughly secured and its doors locked. In spite of this they heard the unmistakable sound of heavy footsteps, as though someone had entered the building and was coming up the steps towards the room where they were playing. Shortly afterwards a message was received that a plane had crashed while trying to land near the airport. Only the pilot was aboard, and he was killed. Some of his personal belongings had been left in the locked building in a room close to the games area where the two women were playing. The dead pilot had lived at King's Lynn, not far from Bircham Newton, and he was duly buried in his hometown. If his flight had gone as planned he would have been flying over his home. The general impression was that the pilot had gone back after death to try to collect the equipment he had left at the camp.

The Construction Industry Training Board (CITB) took over Bircham Newton in 1962 when it closed as an RAF station. One of the first things that the CITB undertook was to make a training film, and the crew was working in what had once been the Officers' Mess. For no reason at all one of the extremely heavy lamps the film crew was using began to fall. One member of the crew was immediately in its path and if gravity had worked in the normal way the falling light could well have killed him. Miraculously it swerved away at the last moment, as though it had been pulled or pushed by an invisible force intent on saving his life.

Very close to the Officers' Mess at Bircham was a squash court dating back to World War I. Another strange episode took place there involving a different member of the film crew. Some years before, three members of the crew of an Avro Anson had been killed when it crashed not far from the Bircham Newton airfield. The three friends who made up its crew had all been enthusiastic squash players and had made a pact that if anything happened to any of them, they would all meet up at the squash court. Perhaps the strange phenomena that some witnesses reported from Bircham Newton RAF camp were connected with that grim final rendezvous of the crew of the crashed Avro Anson.

One of the most interesting reported hauntings concerns a pop group known as the Peter B's, named after its leader Peter Bardens. Back in the 1960s, when Peter was in his twenties, the group had just played a gig at Cobham and was driving in their van in the early hours of the morning. The night was clear but there was no moon. As they rounded a bend they caught sight of a pedestrian on the near side. The figure was walking towards them along the sidewalk but did not seem to be observing them. All four members of the group realised at once that *this was no normal human pedestrian*. It was much larger than a man and seemed to be surrounded by something like a luminous aura. The streetlights were not particularly bright and it did not seem possible that they could have produced the odd aura effect.

DEATH

The apparition had its arms parallel, hanging down by its sides and pointing outwards. It did not seem to be walking so much as gliding or drifting. It looked almost as though it was mounted on very smooth rollers, or a skateboard, and was being pulled or pushed by some invisible force. The witnesses in the pop group described it as yellowish-white tinged with grey. Three of them described the figure as having a very impressive face — looking like a human male aged between fifty and sixty. There was a very long, rather strange, garment — a bit like an overcoat — reaching down almost to the feet, almost like a shroud. Another member of the group described the face as old and vacant-looking — as though it was the face of a corpse. Another witness, the guitarist in the group, described the creature as resembling something out of an early Frankenstein film. Unlike his companions, he did not think that it was *necessarily* a ghost because there were a great many strange and weird "underground" people around at that time and he thought it might have been one of them.

It is interesting to note that Field Marshall Ligonier lies buried in Cobham. Jean Louis Ligonier was a French Huguenot who joined the British army early in the eighteenth century and rose to the rank of Field Marshall. He was a humane commander and treated his soldiers as human beings, as well as hardy fighting men. Ligonier lived to be almost ninety, and was above average height. There is a picture of him in the National Portrait Gallery. When the members of the group went to look at it, one thought there was some resemblance, another thought the likeness was striking, and the other two musicians did not feel able to comment either way.

Co-author Lionel is currently lead singer for a recording pop group called Big John Downes and The Amphibians. The authors know the group members well and work with them frequently. They are typical of pop-musicians and are not in the least inclined to be credulous or imaginative. The Peter B's, who encountered the strange apparition in Cobham, would have been similar types. It seems a good bet that they saw something paranormal that night.

Reports of hauntings come from every age and every country. The great Roman author Pliny the Younger, whose work bridged the first and second centuries A.D., records the story of a spacious Athenian home that remained unoccupied because it was allegedly haunted by the ghost of a repellent old man who moaned and rattled his chains as characteristically as Marley's ghost in Dickens's *Christmas Carol*. A number of courageous, if sceptical, young Greeks

Skeleton in chains: from ancient Greek records of hauntings.

volunteered to spend the night in the house but fled when the weird, moaning old spectre turned up. Even in the beautiful Greek climate the house began to crumble from neglect. Athenodorus, who was a Stoic, saw the place and decided it had the great virtue of solitude. The unbelievably low rent made it even more attractive to him. The honest landlord explained to Athenodorus that the rent was ridiculously low as he was unable to find a tenant because of the alleged haunting. According to Pliny's account, on the first night that Athenodorus spent in the house working on his book he was interrupted by the rattling of chains. A few moments later the ghost of the repellent old man appeared before him and beckoned with a bony finger.

A Stoic philosopher is not easily disturbed. Athenodorus simply waved one hand dismissively and carried on with his work. The spectre persisted in rattling its chains and making hideous noises until, rather wearily, Athenodorus followed him into the garden where the spectre vanished in the undergrowth. The philosopher marked the place with a small cairn of stones and went back to his room. The next morning Athenodorus went to consult the magistrates and a number of leading Athenians returned with him to the spot he had marked in the garden of the haunted house. On their instructions, slaves began to dig. A metre or so below the surface their spades encountered something curious. What they unearthed was a skeleton encumbered with rusting chains. On the orders of the Athenian magistrates these pathetic remains were interred with honour and dignity and the proper ceremonies, and the spectre never again disturbed the house.

Athenodorus was one of the greatest of the Stoic philosophers. The way in which he ignored the persistent ghost that was interrupting his writing was typical of the man.

Bettiscombe Manor in Dorset once belonged to Azariah Pinney, who went to live and work in the West Indies. John Frederick Pinney, the grandson of Azariah, came back to Bettiscombe accompanied by a friend from Africa who had once been a slave. After many years at Bettiscombe, Pinney's African friend asked whether John Frederick would send his body back to Africa to be buried among his own people when the time came. Pinney gave his word. Promises are fragile things, and, as the old aphorism goes, the road to hell is paved with good intentions. When his African friend finally died, Pinney did not send him home. Instead he was buried in the village churchyard close to the manor house. In the days and weeks following the burial, strange sounds, cries, and thuds plagued Bettiscombe Manor during the hours of darkness. With the power and influence that an eighteenth-century squire possessed, Pinney gave orders for his old African friend to be exhumed. The body was then stored in one of the lofts in the manor house, and the strange disturbances ceased immediately.

Slowly disintegrating over the years, most of the body disappeared *but the skull remained*. The lower jaw apparently vanished along with the rest of the corpse. There is a record from the middle of the nineteenth century that tells how the skull was shown to a visitor by a psychic housekeeper at Bettiscombe who believed that as long as it was there it protected the house and grounds from any *other* supernatural presence.

This is reminiscent of the great Zulu hero Umslopogaas in Rider Haggard's famous adventure novels set in Africa. When the unparalleled Zulu warrior finally dies of his wounds after an epic battle in which he was victorious, his body is covered in gold-leaf and set up in a place of honour to guard the city.

EXAMPLES OF HAUNTINGS

Strong local traditions associated the Bettiscombe skull with disasters in the area and especially disaster to the owners of the house if any attempt was made to move it. There are records of thunderstorms decimating crops when the skull was disturbed, and on other occasions livestock fell ill and died.

Not unexpectedly, there is also a totally different version — contradictory legends frequently spring from the same rootstock — which suggests that the skull is *much older* than the eighteenth century. One eminent pathologist who examined it gave his opinion that it was female, and that it was possibly prehistoric. If so, and if some ancient building originally occupied the site of the present Bettiscombe Manor, then it may have been the skull of a sacrificial victim.

Similar tales are attached to Wardley Hall, not far from Manchester. The skull at Wardley is said to be that of a Roman Catholic priest who was killed during the persecution of 1641. There is a tradition that it was displayed as a warning to Catholic sympathisers but was then spirited away to Wardley Hall and preserved there by a devout Catholic family. Over the years thoughtful occupants of the hall thought it would be more respectful to give it proper Christian burial, but whenever it was removed — so the stories go — there were storms or other local disasters, just as there were at Bettiscombe.

Renowned psychic investigator Eric Maple tells how one owner, desperate to be rid of it, threw the skull into a pond but that somehow it made its way back to Wardley Hall. This parallels one of the adventures attributed to the Bettiscombe skull, which was once buried under three metres of earth. The following day, however, according to this tradition, it had somehow worked its way back to the surface and lay gleaming yellow and white on top of the soil, as though asking to be taken back indoors.

Crossing the Atlantic, as the fearless, pioneering Samuel de Champlain did, it is possible to investigate some of the strangest Canadian mysteries. In July of 1609, as part of his second visit to Quebec, Champlain joined the Huron, Algonquin, and Montagnais nations as they set out to make war on the Iroquois. It amazed a brilliant soldier and adventurer like de Champlain that his indigenous Canadian friends — as he noted in his famous journal — slept peacefully beside their campfires in wartime without posting any sentries. His Amerindian companions did not bother with watchmen because of their absolute faith in the skills of their *pilotois* or medicine man. One of these accompanied each camping group of warriors and his function was to foresee the future and warn his soldier-companions if any peril or hazard was approaching.

When they reached Sorrel Rapids, Champlain made a detailed study of the way in which the *pilotois* worked his apparent magic. Part one consisted of the construction of a wigwam covered with beaver robes. The *pilotois* then took off all that he was wearing and lay flat on the ground inside the wigwam that he had just built. He then chanted the words of a secret spell or incantation to the earth. In Champlain's opinion, as he watched the *pilotois*, the man seemed to be trying to call up a powerful spirit: perhaps good, perhaps evil, perhaps elemental. The *pilotois*, like one of the priests of Baal in their frenzied contest with Elijah on Mount Carmel, gradually reached a climax of berserk screaming and writhing — springing suddenly to his feet, covered with sweat. While all this was taking place, the wigwam was vibrating inexplicably. Meanwhile, the warriors were squatting around it and were convinced that the shaking was due to the presence of strange spirits who were communicating with the ecstatic *pilotois*.

Champlain himself was not particularly impressed. He was tough, experienced, highly intelligent, and inclined towards cynicism and scepticism. In his opinion the *pilotois* was probably shaking the tent himself and the strange noises were the result of ventriloquism.

Father Paul Le Jeune was a Jesuit missionary working with the Huron tribe during the seventeenth century. Le Jeune and his fellow Jesuits left behind a number of highly significant and accurate reports — well up to the standard of those produced by contemporary scientific investigators into the paranormal. His work in Quebec began in 1632 and he stayed for almost eight years before going back to Paris. His Canadian work was continued by Gabriel Lalemant and Jean de Brébeuf. Le Jeune learned the Algonquin language and then went out with his Amerindian friends all through the harsh and hungry winter. He stayed in tents that were overcrowded and full of smoke but he felt that all of this was worth it if he could teach his Indian friends the truth of the Gospel, in which he believed so fervently. His main problem was the *pilotois* — the medicine man — who was apparently able to control the weird spirit forces that the Indians held in such awe.

EXAMPLES OF HAUNTINGS

Believing that the best form of defence is attack, Le Jeune set out to find how the *pilotois* performed what Le Jeune believed were tricks. Le Jeune was well educated and he understood the importance of careful objective observation. He was also a logical and rational thinker. Furthermore, he was not content to observe the magical practices from a distance. He did his best to gain the confidence of the *pilotois* and get as close as he could to the apparently supernatural events that focused on the medicine man. As a Jesuit, of course, Le Jeune had no doubt about the reality of the supernatural. He accepted Biblical miracles, dreams, and visions but as a staunch Catholic churchman he refused to accept that anything was valid outside what the church approved. Le Jeune naturally wanted to weaken or totally negate the *pilotois'* influence. He therefore approached all the medicine man's demonstrations with a maximum amount of scepticism in the same way that effective, contemporary investigators work. Le Jeune did his best to explain away as much as possible as mere coincidence, juggling, sleight of hand, ventriloquism, and simple fraud. The problem as he soon discovered was that although some of what he saw and heard could be explained in this way, there was a hard core of paranormal phenomena that stubbornly refused to succumb to even the most scrupulous and rigorous investigation. Being a devout Jesuit, as well as a man of reason and logic, Le Jeune was forced to "explain" the things he could not understand as the work of the Devil and his minions. In his report in *Relations* dated 1634, Le Jeune included a first-hand eyewitness account of a *pilotois* at work.

Le Jeune records that he watched a group of young men building a tent in the centre of a cabin. Six poles went into the ground in a circle, a large ring went over the top of the poles, and blankets completed the structure. The top was left open. There was enough room for five or six men to stand upright inside the structure, which was so high that a tall man would have been hard pressed to touch the top. As soon as the structure had been completed, all the fires were put out and the embers taken outside the cabin because the *pilotois* did not want any flames or glowing sparks to discourage the spirits, whom he called *Khichi-gouai*, from coming inside the structure.

One young man entered at floor level and then replaced the covering as soon as he was inside. It was important for the ceremony that there be no openings apart from the one at the top. As soon as

The shaking tent phenomenon and the Pilotois conducting
the strange ceremony.

he was inside, the young man began to groan and murmur quietly —
as if he was complaining about something. The tent began to shake,
very gently at first and then increasing in intensity.

The young man on the cabin floor started whistling in a strange
haunting tone — like the wind in distant mountains. The sound
seemed to be coming from a very long way away. The *pilotois* then
made a succession of odd noises, some like the hooting of owls, then
a strange singing and howling. The sounds changed in tone, volume,
and pitch, and odd syllables like "*ho — hi — gui*" and "*nioue*" were
recorded. Le Jeune was reminded of puppet masters whom he had
heard at fairs and exhibitions in France. According to Le Jeune the
shaking became much more vigorous and finally quite violent. The
Jesuit was surprised that the relatively flimsy edifice inside the cabin
did not shatter. He was even more surprised by the strength and
stamina that would be needed to continue the shaking at that level
for two or three hours. Le Jeune felt it would be beyond the strength
of most normal human beings — yet he could not bring himself to

admit that the force came from anywhere other than the hands and feet of the young Indian *pilotois*. An Indian who was standing beside Le Jeune outside the wigwam where the demonstration was taking place explained to him that the soul of the *pilotois* was now out of his body and that it had risen to the open top of the wigwam in order to rendezvous with the spirits whom the *pilotois* was summoning.

The voice of the medicine man grew louder, stronger — almost unbearably so. Le Jeune recognised the syllables, "*Aiasé, aiasé Manitou.*" There was a sudden exclamation of rapturous delight from the Amerindians in the circle around the wigwam and Le Jeune saw that they were all pointing to the top of the tent. He followed the direction of their gaze. A shower of sparks was issuing from the opening at the top of the wigwam. The Amerindian friend who was explaining everything to Le Jeune cried exultantly, "One of the *Khichi-gouai* has arrived. One of the *Khichi-gouai* has come to the summons of the *pilotois!*" Then they all began to call out, "*Tepouachi.*" With his knowledge of the language, Le Jeune interpreted this as meaning, "Go and call the others." Several of the men around the wigwam now began to dance; another beat loudly and rhythmically on a drum; the *pilotois* himself spoke in a voice that was harsh, strident, and totally different from the voice that he had used before.

The *pilotois* began by forecasting the death of his squaw before the end of the winter and his own survival. Le Jeune was unimpressed: the poor girl looked far from well, whereas the *pilotois* was well fed, muscular, and looked as if he enjoyed robust health.

Le Jeune also reported subsequently that he had heard reliable accounts from his Amerindian friends of actual levitation — when a *pilotois* rose to the top of the magical structure in which he worked.

In May 1637, Le Jeune was present at a fire-magic healing session. He recorded how stones were brought and made red hot in a specially prepared fire. Le Jeune says that he saw the medicine men taking these hot stones between their teeth while holding their hands behind their backs. He saw them carry the stones in this way for several feet. When those same stones were dropped on the ground from the sorcerers' mouths they were still hot enough to cause sparks to leap from the ground where they had landed.

According to Le Jeune's evidence the sick who were being healed by this strange display with the red hot stones were actually massaged with glowing cinders, during which they showed no evidence of pain or even discomfort.

DEATH

Father Pijart was one of the missionaries doing similar work with the Hurons and he also witnessed a spectacle involving hot stones. He even sent Le Jeune a specimen, one which had been carried red hot in the mouth of a *pilotois*. According to Le Jeune's evidence, although the stone showed marks of having been softened by fire it also seemed to bear the marks of human teeth.

Another fascinating description of the paranormal phenomenon of the tent comes from Alexander Henry. He was a trader in Canada at the time and recorded his adventures for posterity in *Travels and Adventures in the Years 1760-1776*. Alexander Henry was an Ojibway prisoner for some time. In 1764, however, a canoe arrived with messages from the chief Indian agent for the British in North America, Sir William Johnson. His messengers invited the Ojibway to send their representatives to a ceremonial meal with Johnson at Fort Niagara, situated on Lake Ontario. The purpose of the solemn feast was to arrange a peace treaty between the British and the Ojibway. Henry desperately wanted the Ojibway to accept the invitation and to allow him to go with their delegates so that he could make his way back to Montreal. The Ojibway, on the other hand, had great difficulty in deciding whether or not the offer to attend the feast was a trap. The Indians told Henry that they would summon Mikinak — their Great Turtle — who would decide the issue for them.

They explained to Henry that Mikinak was a master spirit and that they would proceed to build a house for him into which their medicine man would invite him, whereupon Mikinak would reveal whether the British were to be trusted or not. Henry begged to be allowed to attend the ceremony, and permission was granted.

For the ceremony the Ojibway warriors built a very large wigwam with a smaller one inside it. The frame was made of five poles, each of a different kind of wood. These poles were pretty substantial, being seven or eight inches in diameter, and the builders sank them two or three feet into the earth. They were secured at the top with a hoop. The skin covering was tied tightly to the poles with rawhide — except for one place where a flap was left to admit the *pilotois*. As soon as it was dark, he crept through this flap into the bottom of the tent. Immediately after he was inside, strange noises began and the whole structure shook vigorously. Henry thought some of the noises sounded like barking dogs or howling wolves, but there were also human cries of despair and pain. In addition, there was a certain amount of intelligible human speech that was evidently a language, but it was a language that neither Henry nor any of his Amerindian colleagues seemed to know.

The voice of Mikinak, their Great Turtle Spirit, when it finally came, was very low and soft — contrasting strangely with the wild animal sounds and the strange voice that they had heard before. When God spoke to the Hebrew prophet Elijah, He was not in the fire or the earthquake but in the "still small voice." After some strange chanting and a period of silence they heard the *pilotois* speaking in what was clearly recognisable as his own normal voice. "Mikinak is now here with us and will answer our questions."

In response to the questions that were put to it, the alleged Mikinak the Turtle Spirit answered that although there were many redcoats with guns, it would be safe for the Ojibway to visit Sir William Johnson, who would receive them as friends and load their canoes with gifts. Every man who went, said Mikinak, would return in safety to his people.

Alexander Henry was then allowed to pose a question. He brought a gift of tobacco, as was customary, and then asked if he would revisit his own country. The spirit answered, "Have no fear, white brother, you shall not be harmed and at last you will return to your friends and from them go in safety to your own land."

There is another extremely interesting record left by J. G. Kohl, a German anthropologist who carried out important research around Lake Superior. A witness told Kohl that thirty years before the anthropologist's visit he had been to see a shaking tent ceremony performed by a *jossakid*, another name for the *pilotois*. The tent shook just as on other occasions and two voices passed on the messages, one from the base and the other from the open end at the top. It sounded almost as if there were two individuals present — although only the one *jossakid* was inside the tent. It could, said the witness, have been very clever ventriloquism, or a genuine spiritualist medium using a guide as was the practice in Victorian séances — and one that is still used in our day.

Thirty years after the event, the man who gave Kohl the information came across the *jossakid* again. The man had been converted to Christianity and had totally abandoned the old pagan magic that he had used in the past. By the time Kohl's informant found him the old Indian was terminally ill. Kohl's informant asked him if he remembered the strange magical performance that he had given thirty years before. He made the point to the old *jossakid* that now that he was dying, especially now that he had become a Christian, he could tell the truth about the method by which the trick in the wigwam-that-shook was accomplished.

"I will tell you the truth," said the old Amerindian. "I did not deceive you and I did not move the tent. What I did and what you saw were real. I said nothing except those things that the spirits told me. I could hear them plainly. The top of the tent was filled with them." This was not the only deathbed corroboration of the truth and validity of the strange shaking-tent phenomena. Wan-Chus-Co had also been a medicine man when he was young and like the *jossakid* also become a Christian some ten or twelve years before his death. When he spoke to Henry R. Schoolcraft he made exactly the same point as the old *jossakid* whose evidence had come second-hand to Kohl the anthropologist. Wan-Chus-Co said that when he was a *pilotois* or *jossakid* he would beat the drum and begin chanting, then he could physically feel the presence of the *manitous*, or spirits, as he thought of them. Although unable to see them he knew that they were there. It was their power, he believed, conducted by currents of air spinning within the tent — almost like a miniature hurricane, tornado, or whirlwind — that made the thing shake and move. Wan-Chus-Co also spoke to another interested researcher named W. M. Johnson. He did his best to explain that in his pagan days he had genuinely communicated with spirits or paranormal beings of some kind, who acted on him and through him and told him the things that he then passed on to his audience.

Fascinated by our research into all these shaking-tent reports, and looking in principle for rational, scientific explanations, wherever possible, we consulted two top-flight professional sound engineers who are currently working at the sharp end of binaural recording technique development.

They were as interested in the shaking-tent problem as we were, and discussed with us how it might have been accomplished by natural means. They explained that sound can be *focused* in much the same way that light waves behave in the presence of a lens. They considered that, under certain circumstances, sound would move in unusual and unexpected ways. If the air near the ground, for example, where the *pilotois* was lying, was colder than the air above it, that might account for some unusual sound effects. They also pointed out that sounds of different frequencies travel at different speeds. Might this have accounted for the high-pitched noises in the vicinity of the wigwam seeming to come from one zone, while the lower, bestial, growling sounds came from another?

Our sound engineers also explained to us that sound tends to follow the shapes of surfaces: the Whispering Gallery at St. Paul's Cathedral in London is a prime example of this. Sound runs around some objects in much the same way that water follows the shape of your hands when you're washing them.

The presence of *tightly stretched* skins over the wigwam frame also interested the sound engineers. They felt that the vibrations might have been sustained by resonance, which would have been easy enough to maintain once the right frequency to shake the poles in the first place had been established. This all sounded reasonable and possible to us, but some of the early eyewitness accounts remain very difficult to explain.

For example, a famous female *pilotois* named The Cloud Woman with Blue Robes also gave evidence to Schoolcraft. Her evidence also supported the genuine nature of the shaking-tent phenomenon. The Cloud Woman with Blue Robes certainly believed that it was the force of the spirits that made the tent shake, and she also believed that it was the voices of the spirits that she passed on to those who came to listen to her.

Cecil Denny was a member of the North-West Mounted Police. He was as sensible, efficient, and fearless as any other officer in that outstanding force. He was camping by the bank of the Red Deer River not far from a Blackfoot Indian camp when he had an opportunity to witness a shaking-tent ceremony for himself. Denny watched with proper detachment and objectivity. The tent shook as inexplicably as on all the previous occasions when witnesses gave their reports of that anomalous phenomenon. Although it is now extremely rare and almost impossible to witness the shaking-tent ceremonies, they were still being conducted during the twentieth century. Records of the ceremony go back for almost four hundred years and provide enough data for a worthwhile analysis. First, the tent undoubtedly shakes and the movements range from a light vibration to shaking of great vigour and duration that is well beyond the power of human muscle to maintain for long. Secondly, on most occasions the medicine man is securely tied. Thirdly, there are incantations accompanied by drumming and rattling. Voices that appear to be different are heard:

some sound human, others sound like the voices of wild beasts. Fourthly, fiery sparks are frequently seen coming from the top of the tent. Immediately after the sparks have been sighted the prophecy and divination begins. The *pilotois* are of the opinion that the sparks themselves are the spirits, a manifestation of the spirits, or, in some strange way, they *contain* the spirits.

This can be thought of as analogous to the idea of what a real personality is. A human being is wrapped in skin that makes him or her visible to the outside world. The personality inside that skin is partly physical in terms of muscle, bone, and organs and is also partly intellectual and spiritual. Some *pilotois* would suggest that the sparks are the equivalent of the skin — the outward appearance of the spirit manifestations. Others would argue the sparks are the spirits themselves.

The messages are the fifth part of the proceedings and these bear a close resemblance to the messages of the Victorian *séance* room. The *pilotois,* or whoever is giving the tent demonstration, proclaims that the spirits are present; sometimes he says that he is going away to fetch them or to consult with them in some other realm, some kind of spirit kingdom.

Occasionally the demonstrator will claim that he is sending someone else to consult them and to bring back messages. Perplexingly, many of the messages received appear to be relatively trivial. They are surprisingly similar to normal human conversation: there is news or advice about hunting or fishing; there are neighbourly comments on whether friends and relatives are well or injured, healthy or sick. The weather is a popular topic, as is a trip or journey.

From divinations about health and sickness, wholeness or injury, the subject of healing comes up as the sixth major common denominator of the shaking-tent phenomenon. In cases of spiritual or faith healing there is much discussion about the extent to which hypnotism or suggestion is involved. The most scientific of medical researchers and clinicians would readily admit that psychological factors play a very significant role in physical health. Connections between stress, anxiety, and illness are well known. An individual's positive belief in his or her own health, strength, energy, and longevity tends to be a remarkably powerful, self-fulfilling prophecy — and massive self-confidence almost invariably leads to major success. Additionally, all these positive factors seem to be reflected in robust physical health and practically inexhaustible stamina.

EXAMPLES OF HAUNTINGS

If the patient is convinced that the *pilotois* or medicine man in the shaking-tent is truly able to summon and receive assistance from powerful spirits who are benign and willing to help, then the patient is likely to show a dramatic improvement.

Several sceptics and cynics have approached the tent phenomenon with a critical attitude. They claim that the shaking has to be the result of some kind of trickery — although none has ever been able to explain it satisfactorily or to demonstrate how it is done. Critics have also suggested that the so-called fiery sparks are either entirely imaginary, or are produced by a hidden tobacco pipe that the *pilotois* has somehow smuggled into the tent.

Others have "explained" the sparks as a strange kind of electrical discharge in the same category as St. Elmo's Fire — or even very minor forms of ball lightning — although there is, of course, a marked difference between those two forms of abnormal electrical illumination.

Critics again attempt to dismiss the strange voices as skilful ventriloquism, but is must be said in defence of the *pilotois* that the level of skill required to produce the vocal phenomena that have been reported would enable him to earn an enviable salary in any major variety theatre.

It is also significant that many of those to whom messages have been given — even if those messages are homely and almost mundane — have confirmed that they have proved remarkably *accurate*. Other critics have suggested that the *apparent* shaking of the tent — if it is not a trick performed by the *pilotois* — is due to mass hallucination, suggestion, or some form of group hypnosis. The idea of collective hallucination is itself open to pointed question.

It was the highly intelligent Sir William Crookes who once said, "The supposition that there is a sort of mania or delirium that suddenly attacks a whole roomful of intelligent persons who are quite sane elsewhere, and who all concur, to the minutest particulars, in the detail of the occurrences of which they suppose themselves to be witnesses, seems to my mind more incredible than even the facts which they attest." Professor Hans Driesch of Leipzig is also on record as saying, "I admit that a single person investigating so-called psychic phenomena can fall victim to hallucination caused by auto-suggestion. But this possibility appears to me excluded in the case of observation by several persons."

DEATH

It may, therefore, be reasonable to conclude that the extraordinary shaking-tent phenomena can safely be added to the mountain of evidence for the existence of a paranormal, spirit universe in which human souls or spirits survive.

Professor Irving Hallowell has witnessed tent-shaking phenomena for himself and has come up with a very interesting theory: in his opinion they are neither deliberate trickery nor supernormal. Hallowell suggests that the *pilotois* of the Saulteaux nation found themselves occupying a role filled with social expectations very similar to the role of the prima donna, poet, or artistic genius in our own society. The man becomes literally inspired and capable of a performance that seems to exceed the normal, *simply by virtue of the sociological expectations directed towards him* and in which he himself participates. The powers are *believed* to be his — and he *believes* that he possesses them.

Another very strange Canadian case was investigated and reported by the famous nineteenth-century artist Percy Woodcock, who lived at Waterniche in Brockville, Ontario. He became a full member of the Royal Canadian Academy in his early forties in 1889. As well as his considerable artistic talents, Woodcock was keenly interested in investigating psychic phenomena. Up on the north side of the Ottawa River, not far from Shawville in Quebec, lived George Dagg. He and his wife Susan had two children, four-year-old Susan and two-year-old Johnny. They decided that it would be a good idea — useful as well as kindly — to adopt an older child from one of the orphanages, so that she could help Mrs. Dagg with the housework and to look after the two young ones.

Dinah Burden McLean was a Scots girl who had recently arrived in Canada and been placed in the orphanage at Belleville, Ontario. Dinah was a few months short of her twelfth birthday when she went to live with the Daggs, and the paranormal occurrences seemed to begin.

When Woodcock heard some of the accounts of the strange events that were allegedly taking place in the Dagg household, he travelled over to Shawville in November of 1889 and then went out some seven or eight miles to the Daggs' farmhouse. As Woodcock described it the building was a single-storey log house with a storage shed at the rear and a small attic at the top. In his opinion the Daggs were ordinary, hardworking, intelligent farm people. He had no reason at all to doubt their honesty or integrity. He was welcomed because many sightseers had visited them over the past few weeks.

They explained to him that they did not really expect any phenomena would take place as Dinah — who seemed to be the centre of the activity — had gone over to see Grandfather Dagg, who lived about three miles away. George and Susan had already noted that when Dinah was not in the house nothing happened. Woodcock was very disappointed. He had undertaken a long journey in the hope of seeing some unusual psychic events. The Daggs felt sorry for him and sent a message to Grandfather Dagg asking him to send Dinah back on the following day. This gave Woodcock an opportunity to have a long talk with the Daggs and to record the experiences that they reported to him. As an artist Percy Woodcock revelled in detail. He was keenly observant and this characteristic approach led him to make lengthy and careful notes of all the events that were reported to him by the Daggs, as well as by their friends and neighbours in the vicinity whom he was able to interview.

Woodcock took particular care over preparing his notes as he had contracted to write an article about the events for the *Brockville Recorder and Times*. The story that George Dagg related to Woodcock began several weeks previously. He recalled distinctly that in mid-September he had given his wife a five dollar bill and a two dollar bill and she had put them carefully in the drawer of their desk. Several local farmers who were as kind-hearted and generous as the Daggs gave a few odd-jobs to a young orphan lad called Dean. It was the Daggs' turn to provide him with accommodation and food in return for some light chores.

Dean was staying in their attic. He got up early and started to light the cooking stove fire for Mrs. Dagg. According to Dean, as he got down low on the floor to attend to the fire he spotted a five dollar bill which, being an honest lad, he took to Mr. Dagg and told him where he had found it. Dagg checked the desk and found both the two dollar and five dollar bill were no longer there. He sent the boy out on an errand, then went and checked the attic. The two dollar bill was in Dean's bed.

It seemed obvious to the Daggs that Dean must have taken them, although they were totally at a loss to explain why he had then claimed to have found the five dollar bill under the stove. The next problem was rather more serious. Excrement had been taken from the outside toilet and scattered about indoors. Criminologists and psychologists who specialise in the analysis of deviant behaviour are all too well aware that it is characteristic of a significant number of burglars to leave excrement at the sight of their crime — almost, in a way, like an animal marking out its territory.

Experienced police officers tend to refer to it as the criminal's "trademark." When accused of the crime, Dean denied it vehemently but Dagg took him to a local magistrate and formally charged him with stealing the two dollar bill. While they were away, more excrement was scattered all over the house. It was perfectly obvious that Dean — who was at this time appearing in front of the magistrate — could have had nothing at all to do with the subsequent problem.

Matters became considerably worse. Milk containers were tipped out, crockery was broken, and a quantity of water was thrown over Mrs. Dagg when there did not seem to be any possible local cause. While George was away, his father, John, and his wife came to stay with Susan and the children. While they were there a great many of the window-panes were broken. Whatever it was that was causing the disturbance then turned its attention to the children's hair. Dinah's long braided pigtail was practically severed, and young John had his hair cut crudely and painfully.

On his return, George went to consult Mrs. Barnes, who lived at Plum Hollow and was generally regarded as a source of folklore and wisdom about the paranormal. "Wise-woman" Barnes told Dagg that in her opinion a woman, a girl, and a boy were involved in launching black magic against him. Dinah was convinced that she could see a huge, dangerous, dark thing dragging the bedclothes away. Grandmother Dagg was nearby, and although she treated the girl helpfully and sympathetically all she could see was that the bedclothes seemed to be lifted into the air as if by an invisible hand.

The next piece of evidence was augmented by a young neighbour named Arthur Smart, who was visiting the Dagg family at the time Dinah thought she could see the large dark object. Grandmother Dagg, like Mrs. Barnes of Plum Hollow, was reasonably well-versed in folklore. She went to fetch a whip, gave it to Dinah, and told her that if she struck at the evil thing she thought she could see, it would be driven away. Arthur was watching the performance and told Dinah not to be afraid but to strike hard at the tormentor that only she could see. All three of them heard a high-pitched shriek that they later described as similar to the squeaking and squealing of a pig. Dinah put the whip down.

EXAMPLES OF HAUNTINGS

"It's gone," she said. Sometime later a message was found on a piece of paper stuck on the wall. The words were, "You gave me fifteen cats." The reference was apparently to the cat-o'-nine-tails that had been used for punishment for many years. The legend behind the nine tails was that nine, three times three, was a triple holy number, like the Holy Trinity, and a whipping with this "sacred" instrument was intended to drive out evil from the criminal or heretic being attended to.

Four-year-old Mary later said she could see the weird, dangerous haunter. She described it as being roughly human in size but having a head with horns, similar to a cow's head, and cloven hooves. The little girl said she saw it standing by the front door. When she saw it again it said to her, "Little girl, would you like to go to Hell with me?"

After this episode, a local minister named Horner was summoned. He was unable to attend but his brother duly went to help them. The brother asked for a Bible and then began to say some prayers with the family. During these prayers the Bible moved — apparently of its own accord — from the chair where he had placed it. It was found a few moments later in the oven. The minister's brother was unable to believe his eyes when, in addition to the movement of the Bible, an inkstand flew from the table to the shed outside — apparently with no visible means of support.

On another occasion, Grandmother Dagg was carrying a bottle of vinegar and remarked, "I daren't put it down in case the goblin breaks it." Even as she spoke a potato flew through the air — apparently without any normal physical cause — and struck her hand.

John Quinn, one of their neighbours, was carrying a halter when he called to see them. He put it down while he was talking and when he went to retrieve it as he left, *it was gone*. A few moments later, while he stood in puzzled conversation with four or five members of the Dagg family, there was a whistling sound in the air and the halter that had vanished fell in the middle of the group. But worse was to come.

Whatever strange presence was troubling the Daggs now began to speak. Like the evil force in *The Exorcist*, the words uttered by the strange voice haunting the Dagg household were usually obscene and full of crudely expressed sexual innuendoes directed towards Dinah. At the end of Woodcock's investigation, a statement was obtained, signed by seventeen local people — including the Dagg family — who had some experience of the strange entity and its voice to report.

DEATH

There may perhaps be a curious parallel between the talking poltergeist that haunted the Dagg family and Gef, the strange "talking mongoose" that haunted Doarlish Cashen, not far from Cashen's Gap on the Isle of Man, in the following century. Doarlish Cashen was well over 200 metres up the western heights, bleak and isolated. The nearest neighbours were out of sight and over a mile away. The family with the mysterious talking mongoose consisted of James Irving, a sixty-year-old retired commercial traveller, who did not make much money from his farm, his rather grim, prim wife, Margaret, and their teenaged daughter, Voirrey, who was the one most closely associated with the weird creature called Gef. The talking mongoose might just possibly have existed in a real, objective sense: it might equally well have been a product of Voirrey's restless, teenaged mind. It could have been a poltergeist. It could have been a harmless deception created in the hope of bringing a little interest (and some much wanted fame and money?) into the boring, rural life of the Irvings.

Reports of strange creatures like Gef and ghostly hauntings of various types are not enough in themselves to provide irrefutable evidence of an alleged spirit world. Is there a case for a mysterious zone in which departed human souls share their psychic existence with curious elemental spirits and strange entities like Gef and the talking poltergeist that tormented the Dagg family?

Co-author Patricia Fanthorpe with a re-enactment warrior in eleventh century costume at haunted Battle Abbey, England.

Phantom armies also have an important place in paranormal research. On 23 June 1744, Dan Stricket, who was one of John Wren's servants at Wilton Hall, saw a phantom army riding up over Souterfell Hill in Cumberland in the British Lake District. He ran to fetch Wren, who also witnessed the unearthly soldiers, as did every cottager for miles around.

Haunted Battle Abbey, near Hastings, England.

Haunted Battle Abbey, near Hastings, England.

The spot where Harold, the Anglo-Saxon king, died in 1066.
Does he still haunt the site?

The battlefield at Hastings, where William the Norman defeated King Harold of Anglo-Saxon England, is also a haunted site. After his grimly won victory, William erected an abbey with its high altar marking the exact spot where Harold fell. Strange apparitions are said to haunt that unique battle site. Thousands of miles to the west, an American Civil War skirmish that took place in Okaloosa County, near the Yellow River on the Alabama-Florida line, is still re-enacted.

When all the cases are taken together, analysed, and evaluated the weight of evidence would seem to support and reinforce the *very strong probability* of human survival of death.

CHAPTER FOUR
NEAR-DEATH EXPERIENCES

Cases of near-death experiences and detailed reports by those who have gone through them seem to indicate the survival of a spiritual body or non-physical soul, a mind that is able to experience things and — when recovery or resuscitation takes place — is able to report what it has seen. The border between life and death is not quite as clear-cut and absolute as was once thought. General medical opinion at one time was that if the brain cells were deprived of oxygen for five or six minutes irreparable damage would occur. An excellent article by Rob Hughes in the *Sunday Times Magazine* of 16 June 1985, entitled "Life after Drowning," included a report from Flight Surgeon Martin J. Nemiroff. On 4 September 1983, the body of Misty Dawn Densmore was rescued from icy waters near the Alaskan coast. Her mother, who had been involved in a boating disaster with three-year-old Misty, described how the toddler had ceased breathing and turned blue almost half-an-hour before the helicopter rescue team saved them. Dr. Nemiroff reported that the child was in full cardiac arrest: her eye pupils were dilated, her limbs were blue and chilled, and he could not detect a heartbeat. He would have been ready to write her off as dead except for the fact that he himself had a much-loved three-year-old child in his own family. Dr. Nemiroff extracted a litre of water from Misty's lungs and then worked tirelessly on mouth-to-mouth resuscitation. Almost unbelievably, after practically three-quarters of an hour of being to all intents and purposes dead, the little girl responded and made a complete recovery. It is difficult to explain quite how the medical miracle happened for Misty, but Dr. Nemiroff among other experts believes that it was due in some way to the action of exceptionally cold water maintaining the oxygen level in the brain.

Misty's case illustrates the very great difficulty of pinpointing an exact time of death. During the 1300s, the brilliant Italian poet Francesco Petrarca (Petrarch) had been laid out, ready for burial. The ceremony was only three or four hours away when the weather changed dramatically. The great Italian poet rose into a sitting position and complained that he could feel a draught. It was fortunate for world literature that Petrarch lived for three more decades, during which he wrote some of his greatest work.

Born on 20 July 1304 at Arezzo, in Tuscany, Petrarch died almost seventy years later to the day at Arqua, near Padua in Carrara. His near brush with death took place in about 1344. Petrarch's father was a lawyer and Francesco had been destined for the same profession, but he developed what he himself described as "an unquenchable thirst for literature." Happily, Petrarch seems to have had an unquenchable thirst for life as well. In view of his very narrow escape from being buried alive, his letter to posterity — which he wrote while in his mid-sixties — seems particularly poignant:

> Greetings. It is possible some of you may have heard of me though I doubt it since a name which is both obscure and insignificant is unlikely to penetrate far either through space or time. If, strangely enough, you have heard of me you may be interested to know what kind of person I was. In truth I was a poor mortal just like you; my origin was not exalted and my birth was humble. My youth had vanished before I realised that it had gone. The strength of manhood swept me away but a riper age gave me common sense and I have learned by experience a truth which I had previously gleaned from my books: youth and pleasure are only vanity.

Back in the 1500s, a couple of centuries after Petrarch's narrow escape, Matthew Wall of the village of Braughing, in Hertfordshire, England, was on his way to a premature burial when one of the bearers tripped up and dropped his coffin. Matthew recovered and lived for several more years. Five hundred years after the event the citizens of Braughing still remember him.

In Philip Aries's book *The Hour of Our Death* there is a gruesome account of a burial at Orleans in France where the corpse revived while a grave robber was cutting off a finger in order to steal a ring. We hope that the effect on the grave robber was salutary!

In book ten of *The Republic* Plato refers to a warrior from Pamphylia named Er, who, assumed to be dead, was placed on the funeral pyre with other victims of a battle. He revived just before the flames got to him and later gave a remarkable account of his experiences. Er was convinced that his body and soul had separated and that his spirit had been one of a large crowd journeying into the unknown together.

If ever a man deserved to be believed by virtue of his holiness and integrity it was Bede. Born in 672 at Monkton, Jarrow, Northumbria, Bede died on 25 May 735. Some twelve hundred years later he was canonized. In the ancient records his name was sometimes rendered Baeda or Beda. His most famous work was the *Ecclesiastical History of the English People*, which related how the Anglo-Saxon tribes became Christian. Modern historians regard Bede as a great scholar, always anxious to check the accuracy of his sources and to write nothing unless he himself was convinced that the evidence for it was totally valid.

Bede's remarkable account of the near-death experience of the Northumbrian Drychthelm is all the more significant because of his scholarly regard for truth and accuracy. Drychthelm appeared to have died during the night. At daybreak he suddenly returned to life and sat up — very much as Petrarch did. The friends and relatives who sat weeping beside his body were so alarmed by this totally unexpected recovery that they fled. When calm and order had been restored, Drychthelm told his story. He remembered leaving his body and described the beauty and light of a heavenly country where a handsome man in a shining robe had been guiding and helping him. When Drychthelm was told he could not stay but must, for the time being, return to the world of mortal men, he was far from happy. In the Northumbrian's own words, "I had no desire at all to go back to my body. The place I had reached was pleasant and beautiful beyond anything I had seen before — as were the people dwelling therein. However, I did not dare to argue with the gracious Being in the shining robes who was attending me and, even if I had had the courage to question him, there was no time, for suddenly I found myself back in my body amongst the men and women of Earth once more."

DEATH

The issue of *The Saint Louis Medical and Surgical Journal* for Spring 1890 relates the remarkable case of Dr. A. S. Wiltse, of Skiddy, Kansas. During 1889, Dr. Wiltse was very seriously ill with typhoid. His own doctor, S. H. Raynes, was convinced that his friend and colleague had died. Wiltse in fact recovered and reported what he had experienced after his apparent death. He felt at first that he was still contained within his physical body but that they no longer seemed to have anything in common. Being a professional physician himself, Wiltse looked at his body objectively — as though he was examining one of his patients — and it seemed to him that he was able to observe the unique process by which the physical body and the immortal soul within it became separated.

As Wiltse moved away from his typhoid-stricken physical body, he came very close to a man who was standing by the door of the sick room. In Wiltse's view his *psychic arm* passed through the arm of the man at the door, *but met no resistance whatever*. He wanted to tell the friends and colleagues gathered around him that he was alive and that there was nothing to fear. None of them, however, were able to see or hear him. The comic irony of the situation made him laugh.

Wiltse's other thoughts concerned his feeling of radiant well-being and he contrasted that with the sickness and discomfort, the weakness and pain, that he had experienced as a result of the typhoid.

During the Vietnam War an American soldier named Bayn was hit simultaneously by the recoil of an anti-tank rocket he was trying to fire, Vietnamese machine gun bullets, and the blast of an exploding mortar shell. It seemed to him that he was looking down on something very much like a theatrical performance to which he was now just a spectator. The Vietcong were all around him, trying to take his boots and gun, but, although he willed himself to do something, there seemed to be an impenetrable barrier between what he wanted to do and what the body that had been his and was now lying helplessly on the ground was able to do. When other Americans arrived, he was placed in a body bag and only narrowly escaped being filled with embalming fluid.

Gilles Bédard was in the Sacré Coeur Hospital in Cartierville, Quebec, near Montreal. Severe illness had brought his weight down to less than eighty-five pounds and the prognosis was not good. With his temperature dangerously high at well over 100 degrees, he slipped into a coma. Gilles remembered sliding in and out of coma, then, when the medical team came back to see what they could do to help him, he observed what appeared to be a circular patch of illumination on the ceiling of the room. It looked more like the moon than anything else. His next experience was the familiar one in out-of-body cases where he seemed to be looking down at himself. Gilles saw not only his own physical body, but also members of his family and the medical team. He described it later as an experience similar to watching television.

Gilles then found himself with a group of dazzlingly white people who did not appear to have faces. There was a tunnel beyond them. They assured him he was not going to die and he was fascinated by the beautiful music that accompanied the experience. Time seemed to have no meaning. It was as though he had stepped out of time and into eternity — like a rider on a merry-go-round stepping off one of the wooden horses and onto the unmoving central platform.

Gilles Bédard later met the brilliantly talented Steve Roach, famous for his electronic music. While he and Roach were chatting he discovered that Steve was a motorcyclist who had also had a near-death experience. He told Gilles that when he was composing the music that fans and critics hailed as exquisite, he was attempting to recreate the indescribably lovely sounds that he had heard during his near-death experience.

When co-author Lionel was writing and researching the HTV programme "Stations of the Cross," he interviewed Gwenllian Buck, an intelligent and vivacious Cardiff teenager who had also undergone an amazing near-death experience that in some ways ran parallel to the accounts given by Gilles Bédard and Steve Roach.

Gwenllian had a very curious experience and one that might almost have been categorised as a premonition of danger. She had a sinister dream twelve or thirteen months before the near-fatal illness that led to her uncanny experience. Gwenllian was in the sea with a great many other people; she was struggling hard to reach land while those around her were being swept away, and she knew that they were going to their deaths. In her dream the waves engulfed her and she described the sensation of being hurled against a harbour wall. She does not recall how — in the dream — she was plucked from the sea, but the dream featured a miraculous rescue of some kind that left her safely back on the shore. She recalled particularly her feelings of distress that the others who had been struggling in the water with her were not going to be saved as she had been. Very close to a year from the day of this weird and stressful dream, Gwenllian was suddenly taken ill. She had gone shopping in Cardiff city centre with two of her teenage friends when she suddenly felt very unwell. The most noticeable of the early symptoms was an uncontrollable cough that made it impossible for Gwenllian to talk properly. Without meaning to be callous or unkind, and with a response that was typical of carefree youngsters, her two friends found it funny rather than worrying when Gwenllian was unable to talk. She went home and went to bed suffering from what she thought were the symptoms of a very severe bout of influenza. Unlike a normal flu bout, however, Gwenllian's illness did not pass in a few days. It got worse. In fact, her entire immune system collapsed. She had been attacked by an extremely dangerous virus that the excellent medical attention available in Cardiff — with its world class University Hospital — had difficulty in treating.

Gwenllian was in a coma for fifteen days. She was so close to death that a priest was called in to give her the last rites. During the long days of her coma, Gwenllian was moving through a series of dark and stressful dreams which, after she recovered, she recorded in picture form. One of the dreams that recurred most frequently and persisted longest was of being in a strange, old-fashioned train on an elliptical track. It went round and round like a toy train in a nursery, getting nowhere. At about three o'clock one morning, just before Gwenllian took her miraculous turn for the better, she was aware of a presence — a benign and massively powerful presence — that entered the room and sat on the end of her bed. She derived great comfort and reinforcement from this presence. It spoke to her, telling her that everything was going to be all right and that she would recover. Gwenllian asked a nurse to come to her and then enquired whether her father had been in the room with her. The nurse told her that as it was between three and four in the morning no one had been in the hospital for several hours, other than the patients and staff. Despite this confirmation that whoever or whatever had been with her was not an ordinary human being, Gwenllian did not feel in the least frightened. The presence had been totally benign and comforting.

Gwenllian subsequently experienced periods during which she described herself as "feeling low," and on these occasions she thought of the presence that had brought her such comfort during that critical point in her near-fatal illness. She wondered whether he or she had actually returned to assist her again, or whether the experience of comfort just came from her vivid memory of their first meeting in the hospital.

David Everson from Thornton Heath in Surrey had a mysterious near-death experience of a similar kind. David had been raised as a Roman Catholic and educated at a Catholic school in Croydon. True to his faith since boyhood, he has nevertheless been interested in — and tolerant towards — other people's attitudes to life's mysteries. In the course of studying his own beloved Catholicism in greater depth, he read around Taoism as well as Amerindian religion and culture — things as mysterious as the *pilotois* and the shaking-tent mystery.

In July 1992, when he was only thirty years old, David was diagnosed as suffering from non-Hodgkin's lymphoma. Treated with chemotherapy, he suffered a severe relapse that brought his weight down to seventy pounds. A tumour formed at the back of his left eye and blinded him on that side. David's only realistic hope of survival was a bone-marrow transplant, but before that could be carried out he needed further chemotherapy on a body that had already reached the limits of its endurance.

David's faith never faltered in spite of all these traumatic medical problems. One night, as he lay alone in his separate hospital room with nothing but his fighting spirit to maintain him, he was not certain himself whether he had blacked out or not, but somehow he found himself walking through attractive countryside. Colours were brighter and more intense there than any he had ever observed in the normal, everyday world. When talking to us about them David compared them to old Technicolor movies from the 1950s. During this experience — whether it was a dream, a vision, or an out-of-body phenomenon — David saw a large fairground merry-go-round with riders on it. They were happy and laughing and the music was bright and jubilant. David found himself drawing closer to it and as he did so he was able to recognise the riders. One was his mother, who had died in 1984; an uncle who had also passed over was on the carousel with her. As he looked more closely he saw other friends and relatives, all of whom had left this world. They shone with happiness and were delighted to see him but as he moved closer to join them on the merry-go-round they said, "David, it's not your time to ride; you are going to be OK." He remembers clearly that they smiled and gave him a cheery thumbs-up sign. He moved away from the ride and saw it slowly fading away, and then

David Everson's vision of the strange, psychic carousel.

— as in so many other reports of out-of-body and near-death experiences — David saw himself walking back slowly towards the hospital. He watched himself getting into bed. Then, in the air above his bed, he saw a glorious vision of the Virgin Mary. She was enveloped in pure white light. Smiling radiantly as she looked down at him, she quietly vanished. When David recovered consciousness again he found himself in his hospital bed crying uncontrollably: his spirit was soaring. He felt amazingly elated and stronger than he had ever felt in the whole of his life up to that moment.

The next day the doctor who was in charge of David's treatment came into his room on an unplanned visit with a group of his students. To the doctor's total surprise, David was out of bed with his back to the door and had not seen them enter. He was wearing his Walkman headset and dancing to a piece of Jimi Hendrix's music. Turning to face the door, David stopped dancing because the medical group had startled him. The doctor joyfully exclaimed, "My God! I do not believe what I am seeing!" Then he took David in his arms and embraced him like a long lost soldier friend who, against all hope, has come safely home from the war. The bone marrow transplant was effective, although David had a slight relapse in 1994. When he first contacted us some three years ago he had been totally clear of cancer for three years. The vision in his left eye was fully restored. Back to a hefty one hundred and eighty pounds, he took up motorcycling and greatly enjoys his bike and his rock-and-roll music. To use his own truly uplifting and inspiring words, David says he has faith in God and faith in himself, and his thirst for life is unquenchable.

David recounted two additional fascinating experiences for us. The first of these happened shortly after his mother died in 1984. He was walking upstairs and felt something that he described as resembling a gentle breeze, a warm breeze that seemed to go right through his body. He could smell his mother's distinctive favourite perfume, and he is absolutely convinced that she was there in the house with him in spirit.

Some six months after her death he had been out clubbing with a group of young friends and was on his way home in a taxi. Immediately before David was due to be dropped off his friend, John, who was sharing the taxi with him, glanced up and saw someone looking out of a lighted window in David's house. John said, "Oh, your mum's still awake. She's looking out of the window." David looked up and saw that she was. He recalled that she had always done that years ago because he was her youngest child, and like any good parent she had tended to worry if he was late coming home. "Oh, yes," he said to John, "so she is." John had no idea that David's mother had been dead for six months, and David did not tell John about her death until a few weeks after the episode in the taxi. *The fact that they had both seen her so clearly could be said to provide further significant evidence for the survival of the human soul.*

When all the near-death experience reports are examined and analysed, including the suggestions regarding hallucinations caused by shortage of oxygen — or by brain chemicals being produced that create hallucinations as well as moods of tranquillity and euphoria — the inner core of survival evidence associated with near-death experiences adamantly refuses to be explained away.

Co-author Lionel had a great-grandmother named Susan or Susanna Tilney. She was the wife of the village blacksmith at Yaxham, near East Dereham in Norfolk, England. Lionel's mother, Greta, told him the story of how when she herself was a girl of eleven or twelve she travelled with her uncle, Fred, to visit Susanna (Fred's mother), who was dying.

As Greta and Fred reached the old lady's cottage, she was already at the point of death. Greta said that Susanna's face lit up with a shining happiness and brightness that was not of this Earth.

DEATH

She turned and smiled at the young girl and then said in a faraway voice, "I can see men in white." The radiant smile displayed an energy too powerful for that frail old body to have generated by any normal physical means. With a sigh and a smile of great happiness and tranquillity Susanna slipped away from this world.

There are limits to the power of hallucinations, as there are limits to what a shortage of oxygen or surfeit of stimulating self-produced bio-chemicals can achieve. In terms of simple probability, it is significantly more likely that the out-of-body experiences reported in such numbers, with such clarity, and possessing such similarity, are genuine indicators of the immortality of the soul, its ability to leave the physical body at or near the moment of death, and its capacity not only for survival but for enjoying its new environment.

CHAPTER FIVE
OUT-OF-BODY EXPERIENCES

Detailed analysis of the out-of-body experience (OOBE) ends at the metaphysical premise that human beings and — very probably — *all* living things may well contain some sort of non-physical component that is capable of separation from the physical aspect of the entity.

A great many witnesses have described their OOBEs in depth, and the common elements seem to be a state of physical relaxation and a temperature that is neither uncomfortably hot nor distressingly cold — mild, pleasant warmth seems to be an important aspect of the opening stages of an OOBE. The drowsiness accompanying the relaxation period of an OOBE is described as seeming to be distinct from the normal, semi-conscious drowsiness that comes naturally prior to sleeping or on moving gently out of sleep before rousing fully. Those who have had an OOBE are convinced that they were neither asleep nor dreaming when it happened.

In those parts of Africa where the care and raising of cattle is a highly specialised task that has been carried on for centuries — so that cattle-farming expertise has been passed on down the generations — there are far more words to distinguish by very fine degrees the various states and conditions of cattle than exist in other languages.

The languages of groups with focused knowledge necessarily expand to cover those particular concepts that are essential in order for the group to perform its skilled functions. For example, this is true of groups of specialists who use computer technology and the Internet.

DEATH

Those who have had frequent OOBEs need to look for and define those mental states, self-perceptions, and particular *awarenesses* that are subtly distinct from one another but are not easy to categorise using ordinary everyday linguistic terms. Those with OOBEs know perfectly well what they mean by a state of relaxation and something akin to drowsiness — but they are also vividly aware this is *not* a simple pre-sleep or post-sleep condition.

We might even manufacture the term *oobiness*, meaning something like the mental equivalent of standing on a railway platform or waiting in a queue at a bus station. It is the feeling that you are in the right place and that something is going to enable you to undertake an OOBE or astral travel. The subject undergoing the experience knows that standing in the bus station or on the railway platform is a totally different type of expectation from standing in a supermarket looking at the shelves and deciding what to buy, or standing in a friendly pub with a pint of lager in one hand.

There are undoubted *similarities*, but the man or woman who has experience of pubs, supermarkets, bus stations, and railway platforms can tell which location he or she is in. The standing aspect is common to all three, but the other dimensions of the experiences are different.

So the relaxation and drowsiness is transformed into our new focused, technical term, *oobiness*. A significant number of subjects then try to describe a feeling of "rolling up or a mental equivalent of physical curling." An analogy here is the woolworker, or expert knitter, who takes wool from a skein and turns it into a ball. It is the same wool, but in one form it is much easier to work with than the other.

The skein, in this model, may be thought of as normal waking consciousness in which the spiritual, or astral, aspects of our lives are prone to over-involvement with the pressures of the here and the now. There is the knock at the door, the bell of the telephone, the beeping of the fax, the mobile phone, or the pager. The skein is the world in which household bills have to be paid, valued customers and important clients have to be looked after, much-loved children have to be taken to school and helped with their homework, meals have to be prepared, eaten, and cleared away.

Such abstract and delicate experiences as *oobiness* and potential astral travel are not at their optimum when the paper-boy arrives at the door for his week's payment or the postman knocks with a registered letter.

OUT-OF-BODY EXPERIENCES

Once the metaphorical human-experience-wool has been transferred from the day-to-day skein to the metaphysical ball, it is a great deal easier to proceed psychically without the distracting entanglements of normal, physical life. In what might be termed his or her psychic ball of wool state, the prospective astral traveller on the verge of an OOBE is in a time or place — and in a sufficiently relaxed physical state — to be safely beyond the reach of mundane interruptions.

It is possible to write good lyrics on the back of an envelope while sitting on the Number 27G streetcar on your way to work. It is more probable, however, that the best lyrics with the most fluent flow, rhythm, and meaning will be written in an isolated cottage beside a Welsh mountain stream with no distraction greater than the jewelled light of a kingfisher diving down from the other side of the water. *Oobiness* is that idyllic writer's cottage; normal drowsiness is the back of the 27G streetcar. *Oobiness* is the strange feeling of being rolled up into a ball, or coiled neatly like a fisherman's line on a reel, so that psychic movement from that position to a distant place is facilitated.

This ties in, of course, with the classical description of the silver cord which seems, in the records of many OOBE adventures, to be the essential link between the physical body and the astral traveller.

There is an excellent family board game called "Flutter," which emulates the activities of investors in a stock market. Part of the mechanism of this game consists of a parent peg and a traveller peg. As the game proceeds and good or bad things happen to the various companies represented on the simulated stock exchange, the traveller peg moves up the board leaving its parent peg behind. As the game proceeds further, the activities of the traveller peg have an effect on the movements of the parent peg.

Those readers who have played "Flutter" will instantly recognise the analogy of the parent peg and the traveller peg with theories concerning the relationship of the physical and astral body (always allowing that such an astral body exists).

Some subjects who have reported their astral travel experiences have described their pre-take off feeling as being coiled up somehow inside their own heads. Others have thought of it as drawing back the string of a bow, or of winding a crossbow into the firing position. Those astral travellers who are old enough to remember windup portable gramophones — popular during the 1920s and 1930s —

have likened their OOBEs to tightening the coiled spring of one of those portable gramophones. When the brake on the old windup turntable is released and the needle lowered carefully on to the brittle old grooves of the 78 rpm record, the experience of speech or music can begin. In the same way with OOBEs the subject is aware after the tightening process of a sudden *release*: the arrow speeding from the bow, the bolt hurtling away from the crossbow, the speech or music emerging (despite its imperfections) from the tinny outlet of the old windup gramophone.

Most researchers and specialists in the OOBE field agree that it is highly probable that some sort of altered state such as *oobiness* is necessary before astral travel can take place. There are, however, interesting cases when an OOBE seems to have taken place while the subject is very much awake and active. Lorraine Parry reported one very interesting case in Spencer's excellent *Encyclopaedia of the World's Greatest Unsolved Mysteries*. Lorraine recalled that as a child of five or six she was at the top of a staircase and felt a sudden urge to fly down the stairs like a swooping bird. It seemed to her that she jumped from the top step, flew slowly and gracefully down, and landed just below the bottom stair. During the astral flight she looked down and saw herself walking slowly down the stairs holding the banister carefully. When her flying-self reached the foot of the steps she re-entered the physical body that she had just seen walking carefully down the stairs, and experienced what she described as "a kind of slight jolt."

This raises the question of how and to what extent the astral body — if, as is generally supposed, it can be regarded as the *true* mind, will, or personality — is able to exert control over the physical body from which it seems temporarily to have become detached. There are numerous interesting cases on record of subjects reporting their OOBEs who have observed their physical bodies walking in the street, crossing busy roads, even conducting conversations.

Enthusiastic model makers can control their cars, boats, and miniature aeroplanes with radio transmissions or with electrical impulses sent along control wires. Does this suggest that the silver cord phenomenon is the psychic equivalent of a control wire? While the astral body is flying to Samarkand is it able to ensure that its physical base is buying the right vegetables from the corner shop or polishing the car? How many of our everyday functions are more automatic and conditioned than we realise? When we *think* we are making decisions, how often are we rolling like a railway carriage along a well-used track?

If I always feed my cat or walk to the news-stand to buy my daily paper at the same time each morning, if I always use the same brand of cat food and purchase the same paper, are there times when I am running on a sort of automatic pilot rather than making conscious decisions to buy that particular brand of cat food or to buy and read that newspaper rather than another one? Does this then mean that as far as simple, daily functions like crossing the road and making toast for breakfast, or pouring coffee into a cup, are concerned, the physical body can largely be left to its own devices — to run satisfactorily and safely on its autopilot? We do not have to think *consciously* about remembering to breathe, or to ensure that our hearts are beating at an appropriate rate for the activity level on which we are working. How much more of our normal, waking, human lives — lived in the everyday world — is running on an automatic pilot of which we are scarcely aware?

In the case of the OOBE in which the astral flyer saw himself conducting a conversation, it is worth noting that many of our conversational phrases are practically automatic anyway. Greetings and farewells almost certainly fall into this category. Many of us have had experiences, additionally, in which we have felt moods of extreme happiness and elation on the one hand or fierce anger and deep depression on the other. In some of these moods, it seemed as if part of the mind had separated itself off from the semi-automatic, emotional behaviour of the elation or anger.

It is almost as though in moments of what *appears to be* uncontrollable anger, or euphoric, ecstatic happiness, there is a distinct, separate, central, rational, and *balanced* part of the personality that is trying to hold down the emotion. This central, balanced mind is well aware that the elation pattern or the anger-depression pattern is following some track that is not under the direct control of the will: *and yet could — by an effort of the will — be recalled and made to obey.*

Is this in some way similar to the automatic functioning — in quite an elaborate and complex way — of the body that has become disconnected from its "real" mind or controlling will and true personality?

As a sagacious writer on the paranormal once said, "If there is one thing in the supernatural realm more terrible than a disembodied spirit it is a body that is still living, moving, and functioning *with no spirit in control*."

Another important and interesting consideration connected with OOBEs is Darwinian. Is there any sense at all in which the OOBE could be said to have any survival value? In a freely adapted film version of Edgar Allen Poe's *The Pit and the Pendulum*, two prisoners of the Inquisition were being brutally tortured. One, who in the story was a genuine witch possessing real paranormal powers, taught the other victim how to perform an OOBE so that she could escape from the pain that was being inflicted upon her physical body. The two astral bodies then found themselves flying high above the pain-racked physical bodies. The less experienced astral traveller made the mistake of looking down to see what the torturers were doing to her and immediately found herself back inside the physical body that they were working on.

Although this particular episode was only a piece of well-made imaginative fiction on the part of the filmmaker, it serves to illustrate a possible survival value of the OOBE. In a less technical and less medically scientific universe than the one we and our contemporaries inhabit, the ability to escape from pain in order to think clearly and devise a means of escape from what would otherwise be a fatal predicament could have been a major survival factor.

In our own century, a farmer found himself trapped by the ankle under a tree that had fallen in just the wrong place while he was working on it. By an almost unbelievable feat of courage he severed the trapped foot with nothing more than a penknife that he had in his pocket. He then managed to put a tourniquet above the wound and drag himself back to his truck. He drove to the nearest farmhouse, where they phoned for medical help and so saved his life.

In explaining how he had found the necessary courage and strength to perform the operation, he said that his main thought had been his determination to get back to the wife and children who loved him and who were financially dependent upon him. This determination to do *anything* rather than let them down seems to have provided him not only with the necessary determination, but also perhaps with some form of self-induced local anaesthesia that made the operation possible.

Imagine a Neolithic ancestor having to do something equally drastic, armed only with a flint hand-axe but, perhaps, having the ability to embark on an OOBE while the desperate action was being done. It could also be argued from the survival perspective of the OOBE that the ability to hover at some vantage point above the damaged physical body would give early warning of predators approaching. Could it also have been the case that thousands of years before the telephone was developed the astral body could have served as the messenger for the trapped and damaged physical unit? Could an astral traveller have reached his Neolithic village, summoned help, and led a party back to the spot where the physical body was trapped?

Researchers have often suggested that telepathy would have been of major importance to early hunter-gatherers. There is a considerable body of evidence to support the hypothesis that telepathy is genuinely functional. Whether telepathy and astral projection served the same purpose, or whether certain apparently telepathic phenomena are actually due to astral projection, is a matter for debate. Either or both, however, possess significant survival value and would have been highly advantageous to our remote ancestors.

"Use it or lose it" is a particularly apposite and relevant aphorism. It applies to both physical and mental faculties. The classical concert pianist who goes without practice for a day or two soon finds that his or her outstanding musical skills are beginning to diminish. The same is true of a keyboard operator, a high-level mathematics teacher, a gymnast, golfer, or hockey star. Unless regularly exercised in the gym, the strongest muscle will inevitably begin to weaken. Unless exercised by challenging and stimulating problem-solving situations, the sharpest mind will also begin to lose its problem-solving abilities.

In contemporary society with its television, radio, satellite links, mobile phones, and the Internet, the need for telepathy and/or astral travel and OOBEs is greatly reduced. We have become conditioned over the last two centuries to think in terms of solving communication problems by having recourse to scientific and technological methods. Like any mental or physical faculty that we may possess — whether it is the ability to solve problems using the differential calculus or to lift heavier weights in competition than the other weight trainers — neglect of telepathic communication or astral travel seems likely to attenuate it. If "use it or lose it" applies to physical thought processes inside the human brain, and to strength and skill performances at the physical level involving nerve-linked co-ordination patterns as well as the muscular strength and flexibility to make those patterns into factual movements, then it seems reasonable to suggest that failure to use certain attributes of the non-physical mind — if it really exists — would lead to a weakening of its powers just as surely as neglect of any other mental or physical faculty will lead to that faculty being diminished.

If, on the other hand, paranormal researchers and investigators of anomalous phenomena try continually to *use* their psychic facilities, including telepathy and astral travel, they may well find that the ability increases with practice, just as any other straightforward mental or physical activity will do.

If astral travel is real and objective, and if OOBEs are real and objective, then they provide massive evidence for survival. If there is a part of us that can truly experience awareness, which can will itself to any part of the globe — and perhaps any part of the universe — as and when it chooses, then its independence of the physical body, and its independence of matter, would seem to provide valuable reinforcement for the hypothesis that the human mind, soul, spirit, or personality can and does survive physical death.

There are critics of OOBE records and reports who would put forward the point of view that the entire experience is subjective and illusory. The human brain, they would say, can be stimulated electrically under certain surgical conditions so that it provides what *seem* to be real experiences as far as the subject is concerned, but which the medical experimenter who is applying the external electrical input to the brain would say are merely the result of stimulating certain groups of neurones.

This is a point that deserves to be addressed and examined very thoroughly. It is the doorway to the far vaster question of the nature of observation. We believe that we are dependent upon our external sense organs for our knowledge of the universe. When we hear a piece by Bach or Beethoven being played, when we see a rainbow, a sunset, or reflections of willow trees on limpid water, we believe that the beauty we are experiencing is coming from an external source. Medical experiments of the kind described earlier, however, would seem to make the counter proposal that the rainbow, the sunset, the reflection, and the exquisite music may all be subjective after all. If a needle carrying an electric current placed at the appropriate point in the brain can produce a sensation of smell, taste, touch, sight, or sound, then it could be argued that the entire universe exists inside our minds.

We, ourselves, do not seriously consider for a moment that this is likely. What we do have to consider, however, is that it cannot logically be ruled out in its entirety. Nor can it be dismissed by empirical means in the laboratory. Certain remarkable characters such as Paracelsus seem to have come extraordinarily close to being able to perform "magic" that worked. If the mind can be electrically stimulated into believing without a shadow of a doubt that it is experiencing music, sunsets, galaxies, moonlight and rainbows, the smell of roses, the touch of silk, the taste of strawberries, and the sounds of the pipes of Pan, *then what kind of link is there between the observing mind and the real, or supposed, external reality?*

The most significant thing that Paracelsus said was, "When the magician believes that his magic is failing to work, it is not the magic that fails — it is the magician's power to imagine the end result in sufficient detail." This realisation is remarkably close to the teaching that faith of sufficient power can literally move mountains. If the internal appearance of a universe that springs into life at the prompting of an electric needle is in some mysterious way harmonised with the "real" objective externality, then it is certainly credible that the human mind can accomplish "magic" and "miracles" beyond the imaginings of the most ambitious magicians.

Bearing all this in mind, may it be asked whether the astral traveller reporting his or her OOBE is journeying through an internal rather than an external universe?

We, ourselves, having considered the evidence over many years of research, would be inclined to the view that astral travel does exist, that the OOBE is a genuinely objective experience, and that some indefinable part of the human personality is able to travel independently of the physical body. If, as we believe, the evidence supports the reality of astral travel in a universe that itself has an external objective reality, then these astral travel records and reports provide substantial support for the human survival hypothesis.

CHAPTER SIX
HYPNO-REGRESSION AND REINCARNATION

Our pioneering researches into the Rennes-le-Château mystery go back to the 1970s. From our very earliest visits to Rennes and our key meetings with such unique informants as Henri Buthion (who then occupied what had once been Bérenger Saunière's luxurious, miniature hill-top estate) it became increasing clear that there was the strong possibility of some involvement between the supposed treasure of Rennes-le-Château and the Albigensians or Cathars. The Cathars were a religious sect who came to prominence in the Rennes area during the thirteenth century.

Supported by many of the political rulers of the Languedoc at the time, the Cathars were extraordinarily popular with the people of the area because of their work as healers. They also seem largely to have led lives of kindness, generosity, and moral integrity. Their heretical beliefs, however, led them into ultimate fatal conflict with the established Roman Catholic Church.

When any organisation — be it clerical or lay — deludes itself into the belief that it is the sole repository of the truth, and that any who fail to share its obsession are wrong and doomed accordingly, conflict and tragedy will follow as surely as weakness follows starvation.

The human mind, and the actions that it motivates, is at its noblest and best when its guiding star is a quest for Truth and its sails are filled with the fresh winds of honest and open curiosity — plus a willingness to change course if necessary. The mind that is

Tower at Rennes-le-Château, in southwestern France.

Father Saunière's luxurious "Villa Bethania" at Rennes-le-Château, France.

closed to all except its own rigid and immutable ideas is a hapless vessel driven rudderless towards a rocky coast. It was the Cathars' tragedy to be the victims of such blind religious obsession, persecution, and mass murder.

Reasonable doubt and openness of mind are the candle flames by which scholars read the Book of Life. Erroneous "certainties" in matters of belief produce no light at all, except the flames around the victims' stakes.

During the thirteenth-century persecutions of the Cathars, they had frequent recourse to their *almost* impregnable line of fortresses. One of the most impressive of these was Montségur, which lay within easy reach of Rennes-le-Château. Perched on the summit of a huge outcrop, Montségur — literally "the secure mountain" — came very close to living up to its name. In 1244, however, its fanatical religious enemies finally overran it, and the Cathars whom it had once defended died in the persecutors' flames.

The great mystery of Montségur centred on four intrepid Cathar mountaineers who escaped before the fortress finally fell, carrying with them "the treasures of their faith." The attackers had made an almost unbelievably generous offer to those doomed Cathar defenders. They had given them a week to think over the surrender

Co-author Lionel Fanthorpe at the Cathar stronghold of Quéribus, in southwestern France.

terms, which were that if they notionally accepted membership of the Church they would not be investigated too closely. Not only would they themselves be unharmed, their property would not even be confiscated. There was, however, one strange condition: no one was to leave the fortress prior to surrender and acceptance of the generous terms. Should anyone attempt to leave *with anything* the generous terms would be withdrawn and the occupants — soldiers, civilians, men, women, and children alike — would all be consigned to the flames.

The four men who chose to leave carrying "the treasures of their faith" also carried with them the responsibility for the agonising deaths of those they left behind. *Could anything on Earth have been as important as that?*

Dr. Arthur Guirdham was generally recognised as one of the world's greatest authorities on Catharism. Co-author Lionel interviewed Arthur at length during the course of our research for *Rennes-le-Château: Its Mysteries and Secrets* (1991).

Arthur Guirdham was born in Cumberland and educated at Oxford. He was for many years the senior consultant psychiatrist for the Bath area of the United Kingdom. A doctor sent one of his patients to Guirdham for help in 1962 because the lady was suffering from terrifying nightmares. She described to Guirdham a dream in which a man entered a room where she lay on the floor. The approach of this character filled her with such mortal dread that she normally woke up screaming uncontrollably. This experience was taking place every few days.

Like any good professional scientific or medical investigator, Guirdham went very carefully through his patient's case history. She had been brought up by Roman Catholic parents and in her early teens had a near-death experience as a result of peritonitis. A priest and some nuns had actually called at the hospital to administer the last rites.

During a period of delirium associated with the peritonitis, she spoke more than once about having a baby. The possibility that this was a memory from a previous incarnation was considered. After making further progress towards recovery she began to experience inexplicable lapses into unconsciousness, almost as though she had acquired some type of epilepsy.

Concurrent with these periods of lost consciousness she began to experience the nightmares involving lying on the floor and being terrified of the man who was entering the room. The patient remained in touch with Dr. Guirdham for several years, during which he learned a great deal about the traumas that she had suffered. It seemed from her clinical interviews with Dr. Guirdham that the patient was able to recall her life among thirteenth-century Cathars in the Languedoc area of south-western France.

Recalling her schooldays, she told Arthur about "daydreams" in which she had been with her French lover, Roger, from her previous life as a Cathar. Arthur Guirdham was already among the most knowledgeable Cathar historians before he began treating the patient with the strange Albigensian memories. There was a small point of detail regarding the colour of Cathar robes. Up until this point in his investigations, Arthur had been under the impression that the Cathar robes were black. His patient, however, described them as dark blue and this led him to consult Professor Duvernoy, who was the leading French expert on the subject. Guirdham's work with Duvernoy brought to light further information indicating that Cathar robes were dark blue during the particular period that his patient was describing.

Another interesting historical comment that the patient had made concerned her beloved Roger using sugar as medicine when he had a problem with his chest. Guirdham's detailed researches produced evidence that loaf sugar was prescribed by Arabian doctors of the period for chest problems. It was also evident that advanced Arabian medical information was available in the Languedoc in the thirteenth century.

Guirdham's patient described a horrendously vivid dream of being burned at the stake shortly after her lover, Roger, had died in prison. Historical research revealed that Roger-Isarn de Fanjeaux *had* died in prison in 1243. To Arthur Guirdham's great surprise *he recognised himself* as a reincarnation of his patient's thirteenth-century lover. It seemed to him, as well as to her, that the nightmares had ceased when she came to consult him — not necessarily because of his clinical expertise and honest, friendly, helpful manner, but because they had rediscovered each other seven centuries after their sufferings at the hands of the persecuting Church.

Guirdham's very well written volume, *The Cathars and Reincarnation*, presents the evidence with great accuracy and clarity. During the lengthy meeting with him, Lionel was particularly interested in Guirdham's opinion of what those Cathar mountaineers had carried down the precipitous rock on which Montségur stood. What *were* those "treasures of their faith" (described elsewhere as *pecuniam infinitam*, or *infinite money*), which were worth not only their own lives but those of all their friends, companions, and co-religionists? Guirdham was absolutely clear on the point, "They were books, my boy, they were books. The mountaineers were undoubtedly carrying *books*."

The great mystery remains as to the secrets that those precious Cathar books might have contained, and whether they finally made their way to Rennes-le-Château to be rediscovered by Bérenger Saunière in 1885 — a discovery that might have led to his unaccountable wealth.

It was a pleasure and privilege to talk to Arthur Guirdham. His fine mind and high intelligence were clearly evident during the interview, as were his honest spirit of enquiry and intellectual integrity.

One of the most striking and interesting of his case histories concerned another patient who had experienced horrendous recurring dreams of walking towards a stake with bundles of sticks heaped around it.

In the case of this patient, there were vivid memories of being struck by her persecutors with a burning torch as they drove her towards the place of execution. When Dr. Guirdham examined her, he found a strange birthmark resembling the blisters produced by burning. He asked her whether the area was the same as that in which she remembered being struck by the burning torch in her nightmare and she replied that it was.

Although open to argument — and Ian Wilson's astute questioning of Guirdham's work has to be taken with the seriousness that it deserves — co-author Lionel's impression of Guirdham was entirely positive. He gave every indication of being highly intelligent, truthful, and reliable. The evidence Guirdham presented, first in *The Cathars and Reincarnation*, then in *We Are One Another*, and finally in *The Lake and the Castle*, is not easily refuted or set aside.

Because of the deaths of many of Guirdham's witnesses from the 1970s, it is now very difficult indeed to obtain first-hand corroboration for the evidence that he presents in his three reincarnationist books. However, when reliable and accurate witnesses have presented their testimony to an honest and dependable researcher like Guirdham, that evidence has considerable validity.

HYPNO-REGRESSION AND REINCARNATION

The intriguing evidence that he uncovered and recorded in *We Are One Another* describes his meeting with another lady who seems to have been an additional reincarnated Cathar.

Angry Cathar supporters assassinated two Roman Catholic inquisitors and their companions in Avignonet in 1242. Guirdham's informant in this episode was apparently a Cathar woman named Helis de Mazerolles, who had been the sister of Guirdham's own thirteenth-century character. Tragically, in the 1970s the allegedly reincarnated Helis de Mazerolles died young, but her mother produced significant evidence on her behalf and continued to be an important data source for Guirdham. She too, it seems, had been a thirteenth-century Cathar, one Bruna, wife of one of the soldiers defending Montségur. Other friends and relatives of those who came to Guirdham with their strange dreams and memories of life as persecuted Cathars all seemed to have been together in the past. Their alleged reincarnation memories concerned not only the turbulent and tragic times in south-western France in the thirteenth century, but they had also known each other during very different periods of history. There were reports of shared memories of their membership of the Celtic Church in the sixth or seventh centuries. Other memories concerned fourth century Roman Britain and late eighteenth century and early nineteenth century France.

One or two critics of Guirdham's work have pointed out some minor errors that could well have been simple typographical mistakes. When he comments, for example, on the peritonitis that almost killed one of his informants he says on one page that she was eleven and on a later page that she was thirteen or fourteen years old.

Total accuracy and strict academic rigour are rare treasures that deserve to be carefully prized. It is, however, an equal and opposite error to worry so much about *precision* that the main thrust of a narrative or an argument can be seriously weakened or deflected. In watching a good crime thriller on the stage, it is only of very minor importance if the villainous former pirate who is suspected of the serial murders enters in act 3 with his black eye-patch over the *other* eye. Of course, if the play is a finely written detective puzzle in which the wearing of an unnecessary eye-patch is germane to unravelling the intricacies of the plot, then the position of the patch is of major significance. However, if the villain with the eye-patch is simply a one-eyed ex-pirate for whose character the eye-patch merely serves to indicate a dangerous and sinister past, then the fact that he has taken it off while having a quick coffee and sandwich between acts and has then mistakenly placed it over the wrong eye ought not to detract in the least from the validity of the final entrance where he is shot by the tough American private investigator who has come in to protect the family that the ex-pirate is threatening.

Details that are not of direct significance to the main flow of the narrative can be irritating obstacles. The age at which Guirdham's informant suffered the near-fatal peritonitis is not of major consequence to the reincarnation argument that he presents in the trilogy. In an ideal world, he, or his proof-reader, would have picked up the discrepancy, checked the record, and corrected it, but even the most thorough and careful researchers (to whom scholarly rigour is second only to godliness) occasionally make mistakes of that sort.

What Guirdham's researches do seem to raise is the whole question not only of the *feasibility* of reincarnation as a viable concept but of reincarnation being in some mysterious way *a communal or group experience.* A number of excellent science fiction stories have been written concerning gestalt organisms. In one of these a group of friends *bleshed.* The author had combined the words *blend* and *mesh* to create the new term *blesh,* which, in his story, described the particular type of close interaction that was peculiar to the members of the gestalt organism: seven or eight individual human beings with unusual psi powers acted as one being. Their degree of co-operation and integration took them rather further than the kind of symbiosis observed in nature. Some of the group members were telepaths, some were teleports, and another served as the "brain" or central processing unit of what amounted to something rather like a biological computer with "limbs."

Is it possible that what Guirdham discovered about himself and his hypothetically reincarnated friends was allied to the concept of a gestalt organism — like the one in the science fiction story? If reincarnation *does* take place — at least for *some* members of *Homo sapiens* — do those who experience it need to travel *together* from one age to another because like the gestalt organism in the story they are to some degree mutually interdependent?

If the concepts of learning and development have anything to do with reincarnation, then perhaps it is by travelling together in groups that the learning and developmental processes are reinforced. Rôles and relationships among such groups also appear to vary dramatically. Marriage partners in one life may recur as father and son, brother and sister, or loyal cousins in a different period of existence.

Adding personal knowledge of the man to close study of his researches into reincarnation, as illustrated in his Cathar trilogy, it is by no means possible to dismiss Guirdham's work and theories without according them the attention that they richly deserve.

A great friend of ours, who is a highly intelligent and well-educated company director, prefers to remain anonymous regarding his regression experiences. We can vouch for his absolute honesty and integrity, and the truth of the following account that he kindly gave us permission to include here:

I came to this really from the stage of disbelief, thinking that I would not believe anything from a medium — in fact, believe nothing unless it came from my own mouth.

The hypnotist asked me to lie on a bed and placed a microphone near to my face in order to record my words. The only question he asked me was my date of birth. We then went into the relaxing programme, which took about twenty minutes to half an hour. Then he asked me to go back to when I was twenty, then sixteen, eight, etc. But I could feel myself calculating the answers. Then he said that it was 1864: where was I? I could then see myself sitting in a Victorian drawing room and I described my life as a shoemaker in Trowbridge, in the West Country. I could see the workshop and the tools and I described my home and my wife.

We then went back to another life somewhere in Europe where I was an assistant at a funeral parlour. Before that I had a life in Roman times and before that a life living in caves. Finally, the hypnotist brought me back to two years before my date of birth and asked me where I was. I said "in spirit," or something of the sort. He then asked if I was going back to Earth and I said, "Yes." He asked me why I was going back and I said, "To learn patience."

I was interested that the hypnotist slipped in one or two trick questions such as asking me my age when I was in caves — a question that I would not have been able to answer. He suggested to me that I should be regressed by another hypnotist because I should find that I gave the same answers regardless of who was doing the hypnotising.

There is no doubt that if you have doubts about life after death before you go in you have none when you come out.

(An item I have left out is that he always asked me how I died. This is important so as to prove that it is not inherited memory.)

This is an extremely interesting, up-to-date account of a contemporary hypnotic regression, recorded by a very able and reliable witness.

Dr. Ian Stevenson, the brilliant Canadian psychiatrist, was born in Montreal and trained at the prestigious McGill University. After qualifying, he worked in New Orleans and Arizona prior to specialising in psychiatry in Louisiana. Before his fortieth year he was Professor of Psychiatry and Neurology at the University of Virginia in Charlottesville and was the distinguished founder and director of their Parapsychology Division.

The data bank that he built up contains cases not only from the United States and Britain but as far afield as Turkey, Lebanon, India, and Sri Lanka. One of the most interesting and significant aspects of Dr. Stevenson's work is that a great many of the most remarkable cases centre upon the evidence provided by very young children, almost invariably less than six years of age. Almost as soon as they are able to talk at all, some of these young informants have told their parents and brothers and sisters that they have come from a different family, based in another place.

Very young children will claim that they recognise particular landmarks, or they will see some location that they have never visited in their present young lives and say that they have lived there during a previous incarnation. On other occasions they will say that they recognise people whom they have never seen before and claim them as relatives.

Just as one of Arthur Guirdham's important witnesses bore what appeared to be a birthmark in the place were she was reputedly burned by one of her supposed tormentors in the thirteenth century, so Stevenson reports that he has studied birthmarks that look remarkably like the scars of old wounds from injuries received during a previous lifetime.

Stevenson's intriguing case histories include an account of Ravi Shankar, born in the 1950s in Uttar Pradesh, the son of Ram Gupta. By the time he was two years old, Ravi, who was an intelligent child and an early talker, recalled a former life as the son of a hairdresser named Jageshwar from Chipatti. His memories of his earlier life as Jageshwar's son were not happy. He had apparently been murdered by a washerman — a dobi-wallah — and another hairdresser called Jawahar, who had cut the little boy's throat.

Young Ravi Shankar's story soon became widely known in the district and reached the ears of a hairdresser named Jageshwar. He called on Ravi's astounded parents and recounted that his son Munna *had* been murdered in his sixth year, in exactly the way little Ravi had described. The suspects were Chaturi, the dobi-wallah, and another hairdresser named Jawahar. They had been arrested and Chaturi had apparently indicated his guilt, but there was insufficient evidence for them to be convicted. The child Munna had been murdered barely six months before Ravi Shankar was born in July 1951. Unfortunately, when Dr. Stevenson began his investigations Ram Gupta was already dead and the boy, who was by that time almost twelve years old, could not remember much of what he had told his parents and other family and friends when he was younger. Fortunately for Stevenson, a teacher had taken the trouble to write down things that Ravi had said when he was five. By studying the teacher's records and questioning relatives and friends, Stevenson found almost thirty impressive items that bore out the young lad's testimony.

Ravi Shankar, when Stevenson saw him, still carried the birthmark around his throat that could reasonably be described as resembling the scar from the other child's murder. Those who remembered Ravi's earlier days told Stevenson that the scar had been longer and rather lower on his neck when he had been very small.

Sri Lanka, famous as the greatly appreciated sanctuary of Arthur C. Clarke, is also home to a significant Buddhist community. Buddhism is particularly sympathetic to reincarnation theory. One of Stevenson's most striking investigations comes from Sri Lanka. The subject of this investigation, a boy named Sujith, was born in August 1969 in Colombo.

As soon as he was old enough to talk, Sujith said that his *real* home was Gorakana, almost ten miles away. In fact, his name in his previous life had apparently been drawn from the name of the town, just as the celebrated Gosport Nancy had been named after the famous naval base. According to young Sujith, everyone had known him as Gorakana Sammy and in his previous life he had been a railway worker who made and sold arrack on the side.

Like other spirits such as rum, whiskey, and brandy, arrack is produced by distillation from something that has already been fermented. The basis of arrack (which comes from an old Arabian word meaning "sweet juice" or "sweet liquor") is molasses mixed with fermented, malted rice. It has a very high alcohol content and is *exceptionally powerful.*

Gorakana Sammy not only made and sold arrack, he greatly enjoyed drinking it. Sammy was fifty years old when he was struck by a passing truck and killed. In his apparent Gorakana Sammy identity, Sujith claimed to remember being married to a local beauty named Maggalin, whom he had ill-treated when hopelessly drunk on arrack.

During his life as Sammy Fernando he had always smoked Four Aces cigarettes and went in for very hot, spicy foods. Those who are familiar with the habits of heavy arrack drinkers report that there is a peculiar type of belch that indicates that the drinker is on arrack, and by which such drinkers can be identified. Another characteristic of arrack drinkers, according to those who know them well, is an appetite for particularly spicy foods.

Young Sujith begged family members to buy him arrack and Four Aces cigarettes. He was never given anything other than soft drinks, but would imbibe these in a manner that those who had known Sammy Fernando said was very characteristic of his drinking style. Young Sujith would also ask for spicy foods and hot curries — not the usual choice of children of his age.

On the basis of Stevenson's case histories and many others, it seems as though the theories of reincarnation cannot be discarded lightly. On the other hand, such apparent memories of previous lives are by no means universal. Numerous investigations, such as those undertaken by the rigorous and incisive Ian Wilson, have revealed that it is *possible* for seeming memories of past lives to have been acquired unconsciously from the pages of vivid fiction that impressed a subject long ago, or from stories and anecdotes provided by an amiable elderly neighbour or grandparent.

Such relevant criticisms of reincarnation theory need to be borne in mind carefully when evaluating its possibility. Undoubtedly, some apparent records of reincarnation can be explained in perfectly natural terms by the methods that researchers like Ian Wilson have used. On the other hand, when the most careful and accurate criticisms of reincarnation evidence have been made, a stubborn core of data refuses to dissolve away into nothingness.

Psychologists and psychiatrists with qualifications and experience to equal Arthur Guirdham's have proposed interesting alternative hypotheses. Can there sometimes be a desire in the hypnotised patient undergoing what is believed to be a regression experience? Desires, frustrations, and inhibitions can sometimes be sublimated by creating "memories" of a previous life. In such a life, the timid man who does not feel sufficiently assertive to ask his burly neighbour to turn down his stereo player recalls a totally imaginary but highly compensatory existence as a tyrant emperor who had but to raise a finger to turn the boldest of his courtiers into a trembling, nervous wreck.

Danny Kaye's performance as Walter Mitty in the brilliantly successful film *The Secret Life of Walter Mitty* (1947) provides an ideal example. A large measure of the script's success sprang from the audience's ability to identify with Mitty. Bullied and browbeaten both at work and at home, Mitty compensated by daydreaming himself into a number of heroic rôles in which he had the strength, skill, and courage of a demi-god.

If we are totally honest with ourselves, and survey our own life experiences closely, we may find that there is a fragment of the Walter Mitty technique hidden in all of us. Stage hypnotists are frequently able to demonstrate their ability to superimpose totally fictitious memories into the minds of their subjects. Asked what he had for breakfast the volunteer from the audience will tell the hypnotist and the others present that it was porridge followed by eggs, bacon, and coffee.

Once under the influence of the hypnotist, however, he can be assured that he had made his breakfast from half a grapefruit, porridge, and a cup of tea. When roused from the hypnotic trance and asked again what he had for breakfast, he will reply perfectly naturally and with every appearance of believing it himself that he indeed had grapefruit, porridge, and a cup of tea for breakfast.

There have been numerous cases in which courts, attempting to settle tragic charges of child abuse, have had to decide whether the "memories" of the allegedly mistreated children were, in fact, genuine. Or were they the traumatic result of strong suggestions put to the children by well-meaning but over-anxious counsellors who were tilling the volatile mental soil in which such false memories might well be sown and take root?

Just as memories are sometimes capable of insertion, so they are equally capable of deliberate eradication. A hypnotist can tell a client that something that causes great pain each time that it comes up into that client's memory *never actually happened*, and the memory can be almost totally eradicated.

It may be asked rhetorically how many psychopathic criminals are able to convince themselves that the atrocities they have committed never took place, or that they merely viewed them on a horror video.

If the memories upon which our human minds rely so heavily for the basic matters of everyday life can be demonstrated to be vulnerable, how much reliance can be placed on those mental experiences that seem to be the merest vestigial traces of events in a *previous* life? Hypno-regression and reincarnation evidence may provide vital clues about the human survival of death, but like all the rest of such evidence they must be approached carefully and circumspectly. We ourselves think that there is definitely something in it — but that conclusion is by no means definitive *yet*.

CHAPTER SEVEN
AUTOMATIC WRITING

Among the vast complexities of the human mind are many facilities for performing complicated functions at levels that do not impinge upon consciousness. The school-age child learning the basic skills of reading and writing has to concentrate on letter formation and the co-ordinated movements of hand and eye, the balance of the pen, the up-strokes and down-strokes. The shorthand writer taking notes at high speed is unaware of anything except the words that he or she is hearing. The transfer of those messages to the paper in front of the stenographer is an almost entirely automatic process.

Jokes about absent-minded professors are manifold. The old fellow will have placed his glasses on his forehead and then gone in search for them: the placing of the glasses on the forehead was an automatic reaction that side-stepped conscious thought and did not seem to have made any impression on that part of the memory that is available to conscious recall.

Just as the young child has to concentrate on the formation of letters, their position on, below, or above, the line, so the new driver or trainee pilot has to concentrate hard on every single movement. The experienced driver — particularly one in a car that he or she knows well — can perform several other mental and physical functions simultaneously. These vary from running through the speech she has to give at the board meeting in ten minutes to surreptitiously eating a sandwich in a plastic tray on the passenger seat.

Before the health problems associated with it were widely known, and smoking was far more common than it is today — in those golden years of driving when traffic regulations were liberal and flexible — it was probably the majority of experienced drivers who could safely negotiate heavy traffic while rolling and lighting a cigarette.

In any open-minded consideration of the phenomenon of automatic writing, these strange, multi-layered control levels of the human mind ought not to be ignored. None of us would regard the ability to smoke, drive, listen to the CD player, and plan the speech in the boardroom simultaneously as being in the least psychic or paranormal. Being able to do two, three, or a dozen things at once is simply part of the function of the normal human mind, and as a skill becomes ingrained from long practice so we become less and less aware of it.

Why then should what is referred to as "the strange, paranormal phenomenon of automatic writing" be regarded as in any way abnormal?

Unlike the span of control that we can readily recognise in the simultaneous execution of an ordinary series of simultaneous functions carried out at different levels of automatic or semi-automatic mental control, the automatic *writing* phenomenon gives every appearance of coming from some *outside* source. If the normal human mind is capable of driving a car, eating a sandwich, listening to music, and thinking about words that have to be said at an important meeting in half-an-hour's time, then all of those activities — although not being specifically thought about with the full beam of conscious attention — are nevertheless under the *same* control.

If we use the analogy of a management structure for these hierarchical levels of activity, we can see what we might describe as the "full beam of consciousness" as the managing director. Sales, production, personnel, communication, and administration are all vital parts of the business. The head of each division or department is answerable to the overall managing director — the decision-making, focal beam of direct consciousness and full awareness. Each department, however, has its own level of autonomy, and if a junior filing clerk in the production office inadvertently misplaces an important blueprint for a new project, this will not readily come to the attention of the managing director. It is only when the vital blueprint cannot be found that a frantic production director reports to the chief that there is a major problem. Contact then takes place in two directions and finally the missing documents are rediscovered and the problem is solved.

Compare this to a situation in which an industrial espionage agent has broken into the company's premises and actually stolen the vital blueprint. This is an intrusive, external factor. It is not something that is under the overall and unified control of the managing director, the production director, and the inefficient junior filing clerk. With all his faults, that filing clerk is still part of the organisation, is still working for the production director and the managing director who is above him. The clerk's error is simply an internal malfunction — what might be termed an absorbable problem that has arisen in good faith — as opposed to the external act of sabotage from the industrial espionage agent who has broken in.

Playing the violin and talking to Dr. Watson are two activities under the control of the same Sherlock Holmes's consciousness. If Holmes misfingers a note on one of the violin strings, that is merely some small fault within the unified organisation of Sherlock Holmes and Dr. Watson Incorporated. However, if Professor Moriarty sneaks in and puts molasses on the bow, that is an *intrusion*. The musical malfunction that will result is of a totally different quality from that which arises from a mere misfingering of the strings caused by a mental aberration of the performer who was solving the problem and talking to Watson while he played.

Into which of these two categories does automatic writing seem to fall?

In "The Shooting of Dan McGrew," the famous poem by Robert Service, the Ragtime Kid, who was playing the piano in the saloon at the time of the action, was having a drink. The piano stool was empty and the Man from the Creeks (who later shot Dan McGrew) lurched across the saloon and took the pianist's place. That provides another analogy for what might be thought to happen during the automatic writing phenomenon. It is not by any means a case of full possession of the automatic writing medium by a disembodied spirit, and it is a very long way removed from the destructive, total possession of the victim, such as the case of the man known as Legion in the New Testament.

It is as if — with the pianist's permission — someone else had come to play the piano while the pianist did not need it, or was not using it while he took a short break. Mediums who are expert in automatic writing cases either go into a full trance or relax completely with their hand holding a pencil or resting on a small trolley like a planchette containing a writing instrument. The medium himself, or herself, does not normally seem to be aware of what is being written, and very often the writing is rapid.

One of the most famous examples of automatic writing as an indication of the probability of departed human spirits communicating via mediums able to produce automatic writing is the complex and ongoing case known as the "cross correspondence." This reportedly involved some prominent founding members for the Society for Psychical Research who had died, and several gifted and perceptive mediums who appeared to be obtaining messages from them from the other side.

Frederick Myers was a classicist, a redoubtable scholar, and a thoroughly open and honest psychic investigator. It was the central part of his life's work to try to share his passionate belief in survival with others. He was, in fact, an evangelist in that area. He died at the beginning of the twentieth century and right up until 1930 the Society for Psychical Research made a carefully annotated and very well-sorted collection of what appeared to be over two thousand scripts that the spirit of Frederick Myers had sent through from the other side.

In addition to Myers himself, Edmund Gurney, who had passed over in 1888, and Henry Sidgwick, who had left this world in 1900, were also involved.

One of the mediums involved was Rudyard Kipling's sister, Alice Fleming, who carried out her part of the work in India. Mrs. Combe-Tennant was another of the mediums, but her work was done in London. The others were Leonora Piper, from Boston, Massachusetts, Helen Verrall, who later became Mrs. Salter, and her mother, Mrs. Verrall, senior.

The outline of the cross correspondence presupposes a strategy that challenges credibility, but its basic outline was simple and straightforward enough. The scheme was that after their deaths, Gurney, Myers, and Sidgwick would contact suitable mediums through whom they would endeavour to send small pieces of automatic writing — rather like fragments of the Dead Sea Scrolls.

These isolated passages would have little or no meaning by themselves — *but if and when they could be brought together like pieces of a jigsaw, they would be fully comprehensible*. If what came through was genuine — and it's undeniably intriguing — the three wily old scholars in the spirit world did not leave their senses of humour behind on the Earth.

Some of the passages were in Latin, others were in Greek. There were also many references to classical Greek and Latin works, largely because Myers had above all things been a classics scholar. An integral part of the Myers, Gurney, and Sidgwick plan was to use classical languages because they would not normally be expected to be within the vocabularies and linguistic ranges of the mediums who were taking part in the amazing cross correspondence.

Helen Verrall and her mother might have been exceptions, but Alice Fleming, Mrs. Combe-Tennant, and Leonora Piper — intelligent and gifted as they were — were not classical scholars.

It seems to have been Myers's idea that using small portions of script that the mediums themselves would not be able to understand would provide a useful safeguard against the counter-argument that either the mediums had composed the words from some deep subconscious level of their own minds or they had somehow put them together telepathically. The fact that both the Verralls might have had the necessary level of Greek and Latin to have enabled them to communicate it to the other mediums — if telepathy was the explanation — somewhat weakens that particular line of argument that Myers put up.

If, as the cross correspondence seems to suggest, Myers thought up the scheme *after* leaving this world, the implications for the existence and nature of the afterlife are massive. If the cross correspondence is genuine it indicates two major facts, both of which are of vital importance. The first is that the *mind* of the surviving, spiritual part of a human being is capable of retaining terrestial information and using it as a data bank when creating new ideas on the other side. The second is that the cross correspondence indicates a deep and continuing interest in — and concern with — the things of this world. Provided that Myers's spirit survived and took with it his knowledge and memories of earthly life, he would have been in a unique position to identify the mediums who would be most helpful for the great new cross correspondence psychical research experiment — *an experiment that he appears to have devised after his death.*

He was a former president of the Society for Psychical Research and as such knew perfectly well which of the mediums that the society had studied were honest, genuine, and expert at producing automatic writing. Frederick Myers's rigorously scholastic mind went to even greater depths in seeking to validate the experiment. The mediums who were receiving and recording the automatic writing for Myers, Gurney, and Sidgwick were given orders to transmit what they received to specified researchers. They were further requested to date their contributions to the cross correspondence, and, if it were possible, to obtain an impartial witness to those automatic writing sessions.

On one occasion, Mrs. Piper believed that she heard a word that sounded like *sanatos*. She changed her mind almost immediately, however, and re-rendered the word as *thanatos* — which, unbeknown to her at the time, was the Greek word for "death" — from which our modern psychiatric term "thanatomania" or "death wish" is derived. The day before Mrs. Piper received her *sanatos/thanatos* message in the middle of April 1907, Alice Fleming (who was working thousands of miles away in India) picked up the Latin word *mors*, — also meaning "death." Does it seem significant that a classics scholar like Myers should have used both the Greek and Latin terms on opposite sides of the world with two different mediums? Approximately a fortnight later, Mrs. Verrall (working in Cambridge) picked up the Latin *pallida mors*, meaning "pale death."

Mrs. Verrall and her daughter, Helen, also received some curious references from the works of the poet Robert Browning. Browning, who lived from 1812-89, was never quite regarded as a poet of the same stature as his wife, Elizabeth. When Wordsworth died in 1850, she was informally proposed as the next poet laureate and the suggestion was widely supported.

Robert Browning's *Sordello*, which was published in 1840, received a very hostile reception that put his reputation under something of a cloud in hypersensitive literary circles for the best part of twenty years. His reputation, in fact, did not revive until *The Ring and The Book* (1868) was very well received. *The Pied Piper of Hamelin* is perhaps the best known of all his work — and it seems more than slightly significant that references to it were received by Helen Verrall — the precise words being "a star above it all rats everywhere in Hamelin town."

Frederick Myers was an enthusiastic reader and admirer of Browning's work. He and the poet shared many similar ideals. It is, perhaps, again more than coincidental — in view of the Browning *Pied Piper* connection — that one of the mediums involved in the cross correspondence was none other than Leonora *Piper* from Boston, Massachusetts.

In the New Testament parable of Dives and Lazarus, the rich man and the poor beggar at his gate, there is a very interesting reference to Dives pleading with Abraham to be allowed to return to Earth. He wished to do so in order to warn his brothers — rich men like himself — to be kind and generous to the poor (men like Lazarus in desperate need) so that they not find themselves in the same after-death predicament that he was in.

A similar thought occurs in Dickens's *Christmas Carol*, when Scrooge's old partner Jacob Marley visits him in order to help him to reform so as to avoid what Marley himself is suffering by virtue of his failure to help the poor during his years on Earth. Dives wants to go back to tell people on Earth what the afterlife is like. Marley wants to talk to Scrooge; Hamlet's father's ghost in Shakespeare's play wishes to impart vital information to his son.

In January 1904, Myers seemed to share this overwhelming desire to say what he knew about the "psychic life" that he was experiencing after death. Through Alice Fleming, the medium his spirit seemed to be working with in India, Myers wrote, "If it were possible for the soul to die back into Earth life again, I should die from sheer yearning to reach out to tell you that all that we imagined is not half wonderful enough for the truth."

Centuries before Myers and his SPR colleagues lived and died, the mystic Saint Juliana of Norwich, Norfolk, England, reported that she had experienced an amazing vision of Heaven. She was asked by the other Sisters in her Order to describe for them what she had seen and heard during that glimpse of the afterlife. Juliana could only reply, "All shall be well, and all shall be well and all manner of thing shall be well!" This is not a million miles away from Myers's assertion, "All that we imagined is not half wonderful enough for the truth."

Browning's poetry was not, apparently, enough for automatic writers from beyond the grave to refer to. There was also a very famous Brazilian medium named Francisco Candido Xavier — known to his many friends and acquaintances as "Chico." Unlike all too many religious leaders, or so-called psychics, Francisco refused to accept any money for his paranormal work, and furthermore, he did a great deal to assist the poor. He is, therefore, well worth serious attention. Xavier frequently produced not fragments but entire books, and his very consistent work has occupied more than half a century.

As we suggested in the general introduction to this chapter, one explanation for the automatic writing phenomenon can, perhaps, be found in the model of the bar room pianist who gets up and leaves the instrument vacant so that someone else in the saloon can play it while he, himself, is having a drink.

Until he retired from his civil service job Xavier worked full-time but still found several hours a day to let the spirits "use" him.

To pursue the analogy of the saloon bar pianist, Xavier was extremely generous in his loan arrangements of his psychic "piano." He is perhaps less well known in Canada, the United States, and Britain than he deserves to be because as a Brazilian writing in very advanced and scholarly Portuguese, his many works are not easily accessible to those whose first language is English.

The best known, most intriguing and exciting of his works is what is probably best described as an anthology of poetry entitled *Parnaso de Alem-Tumulo* (*Parnassus from Beyond the Tomb*). This anthology is well over four hundred pages and contains nearly three hundred poems. Their style and content differ considerably.

Back in the 1950s, co-author Lionel was writing science fiction and supernatural stories for a London paperback publisher who was bringing out collections of short supernatural stories on a monthly basis. This publisher asked if all the stories in the collection could be produced under different pen names with, as far as humanly possible, different styles for each.

One of the ways in which we attempted to solve this problem was to give our pseudonymous imaginary authors different nationalities. Their names, nevertheless, were usually extractive anagrams of Lionel's full name: Robert Lionel Fanthorpe. Tales with an Irish setting were brought out under the pseudonym Peter O'Flinn; Scottish stories were by Neil Balfort; French stories appeared under the pen name Réné Rolant, and there was an amazing imaginary American author called Elton T. Neef. In our humorous short fantasy story "Curse of the Khan," written as a first-person narrative, Lionel actually *met* six of his alter egos!

Even when an experienced professional author deliberately makes every effort to create the impression that a collection of short stories has been written by seven or eight different people, it is extraordinarily difficult to write convincingly in a number of different styles.

AUTOMATIC WRITING

With that vivid personal experience from the past to draw on, it seems to us today that Xavier's *Parnaso* has a remarkable ring of truth and honesty about it. More than fifty very different, talented, Portuguese-speaking writers have what *appears* to be their work included in Xavier's book.

One very striking example of the quality and succinctness of the work comes from a piece allegedly written by Augusto Dos Anjos. Augusto was a Brazilian poet of considerable talent who had been dead for some time when Xavier "received" his words. The automatic writing poem of Augusto's was simply called "Ego Sum," the *ego* being a very emphatic use of the Latin word for "I" and *sum* being part of the Latin verb "to be." "Ego Sum" can therefore be translated simply as "I Am," but a literal translation of the rest would not do justice to the quality of the poem.

> Ego Sum
> Because I am what I am
> And who I am
> There would be no justice
> No truth, no honesty — unless I confessed simply
> And gave you my name — as a man of honour should
> I am Augusto.

Sure enough, the poem is signed — in the same automatic writing — "Augusto Dos Anjos."

Xavier's work continues to impress us favourably because a confidence trickster would have accepted with alacrity the vast fortune that his books — purporting to have come to him as automatic writing — have made for him over the years.

It is also significant that prior to his retirement almost forty years ago Xavier was a local government officer and as such clearly literate and numerate. However, there is a vast gulf between the degree of literacy required for competent letter writing and office administration and that which is required to produce what passes very convincingly as the stylistically different and expertly written poems of fifty talented poets writing in Portuguese.

If *Parnaso* presents a challenging problem and interesting evidence for survival, another of Xavier's works entitled *Nosso Lar* is a great deal more so. Xavier believed that a doctor in the spirit world had — during his earthly life — been a pioneer of tropical medicine. This spirit-doctor was Andre Luiz.

Nosso Lar is eight times longer than *Parnaso* and reads like some well-written science fiction and fantasy of C. S. Lewis or Tolkien in English. If they, or George MacDonald, had claimed to be the author of the automatic writing that Xavier produced it would have seemed credible. In *Nosso Lar*, Andre Luiz, the tropical medicine pioneer, produced a vast novel running to some nine volumes in which the hero dies very early on in the first book, so almost all the events of the novel are set in the world to come. According to what Luiz supposedly dictated to Xavier, this world beyond the grave does not bear much resemblance to the traditional pictures of Heaven or paradise drawn by major religious leaders.

What Luiz supposedly dictated described a country in which life was lived in very much the same way that it is on Earth. Apparently at Luiz's dictation, Xavier wrote, "Death is only a change of clothing. What is to come is the Heaven or Hell which we ourselves have created here."

Much of what Xavier wrote made considerable sense. He claims that Luiz informed him that human beings are the sons and daughters of God and the inheritors of time. According to Luiz, many reincarnations are needed in order to acquire the necessary wisdom and experience to complete the human quest. The ideas Luiz apparently passed on to Xavier make reincarnation a very complicated process.

Bearing in mind that Andre Luiz was a doctor of medicine, his highly technical references to other scientists such as Hugo de Vries (a Dutch botanist who had done outstanding work on the rules of plant heredity) would not have seemed to be within the data banks of Francisco Xavier.

Something akin to the mysterious cross correspondence of Myers, Gurney, and company also took place in Xavier's activities. He was working in Pedro Leopoldo and was taking from dictation — as it appeared — a book entitled *Evolution in Two Worlds*. This remarkable work came to Xavier a chapter at a time — *but his chapters did not follow on from one another*. Meanwhile, Dr. Waldo Vieira (working at a considerable distance from Pedro Leopoldo) was busily taking down the missing chapters from dictation. Finally the spirit guide who was said to be controlling Xavier put him in touch with Dr. Vieira. What is uniquely remarkable about their co-authored piece of automatic writing is that the separate chapters transcribed by Waldo and Francisco have perfect continuity once they're amalgamated.

Matthew Manning is another remarkable automatic writer, and was originally based in Cambridgeshire. His house was at one time the home of Robert Webbe. Manning's powers differ widely from Xavier's in that in Manning's case the writing seems to have appeared spontaneously on his bedroom wall. In addition to the automatic writing phenomenon and the strange graffiti that appeared on his bedroom wall, Matthew Manning also drew some very remarkable sketches in the style of Albrecht Dürer.

The transmission of automatic writing and automatic artwork, however, is by no means the end of the story. The remarkable case of medium Rosemary Brown also deserves at least a passing mention. Rosemary's contacts include Franz Liszt, whom she first thought she saw while she was still a very young child. He informed her that as an adult she would be contacted by numerous composers who had passed over, and they would transmit their music to her. In addition to Liszt, Rosemary believes that she has had musical messages from Chopin, Stravinsky, Schubert, Debussy, Brahms, and Beethoven.

When she had seen Liszt for the first time during her early childhood, she said she had not known who he was. It was not until she saw a portrait of Liszt that she recognised him as the amiable spirit, who, she reported, had visited her so many years before. It was during the early 1960s that she believes the other famous composers contacted her and enabled her to write down their music. Very often her transcriptions have been impartially witnessed, and those who have seen her writing the music down are impressed by the *speed* at which she gets the work onto paper.

The music that Rosemary claims to receive from the great, deceased composers is of a quality that greatly exceeds that of any music that she thinks she could write in her normal waking state. The concert pianist Hephzibah Menuhin viewed Rosemary's manuscripts with great respect and said that the pieces were quite distinctly in the individual styles of the dead composers concerned.

No less an authority than Leonard Bernstein was favourably impressed with what Rosemary showed him. Richard Rodney Bennet, a respected composer himself, said that in his opinion it would not be possible to fake music of the kind Rosemary Brown was transcribing *unless the person doing the faking had had the benefit of long musical training*. Rosemary had not. Despite all his own talent and experience, Bennet said that he would not have been able to fake some of what Rosemary alleged had come to her from the spirit of Beethoven — and certainly not at that speed.

When considering the very real possibility that automatic writing, drawing, and musical composition are being passed through to living mediums via composers, artists, and other talented spirits who have left Earth for the afterlife, we must also consider the interesting theory concerning what is usually referred to as the "Akashic Record."

If every idea and every event are somehow *recorded* in what for want of a better term could be referred to as the *ether*, then is it possible that the inspiration for the music of Rosemary Brown or the art of Matthew Manning are drawn from this mysterious, immaterial, eternal Akashic Record — rather than from the surviving, personal, and conscious minds of artists and musicians who have left this material world behind them?

In our opinion, the evidence from automatic writing, music, and painting tends to point in the direction of the survival of individual conscious entities rather than to a simple reading of the Akashic Record by those like Rosemary Brown and Matthew Manning who are talented enough and sensitive enough to be aware of it.

Taken as a whole, the evidence provided by automatic writing seems to suggest that some of those in the so-called spirit world have found a technique of communicating other than speaking through trance mediums, or making visual and audible appearances to those who have sufficient psychic awareness.

According to the records of some of these strange occurrences — which occasionally resemble the messages that appeared on the walls of Borley Rectory during the time of the Foysters's incumbency — no one was in the house when the writing appeared. For example, several hundred short passages along with the names of the writers have turned up in this way on the Manning wall.

We, ourselves, investigated an interesting case of apparent poltergeistic writing in a house in Cardiff in which unexplained words had appeared underneath the carpet in the front room. There were young people of an age that is typically associated with poltergeistic phenomena in the family, and it is also possible that the so-called mystery of the writing under the carpet was nothing more than harmless teenage mischief. When questioned, however, all the children in the family denied having had anything to do with it. It was in this same house that objects disappeared and turned up again in unexpected and inappropriate places. Shoes and items of clothing were found in the fridge and food from the refrigerator turned up in wardrobes and on top of bedroom cupboards.

Going back to Matthew Manning's experience and the writing on his bedroom wall, it may be interesting to consider the possibility that the automatic writing that comes through a medium has a different level of psychic energy than writing that turns up on a wall or floor. One report, for example, said that Xavier's hand, while he was actually producing the automatic writing, looked like a toy driven by an electric motor and a battery. Is the writing that appeared on the wall at Borley Rectory and on the wall of Matthew Manning's Cambridgeshire bedroom an *extension* of the power that enables the automatic writing medium to produce the scripts by hand? Are there cases where the external source of the automatic writing — if it *is* an external source — is strong enough to manage on its own without a human hand and arm as an intermediary? Or does wall writing work through a very special kind of medium, someone blessed with so much psychic power that there's enough externalised psychic energy to spare to pick up the pencil and make marks on the wall independently of direct physical contact with the medium's fingers? Could this supposed phenomenon relate in any way to the writing on the wall at Belshazzar's Feast? *Mene, mene tekel upharsin* — "You have

A mysterious hand wrote "Mene Mene Tekel Upharsin" on the wall of Belshazzar's Palace.

been weighed in the balances and found wanting." He was killed that night, and replaced by Darius the Mede.

Geraldine Cummings was another very perceptive medium who communicated through automatic writing. On one occasion she was with the great Irish poet W. B. Yeats. Geraldine's spirit guide was allegedly someone called "George." What appeared to happen was that Geraldine's hand and arm were "borrowed" by "George" to produce automatic writing. During the session that she had with Yeats, "George" was writing about some people who inhabited an ancient castle. Geraldine then asked the poet if he wanted her to carry on with it: was he interested in it? Yeats was amazed. *"That's the plot of my current book,"* he said quietly. A situation such as that one, however, would seem to open the possibility of telepathy rather than spirit communication from the other side.

Authors tend to get very closely involved in books that they are writing, especially fiction. When the author is manufacturing characters — and a setting for them to inhabit — his, or her, narrative can on occasion become very real. A number of excellent fantasy stories have been written about characters in literature who have become such an obsession with the writer that they have turned up on his or her doorstep. If Yeats's fictional castle and its inhabitants were occupying his attention it seems possible that the force manipulating Geraldine's hand was coming from Yeats's mind rather than from the disembodied spirit guide "George."

CHAPTER EIGHT
SÉANCE PHENOMENA

Those who have possessed strange psychic powers, or have *imagined* that they possessed strange psychic powers, or have cynically seen the social and economic advantages of persuading other people that they had strange psychic powers, have existed for as long as civilisation — and probably a good deal longer. If the characteristic séance phenomena are the products of an honest imagination, or a dishonest intent to deceive and defraud, they have been remarkably similar for millennia. Their common denominators are an air of mystery, an absence of strong light, and a shared social culture in which gods, demons, djinn, elemental spirits, and the ghosts of ancestors are central members of the *dramatis personae*. Faith in the power of the priest, medium, shaman, witch doctor, enchantress, or other central figure, to produce one or more of the paranormal phenomena that those attending are expecting and hoping to see, seems to be a key factor.

It is only on the rarest occasions that spirits have physically manifested themselves (factually or allegedly) and many of the best of such sightings in the literature tend to have occurred outside the séance room. The witness on these occasions did not always realise that he, or she, had seen a ghost until afterwards, because the apparition had seemed so real and solid at the time.

Far more frequent are communication codes with knocks or raps, the materialisation of a trumpet through which the spirit speaks, or the rather dim and hazy appearance of an arm or a face surrounded by more indistinct or misty substance. There are a number of impressive psychic mediums who will go into a trance at a séance and who will have no conscious knowledge or recollection of what has taken place until they come out of the trance state and talk to those who were present.

Séances are far less popular in our own time than they were a century ago, and the tragic loss of brave young servicemen's lives in the First World War led many grieving relatives and friends to seek the consolation of the séance room. To rob those who mourn seems somehow even worse than robbing the dead. Yet, no matter how many sincere and genuine mediums did their honest best to comfort the bereaved of the First World War, there were undoubtedly too many unscrupulous sharks who were prepared to play on that indescribable sorrow and sense of loss, and to mumble mysterious and expensive platitudes that were alleged to have come from the dead soldier, sailor, or airman.

Serious books on the supernatural, horror films, videos, and even comedies with a supernatural or paranormal setting have tended to provide a stereotypical image of the séance room. Through these fictional presentations, the reader, listener, or viewer has almost certainly come to expect to find a number of tense and keenly interested people sitting around a table with their hands resting purposefully on it.

A few years ago, when B movies were rather more predictable than they are today, there used to be a little game much loved by regular film-goers called "Guess who gets killed." There were certain phrases that must have been employed by every Hollywood scriptwriter of the time that pointed unerringly at any character who would not be around when the film ended. There were immortal lines in war films, such as "Just one more mission, Sarge, and then I'm going home." Another favourite was the old hero or heroine who would remove a lucky charm, bracelet, or necklace and pass it to the favoured youngster and say, "Don't ask me how, but I'm sure this will get you safely through." There was a ninety-nine percent chance that the donor of the talisman would be doing a convincing impersonation of the last dodo bird before the celluloid was put back into its canister.

In the same way as the death of a B movie character could be predicted with almost total certainty once the clichés were known, so in film and theatre presentations of séances the medium has to ask, "Is there anyone there?" If the voice of the medium is theatrically sepulchral, so much the better. If the eyes are staring like Svengali's, or closed in deep concentration, the image of the stereotypical séance is enhanced.

It goes without saying that a contemporary séance attended by perfectly normal people and focused upon the work of a genuine well-known and well-respected medium, or sensitive, is nothing like that image. The difference between the popular picture of a séance and those who attend it and the reality is about as close as brightly coloured pantomime scenery and the real objects that scenery represents. The classical illustration from Plato of the hapless prisoners in the cave illustrates the difference between the popular idea of the séance and the real thing very clearly. The prisoners in the cave all had their backs to the light source and by virtue of the way in which they were imprisoned, all had to look ahead at the cave wall on which flickering shadows of *something* were cast.

A group of bearers with statues and models of real objects on their heads then passed *behind* the prisoners who were looking at the shadows on the wall and *in front of* the inadequate source of intermittent light. Consequently, always assuming (as the illustration never quite makes clear) that the unfortunate prisoners in the cave with the light behind them had been there since the day of their birth, their understanding of reality would be based upon such inadequate data as they were able to draw from beholding the flickering and distorted *shadows* of objects that were themselves only imperfect *models* of reality. Whatever goes on at the séances that are portrayed in supernatural stories, films, and videos, they bear as much relationship to the real thing as the shadowy pictures on the cave wall do to their originals. It is essential to keep this difference clear in our minds from the outset.

In *The Screwtape Letters*, C. S. Lewis has a senior demon telling the junior one that the best way to deceive a human being into thinking that demons do not exist is to conjure up in his mind a sort of pantomime devil with a bright red complexion, horns, hooves, a tail, and a pitchfork. As Lewis then points out, because the human being cannot easily believe in the reality of such a ludicrous and nonsensical figure, *he manages to persuade himself that if that caricature is a demon, then no demons exist.*

Lewis's argument is a good one. If the sceptic tells himself, or herself, that séances are held by oil-lamp or candlelight in heavily panelled Victorian parlours, with nothing more animated than an aspidistra in the room, and a medium who produces all kinds of amateurish psychic frauds by the use of muslin and papier mâché face masks, then the honest sceptic will have the utmost difficulty in believing anything of any value is to be learned from such a performance.

Once the contemporary reality of a session with a medium or sensitive replaces the caricature, the open-minded investigator may be willing to agree that some of the messages purporting to come through from the spirit world are very difficult to explain away. They may be regarded as good luck on the part of the medium, as synchronicity, or as telepathy. Occam's Razor, that valuable instrument of mediaeval argument, stated at its most basic that in order to reach an understanding of a problem we do our best mental work when we simplify. Cut away all that is not essential; prune back all the superfluous shoots that do not appear to have any fruit on them.

The simplest and most direct explanation for the phenomena of the séance room is that the immortal spirits of departed human beings have come to communicate through the medium, who is simply an ordinary, sensible, rational human being — just like the rest of us — but one who is able to see and hear psychic phenomena of which the majority of us are unaware. Other possibilities include the much-quoted Akashic Record in the ether, to which it may be supposed that the people classified as mediums and sensitives are able to tune in. Telepathy cannot be ruled out except in cases where the knowledge supplied via the medium is known *only* to what purports to be the departed spirit who is communicating, and where that arcane knowledge is verified by subsequent events, or subsequent research.

Some simplistic religious theorists put forward the view that all so-called psychic, paranormal, and anomalous phenomena in which researchers are interested are merely the tantalising deceptions of demons and evil spirits and as such ought to be left severely alone. Needless to say, this is not a view that we — as serious researchers since the 1950s — are likely to share!

Mediums who inspire the greatest confidence are those who give what they and their clients believe to be an important and compassionate service to the bereaved *without charge*. One of the greatest of these altruistic and otherworldly mediums was John Campbell Sloan. Sloan was that much sought after type of sensitive known as a direct voice medium. If he was genuine, as he certainly *seems* to have been, then he was a man in whose presence spirits of the departed could hold meaningful conversations with their nearest and dearest. Not only were the words of the spirits characteristic of their vocabulary levels and speech patterns, but their actual, audible voices were also remarkably like those that they had been known for during their lives.

Sloan had received no formal education to speak of — very unusual for a Scot — and for more than half a century, while he conducted fascinating and intriguing séances without charging a penny, he supported himself by working as a tailor, a garage man, and a newsagent. J. A. Findlay wrote a definitive account of Sloan's work entitled *On the Edge of the Etheric*. Findlay was massively impressed when a voice that he believed to be that of his father, the late Robert Downie Findlay, spoke to him distinctly at the first of the Sloan séances that he attended. Findlay's father passed over some information to his son that the younger man knew was shared by only one other person, and that other person — like Findlay senior — had been dead for several years. The son, Arthur, was, therefore, the only *living* man who had that information.

The late David Kidston was the only other person who had had access to it, *and Kidston was the next speaker through the apparent mediumship of John Campbell Sloan at that séance.* When Findlay wrote up the report he made the point that he was unknown to people at the séance, and he did not give his identity when he joined them. He was convinced beyond a shadow of a doubt that he knew no one in the séance room and no one in the séance room knew him. He was equally certain that the explanations normally put forward regarding accomplices and ventriloquism were totally irrelevant to the experience that he described. Reading the detailed records that Findlay left in *On the Edge of the Etheric*, the researcher is reminded of equally detailed reports of the mysterious shaking tent phenomenon of the *pilotois* of North America. The American medicine man producing the shaking tent demonstration seemed to have the ability to create two or three distinct voices either simultaneously or with so little space between them that they *sounded* simultaneous. On more than one occasion John Campbell Sloan was also able to produce two and sometimes three alleged spirit voices at one and the same time. Sloan was certainly a very remarkable man and the phenomena that accompanied his séances are very difficult indeed to explain other than as the spirits of departed human beings who had returned to speak with their families and friends once more, with the help of whatever curious powers Sloan was able to place at their disposal.

Admiral Usborne Moore was deeply impressed by Mrs. Etta Wriedt, an American medium based in Detroit, Michigan. Where all too many mediums who fell under suspicion liked to work at some distance from those who were working with them, and a fair proportion of them favoured using a cabinet or cubicle of some sort, Etta joined those who were attending the séance as readily and as simply as if they were merely having a tea party.

Just like John Campbell Sloan, Etta Wriedt somehow seemed to be able to produce two, three, or even four voices *simultaneously*. The Admiral was not the kind of man who is easy to deceive. Once Mrs. Wriedt got fully into her stride and the spirit voices were flowing all around her, the Admiral testified that with two or three voices talking at once from different parts of the room he forgot that those with whom he was in conversation were supposed to be "dead," whatever "dead" means.

Lionel's grandmother, Phoebe Christian Garbutt, was born Phoebe Christian Tilney in the village of Yaxham, just outside East Dereham, England. Her father was the village blacksmith. Like many Norfolk girls of her generation, she was intrigued by the scandals that frequently surrounded King Edward VII. With typical Victorian propriety, Phoebe would look knowledgeable and hint — very politely — that there were a number of families in the district who had a strong (but quite unofficial!) claim to royal blood via the lusty King Edward. The scandal reached the Dowager Duchess of Warwick at one time, and those who dared claimed that she had been one of Edward VII's many lovers.

The dowager duchess invited Mrs. Wriedt to come and stay with her because Warwick Castle seemed to be the site of a number of curious paranormal experiences. When Etta was taken up to her room and helped to settle in, one or two of her items of luggage were temporarily left outside her door as the unpacking proceeded. The dowager duchess, waiting like a good hostess outside Etta's room so that she would be available as soon as her guest emerged, noticed one of the direct voice medium's trumpets among the items in the corridor outside the guestroom.

Idly, she picked it up and did the most natural thing in the world: she held it against her ear to see if she could hear anything. What she heard made her blood run cold. According to the report she actually heard the voice of the late King Edward through the trumpet. As soon as she recovered from the initial surprise, she began a conversation with her former lover — part of which was in German.

While Mrs. Wriedt was staying at Warwick Castle with the dowager duchess, a number of direct voice séances were held. The late king came through volubly at a great majority of these. He was, in fact, so dominant a psychic presence that the dowager duchess lost her nerve and asked Mrs. Wriedt to return to the United States.

The Dowager Duchess of Warwick and King Edward VII are by no means insignificant witnesses and participants from what might be termed both sides of the séance experience, but celebrated as they were they pale into insignificance beside a New York séance that took place in the 1920s involving the great oriental scholar Dr. Neville Whymant.

If any man enjoyed the reputation of being an expert on ancient Chinese history, philosophy, and literature, that man was Neville Whymant. At this particular séance, what sounded to him like authentic ancient Chinese flute music preceded a quiet, polite, scholarly voice that gave the name K'ung-Fu-T'zu, which is Confucius in Chinese.

In order fully to appreciate the importance of this particular communication, it must be borne in mind that Neville Whymant in the 1920s was rightly regarded as one of the top ten scholars in the field. Such men and women know one another well and respect the abilities of their own small, elite group of top experts who understand the subject at a depth other researchers have not plumbed.

A chess anecdote illustrates the point. An international grand master was sitting in a train, using a small portable chess set to work out some very erudite moves. He was on his way to an important world tournament. A stranger entered the compartment, watched the international grand master for a moment or two, and then said casually, "Would you like a game?"

The grand master sighed wearily, but politely. "All right, I'll give you a queen and a rook handicap."

The stranger who had asked for a game looked deeply offended. "You don't know me!" he exclaimed indignantly. "How on earth do you know that you can give me such a massive handicap?"

The grand master smiled ruefully. "It is simply *because* I don't know you that I feel certain I can afford to give you a handicap of that size," he replied rather sadly. International grand masters all know one another, and know each other's strengths and weaknesses on the board.

It was the same in the 1920s with Neville Whymant and the other experts in ancient Chinese language and culture. The great orientalist made a reference during the séance to a particularly obscure passage from the brilliant old Chinese sage, which seemed to Neville to have been incorrectly translated.

It was his feeling that, perhaps, it had been incorrectly written at the start. Was it possible that Confucius's amanuensis had made an error? What happened next was little short of electrifying. Neville referred to the problematic passage and recited the opening words. The Chinese voice, which identified itself as Confucius immediately after the strange flute music, went through the passage twice. Reports of the séance record that the first rendition was exactly as the quotation was found in all the best standard works of reference. The second time Confucius's words were recited by the disembodied Chinese voice there were minor changes and emendations that made the passage clearer than the definitive textual versions known to the top scholars.

Finally, the mysterious voice asked, "Does that not make the passage clearer?" Neville was certain beyond a shadow of doubt that only a handful of other Chinese scholars could possibly have explained the quote from Confucius as that disembodied voice in the séance room had done. Because the scholars at Whymant's level all knew one another so well, Neville was certain that none of them were in the United States at the time that the séance involving the Confucius episode took place.

Towards the end of the nineteenth century, the famous medium D. D. Home collaborated with William Crookes, who was widely recognised as outstanding by his fellow scientists. A Fellow of the Royal Society, Crookes was the discoverer of thallium. Scientific accuracy was extremely important to him and after almost thirty scrupulously documented experiments, Crookes was convinced that D. D. Home really had the ability to alter the weight of various objects — including people — and to induce table rapping. So accurate and consistent were the measurements that Crookes recorded that he himself explained the phenomenon as an entirely new form of energy to set alongside light, heat, electricity, and the other energy forms already known to physics. Analysing his own observations, Crookes called the new force that they appeared to show *psychic force*. As a contemporary of Sigmund Freud and Carl Jung, Crookes was interested in studying the states of mind and psychological factors involved in the manifestation of this new psychic energy. He became particularly interested in the idea that the existence of such energy — which he felt he had proved to his own satisfaction at least — indicated the existence of other dimensions, *psychic dimensions*.

Of particular interest as far as the Crookes's and Home's experiments were concerned is that a number of them, like valid laboratory experiments in the natural sciences, appear to have been repeatable. The physicist Sir Oliver Lodge was one of the contemporary scientists who seemed to have above average success with the experiments that Home and Crookes had pioneered. Additional work was conducted by Everard Feilding, who did a number of tests involving the medium Eusapia Palladino. Feilding later met and married Stanislawa Tomczyk, who was one of the most remarkable young mediums of the time.

In her normal, waking state Stanislawa produced all kinds of séance and poltergeistic phenomena in a rather haphazard, unexpected, and spontaneous way. Feilding discovered that under hypnosis she seemed to be able to produce the same phenomena practically at will, and much more frequently. There is good evidence that Stanislawa was able to make small domestic objects such as buttons, spoons, and matchboxes move without touching them, and there are reports that she was also able to cause them to levitate simply by making a gesture close to them.

If ever a good and honest man did not deserve the criticism and controversy that surrounded his work, that man was J. B. Rhine of Duke University in North Carolina.

The brilliant Francis Bacon — whose connection with the famous Oak Island Money Pit mystery may one day be proved, if some of his alleged "missing manuscripts" are dredged from its murky depths — was a pioneering scientist in his own way, as well as a writer and statesman. One of Bacon's most interesting theories was that random, or apparently random, events such as shuffling and dealing a pack of cards or throwing dice could be controlled by using what he described as "the binding of thoughts." This was his sixteenth-century term for what we would today call telekinesis. Bacon's sixteenth- and seventeenth-

Sir Francis Bacon was alleged to have hidden some of his greatest secrets in this mysterious watermark code.

century experiences and ideas were remarkably close to Rhine's later thoughts in the 1930s.

It was Collingwood, the historian, who came up with the aphorism that all history is the history of thought. The idea behind that profound wisdom of Collingwood's was that the human mind is a receptacle, an environment, perhaps, in which thoughts live. Collingwood's statement is rather like the geneticist's joke that a chicken is only an egg's device for creating another egg.

So the idea that had once dwelt in Bacon's wide-ranging and fertile mind now crossed the centuries to North Carolina and Rhine's laboratory. He decided to follow Bacon's suggestion rather than comb through volume after volume of evidence from earlier séance phenomena. With the advantages of early twentieth century technology, Rhine was able to throw dice mechanically with a degree of randomness that Bacon had not been able to use in the sixteenth and seventeenth centuries. After many years of rigorous work, Rhine produced results that in our opinion are statistically significant despite criticisms that were levelled at him later.

So where does Rhine's work fit into the overall exploration and examination of typical séance phenomena? What implications does psychokinesis (PK) have for the validity of séance room evidence as a pointer to the immortality of the soul and its ability to communicate?

No analysis of séance phenomena would be complete without reference to Eileen Garrett, one of the most amazing mediums of all time. To say that Eileen Jeanette Vancho was a larger than life character would be a crass understatement. Mrs. Garrett had been born into the Vancho family in County Meath, Ireland. Much of her childhood was spent in and around the famous Hill of Tara, which had mystical associations going back millennia.

Eileen grew up with the firm expectation of seeing and hearing the "little people," as though they were as much a part of the Meath landscape as the hills and trees. Talking about her own psychic abilities and expectations of the paranormal, young Eileen attributed her talent and her attitude, to a significant extent, to the *familiarity with death* that so many of her friends, neighbours, and family shared. Her own parents died when she was a very young child, her husband was killed in the First World War, and three of her four children did not live to reach maturity.

Eileen had amazing powers of survival. She was very much what Americans mean by their very positive and complimentary epithet "unsinkable." She came to New York and American citizenship via the south of France and London, and on the way she met many literary giants who greatly enjoyed her friendship. Aldous Huxley, Robert Graves, H. G. Wells, Bernard Shaw, D. H. Lawrence, and W. B. Yeats were all proud to count themselves among her circle. There is small wonder then that her publishing career was such a great success.

When Eileen conducted séances herself she used a number of spirit guides, including an Asian man named Uvani. Whether or not he had been a martial arts master in life, he certainly seemed to be a very potent minder and guardian of the door to the spirit world. What purported to be other souls attempting to speak through Garrett's mediumship had to get past Uvani first.

It was none other than Eileen Garrett who was involved in the famous London séance of 7 October 1930, which was organised by the notorious Harry Price, at that time Director of the National

Laboratory of Psychic Research. The other people present included Ethel Beenham and an Australian journalist, Ian Coster.

On 5 October, two days before the famous séance, the R101 airship had crashed in northern France on its maiden voyage. Six people survived, forty-eight were killed. The alleged spirit messages began with a flood of tears from Eileen Garrett, then what purported to be the voice of Flight Lieutenant Carmichael Irwin. He reported that the dirigible had too much bulk and mass for her engine to handle. She was drastically under-powered. The lifting power, said Irwin, was far too small: it had been wrongly calculated. An elevator jammed, an oil pipe became plugged. One technical detail after another came through in what seemed to be the anguished commentary from the dead aviator.

It is relevant to note that although Eileen Garrett was a highly intelligent, widely travelled, and very successful businesswoman, she knew little or nothing about the technical details of the construction and operation of airships. What she did know a great deal about, however, was the experience of psychic mediumship.

Concerning her sensations in trance Eileen said, "The space behind the forehead clears and becomes suffused with soft light in which changing colours play an important part, and I actually see a dimension that is colour."

Price sent a transcript of the notes apparently supplied by the dead Irwin via Eileen Garrett to an acquaintance of his by the name of Charlton. Price described him as an expert on dirigibles. Charlton said that Irwin's testimony was amazing and showed a high level of specialist technical knowledge. Charlton himself, however, was not quite the expert that Price made him out to be. He did work at Cardington, where the R101 was built, but only as a member of the ground crew. He was not known to have been an aeronautical engineer, neither was he a pilot nor a member of the aircrew test staff. It is also important to note that he, like Price and Mrs. Garrett, was an enthusiastic spiritualist with a message to proclaim.

Others with a better knowledge of dirigible science also saw the transcript that had been shown to Charlton and were far less impressed by it than he had been. It should also be noted objectively that since the disaster every national newspaper had contained detailed reports of the tragedy, which might well have been embedded in Mrs. Garrett's subconscious. As a publisher she well knew the importance of keeping up with news and current affairs. Even allowing for the problems with Charlton, as a rather dubious "expert," Garrett's R101 séance and apparent contact with Irwin cannot be dismissed or discredited lightly.

Traditional séance phenomena often seem to be centred on larger than life characters like Mrs. Garrett. The question then arises as to whether psychic sensitivity — far from being the prerogative of quiet, meditative introverts — is in some way positively correlated with forceful, ebullient, outgoing personalities.

A remarkable Frenchman, Hippolyte Leon Denizard Rivail, was born in the city of Lyons in France very early in the nineteenth century. It was young Hippolyte's good fortune to be sent to the Yverdon Institute in Switzerland, which was then in the care of the pioneering educational reformer Pestalozzi. The vast and benign difference between Pestalozzi and other educationalists of his time was that Pestalozzi did not believe in repressive discipline and the idea that children should be seen and not heard. Above all else Pestalozzi wanted the children in his care to be able to develop their *individuality*. For him, *personality* was king. This did not mean, of course, that the educational freedom to develop that he advocated in his Institute went with a slack ethos: far from it. Children were taught for nine or ten hours each day and their curriculum would have delighted British educationalists two centuries later.

Pestalozzi's teaching covered a complete spectrum of both the sciences and the arts, and students like Rivail with Catholic backgrounds were also able to study their religion. Hippolyte liked Pestalozzi and the Yverdon principles so much that he himself decided to become a teacher, mainly so that he could follow in Pestalozzi's footsteps and spread his ideas further. By the end of the first quarter of the nineteenth century, Rivail had achieved his ambition to open a Pestalozzi-style school in Paris, and had written the first of over twenty educational books dealing with mathematics, the French language, and general educational ideas.

Like many idealists of that period, Rivail was not able to make a financial success of his educational establishment. Within ten years budgetary difficulties had forced him to close the school, and he worked as an accountant simply to bring in enough money to support his wife and himself.

Anna Blackwell, the translator of a number of Rivail's works into English, described him as a man with colossal energy and stamina who never gave up. She also found him to be cold and lacking in imagination.

Hearing of what had taken place in Hydesville, New York, had a profound life-changing effect on Rivail. Around the middle of the nineteenth century, reports reached Paris of séances in the United States during which tables had moved around of their own volition — rather like the Barbados coffins — and mysterious sounds were heard.

It is interesting to note in passing that there were mysterious sounds from the Barbados vault as well. Although the evidence is scanty as far as the Barbados noises were concerned, it was said in some of the earliest reports that the vault, although constructed much earlier, was not used until 1807 primarily because of the mysterious noises reported to be emanating from it.

The mid-nineteenth century séance episodes, which centred on the home of the Fox family in New York, caused such a sensation that news of them raced round the European capitals, including Paris.

Rivail had a healthily sceptical Fortean attitude to this strange new séance phenomenon, which was one of the most fascinating novelties in mid-nineteenth century Europe. In one of his early texts he had expressed strong disbelief in ghosts, and had followed this up by declaring publicly that he would believe in such phenomena only when he saw them for himself.

Lionel and Patricia Fanthorpe inside the haunted Chase Vault at Oistin, Christchurch, Barbados.

SÉANCE PHENOMENA

The lucid mind of Charles Forte would have applauded loudly. Few things are as valuable to human progress as healthy scepticism.

A technique widely practised by the early spiritualists of Rivail's day was referred to as "basket writing." Rivail saw this in operation and was moderately impressed by what he saw. While regarding most séance phenomena at surface level as somewhat trivial, Rivail was nevertheless sufficiently impressed to want to investigate it further.

He had a great friend named Victorien Sardou, who had been involved with séance work for five or six years. Being a professional dramatist, Sardou was one of those who had seen to it that records had been kept during that time and those notes were now shown to the formerly sceptical Rivail. Hippolyte was duly impressed. It was part of his serious and determined nature to follow things through, and now that he was impressed by séance phenomena he, himself, engaged the services of a medium by the name of Japhet — the kind of mystical pseudonym reminiscent of the era of the patriarchs like Noah.

Rivail himself was not averse to using pseudonyms when it suited him. Based partly on the information that he had received from Victorien Sardou and Japhet, Rivail brought out a book entitled *Le Livre des Esprits* (*The Book of the Spirits*) in 1857. He produced it under the name of Allan Kardec. There is some evidence that a genuine Kardec had been a Breton ancestor of Rivail's of whom Hippolyte was quite proud.

Rivail did not live to see 1870, but during the last fifteen or so years of his life he produced a flood of books dealing with psychic phenomena based upon his own experiences and upon the tenets of spiritism, which he founded.

It is important to understand that spiritism, which was Rivail's brainchild, differed very considerably from the *spiritualism* that could be said to have begun in 1848 in the Fox home in New York. The differences between spiritism and spiritualism were very important to the followers of both movements.

In its broadest and simplest form, spiritualism as a creed could be described as the basic philosophy that human beings contain an immortal essence that survives death, and true personality, soul, or spirit, goes on to another realm of existence. Spiritism, on the other hand, as might have been expected considering the character of its founder, begins with the premise that two worlds — the *invisible* and the *visible* — both exist. The former, according to Rivail and his immediate followers, contains what they describe as incorporeal beings. The visible world, on the other hand, contains beings like us.

The followers of spiritism also believed that what they referred to as spirit was a *substance*, like liquids, solids, or gases in our physical universe. They argued, however, that this spirit in which they believed — despite being substantial in a very odd sort of way — was composed largely, if not entirely, of quintessential matter, and as such could not be perceived by the five human senses.

Just as Descartes wrestled with the metaphysical problem of the manner by which mind and brain made their connections, so Rivail, alias Allan Kardec, and his followers in the spiritist movement argued about the way in which the quintessential matter of spirit made contact with the physical body of a human being. They postulated that there was some sort of half-way substance, for which they proposed the term "perispirit."

In the view of Rivail and his spiritist movement, human beings acquire a physical body at birth, which disintegrates when it is overwhelmed by physical death. In their doctrine, the immortal essence, or spirit, stays behind when the normal flesh and blood physical body disintegrates and the spiritual essence finally returns in another body. Spiritism, therefore, embraces reincarnation as an integral part of its conceptual structure. Although he investigated so many well-authenticated cases of what seemed to be thoroughly genuine mediumship, Kardec was never fully convinced of the importance of the messages that were received at the séances that he attended and investigated. He concluded that some of those on the other side who were trying to communicate with friends and relatives through the services of a medium were just as mixed a bag as mortal men and women are on this planet.

He said on one occasion as he ploughed through mountains of investigative reports and alleged psychic messages, "Those who have passed over are like those of us who remain behind. Some produce exceptionally good work, others produce trivia." It was always his contention that researchers into the paranormal had to be on their guard and should invariably enter an investigation with what Kardec referred to as "their critical and logical faculties" in full operation.

At its peak, mediumship, the séance room, and different approaches to the subject — such as the wide gap that existed between spiritism and spiritualism — sometimes extended to savage and bitter feuds between rival mediums. These led on occasion to accusations of sexual impropriety and even prostitution. There were those critics of the séance industry boom who hinted darkly that the gloomy lighting and emotional tension among those of the bereaved who sought consolation in séance phenomena might also have made them vulnerable to sexual impropriety. One classic example was the on-going and very heated feud between an attractive young medium named Florence Cook and her rival Mrs. Guppy. The nubile young Florence Cook operated through a "spirit guide" who was known as Katy King. In life, according to the legend, Katy had been the daughter of Henry Morgan, the swashbuckling pirate commander who later became Governor of Jamaica. Mrs. Guppy attempted to outdo Florence by materialising Florence's Katy King. The Guppy camp did their best to undermine and destroy Florence Cook's work, while Florence retaliated by publicly accusing Mrs. Guppy and her entourage of running what the Victorians so quaintly referred to as "a house of assignation." Examined seriously and objectively, there do seem to be undeniable links between sexual energy as expressed in tantric practices and those of certain self-proclaimed black magicians like Gregor A. Gregorius, who called himself Master Saturnus and believed that magic and sex were inextricably linked. What seems far more probable, however, is that what Sigmund Freud would have referred to as libido, psychic or nervous energy, is capable of expressing itself both in sexuality and in other aspects of life where the energy seems directed to power-seeking or control. Politicians like Lloyd George and Kemal Ataturk were both notorious to different degrees for their unbridled sexual appetites, as well as for their leadership, dominance, and political acumen.

Evidence for this link between libidinous energy and the world of the paranormal inevitably turns in the direction of poltergeist phenomena. It may, perhaps, be theorised that there is some sort of two-way communication between human psychosexual energy and the objective, external world. If it is the libido that causes poltergeist phenomena — movements of matter in the physical world — is it equally possible that aspects of the physical world can in turn revitalise and enhance the libido? It is debatable whether self-styled magicians like Louis Culling really obtained the benefits they thought they had acquired from their mysterious Mexican herbal infusions, or whether it was largely a matter of wishful thinking and overwrought imagination.

The main point of this particular argument in so far as human survival is concerned is the question of whether the ability of libidinous psycho-dynamism to affect the material world is indicative of its independence of the material body. In other words, if it is the libido under certain circumstances that produces poltergeist phenomena quite apart from any physical contact with the human being associated with those phenomena, then, perhaps, it may be suggested that an immaterial psychic *something* is not only able to operate outside the physical body in which it was generated *but might go on to survive the dissolution of that physical body.*

CHAPTER NINE
POLTERGEISTS

We concluded our examination of séance phenomena with the suggestion that poltergeist activity may be associated with an aspect of human personality that is non-material and which, therefore, has a strong chance of surviving bodily death. Poltergeist phenomena are among the most persistent and spectacular of all paranormal cases.

If ever one individual seemed to encapsulate within himself almost *all* poltergeist activities, that man was Carmine Mirabelli. So many incredible reports were made about him, so many amazing stories told of his astounding abilities, that his connection with poltergeist activity was almost a backwater to the great, surging, tidal river of his dynamic life.

Two of the most reliable and impressive witnesses to Mirabelli's vast range of paranormal abilities were Eurico de Goes and Miguel Karl. De Goes was a particularly well-read intellectual and an academic librarian who became interested in psychical research after the tragic death of his beautiful young wife. His attraction to investigations of paranormal phenomena was based almost entirely on his hope of being able to reach her in the spirit world.

Some of the materialisations that Mirabelli is alleged to have been able to perform were said to have been so realistic and durable that doctors were able to examine them. Mirabelli seems to have attracted as many rumours, myths, and legends as King Arthur and Robin Hood put together. But even when the most dubious of these have been discarded, there still remains a granite core of Mirabelli fact, particularly concerning poltergeist-type phenomena, which obdurately refuses to dissolve away.

Mirabelli was born towards the end of the nineteenth century in the little town of Botucatu, about one hundred and fifty miles from São Paulo. His father was a Lutheran pastor who was remembered mainly for his kindness, sincerity, and generosity. Generosity and kindness were also characteristic of Mirabelli himself. His first job after leaving school was in a shoe shop in São Paulo, where boxes of shoes flew off the shelves in poltergeist fashion while he was attempting to serve customers.

This report about him is remarkably similar to our own experience in the haunted bookshop that we investigated in San Antonio, Texas, close to the site of the Alamo. Books moved around in that shop apparently of their own volition and those who knew the background of the strange episodes there were of the opinion that the shop had been built over the site where the Mexican soldiers, having stormed the Alamo, had cremated the bodies of the defenders.

It is equally possible, of course, that a member of the staff unwittingly produced the phenomena, much as Mirabelli apparently did in the shoe shop where he worked in São Paulo. So much wild talk followed Mirabelli when he was forced to leave his job at the shoe shop that it was generally suspected that he must be clinically insane, and the unlucky young man was incarcerated in Juquery Asylum. There Dr. Franco da Rocha wrote a report on him, as did his colleague Dr. Felipe Aché.

Lionel Fanthorpe at the Alamo in San Antonio, Texas, USA. Do the ghosts of the fearless defenders haunt Brentano's Bookshop nearby?

Patricia Fanthorpe at Brentano's Bookshop in San Antonio, where poltergeist activities have been reported.

Dr. Aché came very close to the theory of libido, or nerve energy, examined earlier on. He believed that the strange phenomena that appeared to accompany Mirabelli were "the result of nervous forces radiating. We all have them," he wrote, "but Mirabelli has them in excess."

Dr. da Rocha gave a detailed description of the kind of telekinetic, poltergeist-type displays that he witnessed while with Mirabelli. A skull was placed on top of a glass and when the doctor asked Mirabelli to make it rotate, *it did*. Both the glass and the skull balanced on it then toppled over on the table. Dr. da Rocha picked them up again and the display continued. In his opinion, some sort of *psychic radiation* seemed to have come from Mirabelli and entered the skull.

In addition to the careful observations of Mirabelli that de Goes carried out over a long period, the medium was also examined and his work observed and analysed by the professional conjurer Carlos Gardonne Ramos, who was widely regarded as an expert in the field of stage magic and illusions. In Ramos's opinion it was not possible for the things that Mirabelli did to be done by a professional conjuror by trickery or by sleight of hand. In other words, as far as one expert stage illusionist was concerned, whatever Mirabelli did was due to some strange psychic power and *not* to prestidigitation.

DEATH

Poltergeistic apports were part of Mirabelli's stock in trade. Sir Douglas Ainslie was attending a mediumistic session with Mirabelli in 1928. As he entered the house, there on the hall table was the small travelling clock that Sir Douglas had left safely *inside his suitcase in his bedroom at his hotel.*

Some expert psychic investigators tend to the view that the *character* of the medium is to some extent, perhaps, reflected in the phenomena that he, or she, attracts. Occasional minor pranks and simplistic practical jokes are often associated with poltergeist phenomena. These minor events are by no means dangerous or malevolent. It is almost as if a schoolchild's sense of humour still clung vestigially to the adult. The most sombre and solemn among us may occasionally have minute humorous quirks that seem totally out of character.

Did a powerful, serious, benign, and highly intelligent medium like Mirabelli have a tendency to perform one or two of these minor practical jokes integrated into his personality? At some of his sessions things moved about the room from one shelf to another. A pair of glasses was mislaid and turned up again. Flowers drifted into a room through a window that was not only locked but *sealed,* and a religious carving weighing a good twenty pounds came in by the same route without damaging the window at all. It floated, much as the flowers had done, toured the room — according to the report — like a sergeant-major inspecting his troops, and then drifted out again as quietly as it had entered.

Whatever Mirabelli seemed to attract in the way of psychic forces, he was himself quite benign. If there is anything in the theory that mediums who have a sinister side to their nature are capable of attracting and, perhaps, using evil forces, a man with Mirabelli's massive psychic energy could have caused as much damage as a stick of dynamite going off in a confined space.

One of the most gruesome reports recorded by de Goes concerned parts of a decomposing corpse that filled the séance room with an indescribable stench and grotesque visual effects that would have gladdened the heart of any Hollywood horror director. De Goes himself described it as reminding him of some of the worst excesses of Edgar Allan Poe.

If poltergeist movements of objects are well documented, carefully reported, and almost impossible to explain away, then teleportation is more remarkable still. It is said of Mirabelli that on one occasion he was on the Luz station platform in São Paulo where he was waiting with a group of friends and acquaintances to catch the next train to São Vicente. According to the witnesses who were with him, Mirabelli *disappeared* as suddenly and mysteriously as the ill-fated captain and crew of the *Mary Celeste*, or Benjamin Bathurst (the missing diplomat of Napoleonic times, who walked around the horses and was never seen again).

Time passed. Mirabelli's companions became extremely anxious. They telephoned the house in São Vicente where he was known to be heading, and which was at least fifty miles from São Paulo. Mirabelli was already there, and had been there for ten or fifteen minutes. Could it possibly have happened?

If it did, it is not unique in the literature of paranormal phenomena. All over the world people have appeared and disappeared without seemingly having used any of the normal means of transport open to human beings. De Goes recorded the teleportation episode as a simple and straightforward factual one, and not as part of the Mirabelli mythology or one of the strange legends surrounding him. It has to be said on de Goes's behalf that Mirabelli was by no means the only person with abnormal powers whom he had investigated with great care and thoroughness. No other medium had impressed him at all. He was inclined to be sceptical and cynical; he was also rigorous and thorough. He believed in examining everything himself, searching for means of entrance, or exit, which would make fraud or deception possible.

In Mirabelli's time the Roman Catholic Church establishment in Brazil was vituperatively antagonistic towards almost any form of spiritualism or spiritism. But one wise and broad-minded priest, Jose Maria de Castro, was favourably impressed after he had actually met Mirabelli for himself and had learned something of his strange powers at first hand. De Castro said categorically that Mirabelli was a good man, and a man of faith, whom the church leaders ought not to criticise until they had seen him for themselves.

A question mark of the first magnitude still hovers over the marvellous Mirabelli. If even a fraction of what was reported of him and his immensely strange powers is true, then, almost unaided, he points unwaveringly to the strongest possibility of the survival of the human soul and to the existence of a parallel realm that is not material.

We, ourselves, have had considerable first-hand experience of the so-called "haunted car" of Eastbourne in England, the one with the weird ARK 666Y licence plate, which we featured in one of our "Fortean TV" shows on Channel Four in Britain. Having not only exorcised this car but driven it near the precipitous cliffs at Beachy Head as well, we were intrigued by the account of another haunted car from over three thousand miles away.

The haunted Ford Capri with the strange licence plate ARK 666Y. Lionel Fanthorpe exorcised this car.

It was the night of 18-19 September 1960 when this parallel Brazilian event occurred. One of the six people in the car at the crucial time was a witness of unquestionable character and total veracity, the famous Dr. Olavo Trindade. Dr. Trindade had distinguished himself and benefited patients throughout the world by his pioneering work in the treatment of meningitis. The vehicle concerned was a big station wagon, and it was travelling along the main road between Brasilia and Belo Horizonte. The car was in the Cidade Livre district (a suburb of Brasilia) when it faltered as though it might be overheated. The driver and passengers checked the car, but everything appeared to be normal. Suddenly out of the velvet darkness — for it was a pitch-black, moonless night — a small volley of stones came whistling towards them.

In addition to Dr. Trindade, the occupants of the car included the driver, a young couple who had been married earlier that day in nearby Luisiania, and the bridegroom's parents. When the bombardment began, at least one stone as big as a man's fist hit the bride and her new mother-in-law and finished up in Dr. Trindade's lap.

The infuriated driver drew his gun and began shooting into the darkness in the direction from which the stones appeared to be coming. This had no effect.

As Dr. Trindade and his friends knew the area well they decided that their best bet would be a police station less than two miles away. They reached the police station without further incident and one of the officers returned with them to the scene of the strange attack on their car. As soon as they reached it the bombardment started afresh. The driver attempted to fire as he had done before, but his gun did not work. This is strangely reminiscent of those UFO reports in which car engines and mechanical devices like guns suddenly become inoperative.

Very bewildered, the police officer escorted Trindade and his friends back to the relative safety of the police station. Dr. Trindade had already left two stones with the officers as evidence before returning to the scene of the attack with their protection officer. When they got back to the police station an inexplicable rain of sand, and what appeared to be gravel, dropped on to the chair where the stones had been left on their first visit.

After a short rest and coffee, which the perplexed police officers provided for Dr. Trindade and his companions, they resumed their journey towards Belo Horizonte. The rain of stones started up yet again. Sand somehow found its way inside the car, although the windows were shut tight apart from a very small gap at the front. The bridegroom's father was driving now and the driver was taking a short rest sitting in the right side passenger seat at the front. He gave a sudden startled shout and said that somebody or *something* outside was trying to force the door open. Dr. Trindade fearlessly reached forward and took a strong grip on the door to help the driver to keep it shut. In his report Trindade said that despite his strength, and that of the driver, the door was slowly being forced open.

When co-author Lionel performed an exorcism on the haunted car near Eastbourne in England, the holy water that he was using as part of the ceremony began to get hot. *It was almost as though it was meeting some kind of opposing energy field.* It did not become scaldingly hot but was certainly as warm as a freshly made cup of tea.

DEATH

Dr. Trindade used all his strength to hold the door in place. The driver used the lock to secure the handle, which promptly unlocked itself again *as though an invisible hand had touched the controls*. According to Dr. Trindade's report this occurred on a number of occasions.

The driver told Trindade that he could see a dark, amorphous form outside the window. He did his best to fire at it but the gun again refused to work.

Trindade, an eminent medical scientist with an international reputation, was a calm, rational, and sensible man. He reported, however, that even he was frightened by what was happening. His hands were now painful and aching and he no longer felt able to keep his grip on the sinister door against whatever power was trying to force it away from him.

They stopped the car and Trindade changed places with the bridegroom's father, also a powerful man, who did his best to hold the door shut to help the driver. The family were devout Roman Catholics and were now convinced that some sort of demon or evil spirit was attacking them. They prayed that it would return to its own place and leave them alone. Stones continued to rattle against the side of the car. Their prayers, so it seemed, were finally answered and whatever or whoever appeared to have been attacking the door withdrew. The bridegroom's father then observed that the glass from his wristwatch had come off in the struggle, and although it was not broken it was now wedged between two of his fingers. Eventually, and very thankfully, they reached Cidade Livre in the early hours of the morning. The newly-weds went to their room and took the broken watch with them. The wristband had been wrenched beyond its normal width by whatever force had caused the glass to come out. The young couple left the damaged watch and its dislodged glass on the table in their hotel room. The driver went into a safe, empty spot in the hotel yard and tried his gun once more. It was working perfectly again.

In the morning, according to Dr. Trindade's astounding report, the watch glass was back in its proper place and the damaged metal wristband looked as good as new. When they examined the station wagon they were in for an even greater surprise. There was not a mark anywhere on the paint of the car. There was no broken glass, and there were no holes or dents.

POLTERGEISTS

From these strange accounts of haunted cars, the trail of the poltergeist leads on to haunted drums and to the town of Tedworth in Wiltshire, England.

In the mid-seventeenth century, John Mompesson, one of the Tedworth magistrates, paid a call to Ludgershall. A vagrant named William Drury, who was walking up and down the street banging his drum, was disturbing the district. It appeared to be some kind of protest on William's part, the object of which was to persuade the local constables to pass some public assistance money in his direction.

Never keen at the best of times, the constables were extremely reluctant to shell out for the rather dubious Mr. Drury on the grounds that they suspected that the document that he was carrying (which purported to be signed by some distinguished magistrates) was, in fact, anything but the genuine article.

Mompesson took his duties seriously and probably rather pompously. He duly ordered the constables to bring Drury before him so that his case and his documentation could be properly examined. In Mompesson's opinion the pass *was* a forgery. Drury's drum was confiscated and he was held in custody overnight, but he promptly escaped the next morning.

In due course the missing vagrant's drum was sent to Tedworth so that Mompesson himself could decide what to do with it. He was either on his way to London, or just about to leave for London, when the drum reached his house. His business in the city was urgent and he did not delay on account of Drury's percussion kit. When Mompesson got back from London a few days later, he was greeted by excited reports from his family and servants to the effect that there had been strange drumming noises all over the house all the time that he had been away. Mompesson may have been pompous and officious, but he did not lack courage. Rather like the Cranswell boys during the famous episode when the Croglin Grange vampire allegedly attacked their sister Amelia at around the same period, Mompesson raced outside with his pistol at the ready as soon as the weird noises started.

Whatever the cause of the disturbance was it was as elusive as will-o'-the-wisp. As soon as Mompesson thought he had reached the room from which the sounds were emanating, they began again from somewhere else.

A few years ago co-author Lionel was asked to exorcise the ghost of a lady in Victorian dress that was troubling the occupants

Patricia Fanthorpe at Croglin Low Hall — where Amelia Cranswell was allegedly attacked by a vampire.

Lionel Fanthorpe at Croglin Low Hall — where Michael and Edward Cranswell allegedly fought off the vampire that attacked their sister, Amelia.

of a house in the Adamsdown area of Cardiff, Wales. The occupants of the house who had reported being troubled by this particular phenomenon had very similar comments to make about it. Both tenants were young, single-parent mothers, who had become friends as well as neighbours, and were supporting and helping each other during the stress they were experiencing because of the apparent psychic phenomena in their house.

They would report hearing footsteps upstairs, bravely ascend the stairs to investigate, and then hear other footsteps sounding in the room below that they had just left.

Mompesson's quarry behaved in very much the same way. As soon as he felt that he was getting closer to the source, *it moved*. Sounds came from outside the house as well as the interior. The noise was chronic and persisted for several months. Oddly, according to some of the earlier reports, when Mrs. Mompesson was in labour and actually being delivered of the newest member of her family, the noise stopped and the house remained silent for three or four weeks. Could this possibly have indicated that whoever, or whatever, was responsible for the noisy disturbances was merely *mischievous* and had no serious evil intentions?

If, as several theorists have suggested, it was some kind of psychic power that Drury himself was putting out, it seems to have been a very similar power to the one that the amazing Mirabelli apparently controlled in Brazil centuries later.

Once Mrs. Mompesson had recovered fully and the baby was thriving, the disturbances resumed with more force than before. This new outbreak, like so many other poltergeist cases on record, seemed to focus around the Mompesson's *children*. The noises seemed now to issue from around their beds, and the beds themselves often moved quite violently. In the Esther Cox case in Amherst, Nova Scotia, the first indication that Esther and her sister had that any inexplicable supernatural force was being directed against them and the house *was centred on their bedroom*.

According to early accounts of the Tedworth drummer-poltergeist, he also seemed to have something in common with the "talking mongoose of Cashen" on the Isle of Man. Whatever it was that caused the disturbances in Tedworth made weird animal noises, sometimes like a dog, sometimes like a cat, sometimes like neither.

The Tedworth case was investigated in some depth by a clergyman named Glanvil. Having studied the area in which the children were sleeping, he went back to the yard and found that his horse was trembling and terrified. The unfortunate animal died shortly afterwards.

Did whatever spirit or force that was responsible for the Tedworth phenomena have some particular dislike for horses, or exercise some strange power over them? Mompesson's own horse miraculously survived an exceptionally unpleasant attack. It was found in its stable with a rear hoof jammed into its mouth, and was only rescued with a great deal of difficulty.

The weird attacks did not confine themselves to horses. A plucky young servant girl sensed where the force was, took a stout stick, and tried to bar its way. The force tore the stick from her hands. A guest in Mompesson's home, who also tried to oppose it, had his sword taken from him, according to the contemporary reports, and the Tedworth blacksmith was allegedly attacked with a pair of his own formidable blacksmith's pincers!

The tale of the blacksmith's being attacked in that way is reminiscent of the legend of the good (and fearless!) St. Dunstan, who was also traditionally a blacksmith and was a very holy man. According to the legend, Dunstan persuaded Old Nick to pay his bill by using a pair of pincers on him. The outline of the story was that St. Dunstan was working in his forge one day when the Devil appeared in the guise of a rather handsome member of the aristocracy, and politely enquired the price for having his hooves shod. The mighty Dunstan, who had no objection to carrying out the work, named a fair price for the task. After the hooves were shod the Devil laughed at Dunstan and prepared to skip off without paying. Dunstan, whose physical strength and courage were as great as his spirituality, had a pair of hot pincers in the forge fire at the time and seized Satan's nose in them. Predictably this was accompanied by screams of agony, but the powerful saint refused to let go until the Devil had paid in full for the shoes. Some historians of aphorisms have suggested that this may have been the origin of the metaphor "to pay through the nose"!

The Tedworth blacksmith does not appear to have been cast in St. Dunstan's mighty mould. He was apparently rather disconcerted at being set upon with his own forge pincers.

The saga of William Drury continued with his arrest in Gloucester for the crime of purloining one of the famous Gloucestershire pigs. During his time in jail he asked a Wiltshire man what news there was in Tedworth. As they discussed the trials that the Mompesson family were suffering, Drury boasted that he was responsible and that he would continue whatever strange, psychic attack he was using until Mompesson had made full restitution for the confiscated drum. According to one version of the story, as a result of that conversation Drury was deported for witchcraft. As soon as there were a few miles of sea water between the convict ship and Britain, Mompesson's troubles at Tedworth went into remission.

Whatever his other weaknesses and shortcomings, Drury seems to have been something of an escapologist. He got back from his transportation sentence and, according to this early account, the disturbances in the Mompesson household started up again as soon as Drury's feet touched English soil. Like all poltergeist cases, however, the Tedworth trouble slowly lost its intensity and finally died away altogether.

If, as a great many investigators believe, poltergeist phenomena are the result of some kind of psychic force associated with children and adolescents, it could be suggested that the gradual fading of the phenomena coincides with the growth from childhood to adulthood. Drury himself was no adolescent, of course, but is it possible that he had some means of directing the power of the adolescents in the Mompesson household by some sinister form of psychic remote control?

Joseph Priestley, an eighteenth-century scientist, investigated a remarkable case reported from the rectory of Epworth in Lincolnshire, England. At the time of Priestley's investigation the rectory was the home of the Reverend Samuel Wesley and his wife and children. Samuel was the grandfather of John Wesley, the founder of Methodism.

The problems that Samuel Wesley and his family encountered began just before Christmas in 1716. One of their maids heard terrible moans and groans, almost as though someone was dying, which appeared to be coming from the family dining room. The Wesley's took it quite lightly and even made jokes about it. Not long afterwards, however, heavy thumps and knocks woke them in the middle of the night. These sounds seemed to be emanating from a loft or garret above the rest of the bedrooms. It may have been significant that everyone in the house heard the noises except the Reverend Wesley himself. For a time it was felt to be appropriate not to inform him in case he became nervous and anxious and decided that the poltergeist phenomenon was a harbinger of his death. (Would it be cynical to ask why a clergyman who preached frequently about Heaven was apparently so reluctant to go there?)

When the noises persisted, the family changed its mind and decided that Samuel must be informed. When he was duly informed, he did not believe them. If poltergeists exist and if they are purposeful, this one seemed to want to make its presence felt and to correct any illusions under which the Reverend Wesley might be labouring.

That night it produced nine inescapably loud knocks close beside his bed. From then onwards the disturbances got worse, louder, and more frequent. For several weeks the house could well be described as being in a state of chaos and uproar. Empty rooms resounded with footsteps, as did the staircases. Frequently several sets of footsteps sounded *simultaneously*. Whatever was causing the disturbances in the rectory seemed to have a wide repertoire of sound effects available in its studio! There were convincing reproductions of bottles being broken and another curious woody noise, rather as though someone was winding up a ratchet or planing rough and difficult knotty pine.

Mrs. Wesley seems to have been a rather more spirited character than her husband. On occasions when noises, thuds, bangs, and knocks came from the direction of the nursery, she repeated them like an echo. It became a sort of audible forerunner of those computer memory test games where you are shown a series of colours in order and then have to transmit the exact sequence back again to pass the test. Mrs. Wesley's efforts at repeating the knock sequence either pleased or entertained the poltergeist — *or whatever it was* — because the pattern of knocks then sounded from the floor immediately under the place where she was standing. It was as if someone in the room below was striking the ceiling with the end of a broom, or a long pole.

The intrepid Mrs. Wesley then looked under the bed and reported that an animal about the size of a badger fled from the room. On a later occasion one of the servants reported to the Wesleys that he had also seen a strange animal that he described as whitish in colour and about the size of a large rabbit. When he had seen it, it had been warming itself, catlike, beside the large fire in the dining room. Epworth in Lincolnshire in 1716 was a pretty rural area, where wildlife was far more plentiful and varied than it is today. It is by no means impossible that a cat, a badger, or a very large rabbit had made its way into the house and under the bed where Mrs. Wesley saw it, or in front of the dining room fire where the servant had seen it. But it does seem to be something of a coincidence that the creature under the bed should have wandered into the house at precisely the same time that Mrs. Wesley was playing the rap-for-rap game with whatever was causing the disturbance.

Co-author Lionel's very rural Norfolk grandmother, Phoebe Garbutt (née Tilney), daughter of the Yaxham blacksmith, was steeped in old country lore and legend. She certainly believed in the existence of the Devil and demons. Phoebe was firmly convinced that she had on more than one occasion seen Satan, or one of his minions, in the form of a little black pig.

Whereas Mrs. Wesley had seen the beast under the bed, Phoebe Garbutt reported that she had seen it running under the family car (a 1939 vintage Series E Morris 8) in the garage. It might have been significant that the garage was far from being new, and was in fact an old stable with a hay loft above it that had been there since the days of horses and carts.

The Wesley family was anxious because the Reverend had recently preached a vehement sermon against witchcraft. Had his words struck home in the parish? And had one of those against whom he had preached practised some sort of evil magic against the family? Their other thought was that these strange knocking noises, and the appearance of these inexplicable small animals, somehow presaged a tragedy or a death in the family. Early deaths were all too frequent in the eighteenth century.

The Wesleys were very relieved, of course, when nothing untoward occurred. The poltergeist was a puzzle and a nuisance, but did not appear to be dangerous or malevolent. The observant Mrs. Wesley began to see a connection between the strange noises and the sleeping patterns of her nineteen-year-old daughter Hetty.

As Hetty lay asleep, with her mother watching, the girl would begin to tremble slightly as though she was experiencing an unpleasant dream. It was at these times that the strange sounds manifested themselves in other parts of the house. Within some ten weeks, by about the beginning of February 1717, the disturbances had died away almost entirely.

There were very rare recurrences in the years that followed but nothing of the same duration or intensity. The thoughtful Mrs.

Wesley, who would have made an ideal housekeeper for Holmes and Watson, worked out another interesting theory in connection with her brother. He had once worked for the East India Company, but had disappeared mysteriously. When compared to the majority of poltergeist reports the Epworth mystery is unusual in its apparent lack of psychic energy. Nothing was thrown around, the furniture did not dance, and no dangerous showers of stones sailed in through the rectory windows.

If the poltergeist phenomena at Epworth were projected from Hetty's subconscious mind, the fact that she was nineteen, almost twenty, rather than at the younger end of her teenage years may have had something to do with the weakness and limited duration of the phenomena.

By way of contrast with the very weak and attenuated poltergeist manifestations that Hetty produced — if Hetty was, in fact, the source — was the case of a French weaver by the name of Angelique Cottin. Angelique was at her usual work of making silk gloves on her loom on a January day in 1846 when she was amazed and frightened when the loom began to move around of its own volition. The other weaving girls working with her were also terrified and retreated as far as their weaving room would allow.

As their curiosity overcame their fear and they tiptoed back to examine the loom, it remained normal and motionless. Then Angelique came back. The moment she was in range of it, the loom began to move again. Angelique next began to give out quite powerful electric shocks. People avoided her as they would have done the bare wires of a dynamo. Some reports described her as "a human electric eel."

In the episode in our British Channel Four "Fortean TV" show in which we examined the Case of the Mongolian Death Worm, we received reports of a snake-like creature some five or six feet long and about the thickness of a man's arm. It was alleged to live below the sands of the Mongolian desert and to be capable of delivering a violent electric shock from its tail, as well as spitting toxic venom from its mouth.

One of its victims, who was interviewed on the programme, had a series of curious electrical burns across his back that he testified had been inflicted by a Mongolian Death Worm. If his report was true, and there seemed no reason to doubt him, he had been attacked by the equivalent of a land-dwelling electric eel.

POLTERGEISTS

Angelique Cottin seems to have suddenly acquired similar powers. When a group of contemporary scientists investigated the strange effects that she was producing they found that unlike most pioneering electrical work with which they were familiar, the "electricity" — if that's what it was — that Angelique was generating did not seem to be conducted via metal.

Just like an electric battery or cell, however, when Angelique felt physically tired whatever strange energy she seemed to be able to produce would subside. There were also some common factors between her surges of energy and normal electromagnetism. If she were standing on a carpet, the effects would be diminished. When she was standing on soil, they reached their maximum potential. Was this some sort of clue suggesting that whatever force she was in touch with was amplified by the earth itself? Could it have been linked in any way with the mysterious forces that are claimed to be found in or near ley lines and the old stone circles?

If the poor girl was to sleep at all, she found it necessary to lie on a cork mat — another very effective insulating substance. In less than six months, however, all Angelique's strange electrical phenomena died away and did not recur.

If the majority of poltergeists seem to confine their activities to noise, mischief, and the movement of heavy objects, the famous Bell Witch of Robertson County, Tennessee, was a very different proposition. The problems began in 1817, and, in traditional poltergeist style, they began in a very limited, almost imperceptible, way. There were scraping and scratching sounds as if rats or other rodents were gnawing at the farmhouse walls. When the family investigated to try to get rid of the vermin that seemed to be causing the trouble, they found nothing.

These animal noises became more varied and grew louder and more frequent as days passed. Something that no one could see was scratching and clawing away at the floor. Something invisible seemed to be flapping its wings around the room and beating them against the roof as though trying to get out. Then came the sound of two dogs trying to fight despite being chained. The rattling of the metal and snarling were very realistic.

The next stage was the well known and frequently recorded one of sheets and blankets being pulled off the beds, and whatever was causing the disturbances graduated from animal noises, scratching, and snapping sounds, to something approaching a human voice.

DEATH

It was the voice of someone in great distress. There were odd swallowing noises, gulping, choking, and then a strangled gasp as though someone was being murdered. The phenomena grew stronger, chairs were overturned, and the usual stones were thrown in showers.

One of Farmer Bell's nine children was a twelve-year-old girl named Betsy, and it was around her that the events seemed to be centring. As was suggested with the case of the Epworth poltergeist, where Hetty was almost twenty years old before the phenomena began and ended relatively quietly, Betsy seemed to be of just the right age to produce, or to act as a focus for, classic poltergeist activities.

A year passed. It was now 1818. A state of almost permanent disturbance reigned in the Bell household. It was practically impossible to sleep at night, and, as in the case of the Epworth phenomena, this force in Tennessee was able to manifest itself in several places simultaneously.

Richard, one of the sons, was sleeping in the room below Betsy's. He and his sister both screamed with pain simultaneously as something pulled their hair savagely. Driven to their wits' end by the constant phenomena, the Bells called in a friendly neighbour, James Johnson, to help them. He was a powerful, direct man and when he heard a strange hissing sound that was apparently emanating from the entity causing the disturbances, he promptly told it to shut up. The hissing ceased.

In one of our own poltergeist investigations in Cardiff the family concerned were Muslim. They had called in their own holy man from a local mosque to drive out whatever evil force they believed was tormenting them and then, as it persisted, asked us to assist as well. After conducting an exorcism in the area in their loft from which the phenomena seemed to be projected, we asked the family concerned to let us know whether things were any better.

The mother of the family, in which there were several children of an age that is associated with poltergeist phenomena in most of the literature, said resignedly, "When our holy man calls it seems to be terrified of him and does nothing while he is here. When you call, the same thing happens: it is equally terrified of you. But as soon as he goes, or you go, it redoubles its efforts and makes life very bad for us."

Something like this seems to have been the case in the Bell household. It is a little like the anecdote of the man who was afraid to fight the milkman, but kicked the milkman's horse instead while its owner wasn't looking. After James Johnson had commanded it to be silent, whatever was causing the problem for the Bells began to hurt Betsy quite severely. Witnesses would hear a sound like a hand slapping someone's face and the girl's cheek would turn bright red as though it had been struck.

Johnson himself was still not convinced that the children were not playing some strange mischievous games of their own and he recommended that the Bells should call in more friends and neighbours as observers. This they did. The next step was to send Betsy away. As soon as she was safely ensconced with a reliable neighbour, the noises and other disturbances at Bell's farmhouse ceased but the girl herself was physically attacked with redoubled vigour and suffered a rain of blows and scratches.

This is in close parallel with the world famous case in Amherst, Nova Scotia. Esther Cox, who was the centre of the poltergeist phenomena in that case, was in her brother-in-law's restaurant kitchen a long way from the Cox home when a heavy iron oven door flew off, despite her brother-in-law's having wedged it with a hickory axe handle.

The Tennessee phenomena grew worse and worse. The poltergeist — or whatever it was — found a human voice and uttered threats against John Bell. By 1820 the constant tormenting had made him seriously ill. The climax came when John, junior, found a weird bottle of dark, evil, oily-looking liquid in the family medicine cabinet. The poltergeist voice said that it had already given John, senior, whom it referred to as Old Jack, a fatal dose while he was asleep. The doctor was immediately summoned and the foul black liquid was tested on the cat. The poor beast leapt up into the air, spun around madly, collapsed, and died instantly. John Bell, senior, died the following day.

There is an interesting coincidence, or piece of synchronicity, associated with this remarkably sinister liquid. Edgar Cayce was an amazingly gifted psychic healer. A generous and good-hearted man and a sincere and devout Christian, Cayce never charged a cent for any of his healing work. His exceptional therapeutic gifts were used unsparingly, and it is a great tribute to the man to record that there is little doubt that Cayce burned himself out in the service of others during the Second World War. Full information about this remarkable man can be obtained from the Association for Research and Enlightenment, Virginia Beach, Virginia, or from the many Internet sites showing the life and work of Edgar Cayce.

In *The Sleeping Prophet* there is a reference to Cayce carrying out a remarkable healing of an intransigent skin disease that refused to yield to orthodox medicine. He prescribed "Oil of Smoke." The remedy proved very difficult to track down, but was at last run to earth. Is it possible that some strange and powerful tinctures like the semi-legendary "Oil of Smoke" can be used successfully as strictly *external* applications, but are fatally toxic if *ingested?* Was it "Oil of Smoke" — or something very like it — that killed John Bell and his cat?

The next dramatic manifestation came one evening after John's death and approximately four years after the poltergeist phenomena had first begun to show themselves. As Lucy Bell and her children were sitting together at supper there was a terrifyingly loud sound from the chimney of the dining room. It sounded to the family as if a heavy sphere filled with gunpowder had smashed its way down the chimney, burst out through the grate, and exploded in the middle of the room. There was smoke everywhere. A voice that the family believed to be that of the poltergeistic entity screamed out, "I shall be gone for seven years. Goodbye." Sure enough, almost seven years to the day, when only the widowed Lucy and two of her sons still lived in the old Bell farmhouse, the manifestations began again. On this occasion, however, they were reduced to something relatively minor. Bedding was pulled away and there were faint but irritating scratching sounds from behind some walls and from below certain floors. Lucy and her sons ignored them, and after three weeks or so the manifestations ceased altogether.

Poltergeist theories are many and various. One group of speculations suggests that poltergeists may be spirits of the restless dead who have returned and who are using the energy fields of the young people in the house in order to perform their tricks. The poltergeist in this model can be thought of as a conductor — a psychic pipe, or channel — along which the strange force flows, having little or no energy of its own to move material objects or to create the characteristic, loud sounds. The poltergeist spirit is nevertheless able to direct the energy of the teenager that it is borrowing in its own chosen direction.

Another group of theories suggests that poltergeists are not the returning spirits of dead human beings but are elemental spirits of some kind. They were never human, and are not particularly intelligent — at least in the way in which human beings would recognise intelligence as a rational response to an environmental stimulus.

Some poltergeists, and quite often it appears that more than one is simultaneously involved in a specific case, could be regarded as the psychic equivalents of snakes in a pit or chattering monkeys in trees. Is such a group what possessed the man called Legion in the New Testament?

Yet another group of theories suggests that a poltergeist is part of a human personality that has somehow come adrift from the rest of the person concerned and is acting independently. Where there are strong psychological tensions within a personality, such as ambivalent feelings towards an objective like sex, which in some cultures is both desired and forbidden, then there seems to be a reasonable possibility that the personality's response to this ambiguity of emotion will be to split. It is, of course, one thing to hypothesise that poltergeist phenomena are the result of a psychological loose cannon that has torn itself away from an otherwise rational mind. It is an entirely different problem to surmise *how* such a mental maverick could be capable of producing the effects that are reported. Many honest and sensible observers report their undeniable experiences of poltergeist phenomena. Something quite real and objective is actually happening.

Wanting, consciously or subconsciously, to make a plate fly through the air or to turn a heavy couch upside down and spin it around the floor is a very different thing from being able to *do* it. It is perfectly feasible that a subordinate personality may indulge in a little window-shopping. The question is where does it get its purchasing power? Mountainous archives of poltergeist reports going back many years still fail to answer those three central questions. They provide valuable clues but no definitive conclusions. That poltergeist phenomena have been seen and heard and that such phenomena have a genuine objective existence is beyond dispute. Whether they are psychokinetic manifestations, or the spirits of departed human beings, or weird elemental spirits of mischief remains undecided.

It may reasonably be deduced, however, that records of poltergeist phenomena point more in the direction of the ability of an immaterial element to survive physical death than in any other direction. If poltergeist phenomena have an immaterial cause, as they appear to have, then it is not wrong to envisage a connection between such immateriality in these poltergeist cases and the survival of a conscious, immaterial personality when the physical human body ceases to function.

CHAPTER TEN
RELIGIOUS TEACHINGS AND BELIEFS
ABOUT THE AFTERLIFE

The revelations of religious leaders, prophets, priests, and spiritual teachers concerning the afterlife vary widely, and seem to have varied widely since the beginning of human history.

To those who accept that their revered holy men and women are, or were, actually in touch with God, or with a pantheon of gods, angels, or spirits, in some unique way, the statements made by such great charismatic religious leaders as Moses, Jesus, and Mohammed obviously carry major life-changing significance.

Almost 5,000 years ago, for example, a number of Sumerians joined their dead king in a mass grave lined with reeds. His Majesty's beautiful young dancing girls, concubines, and courtesans; his musicians, soldiers, and servants; his guardsmen and grooms, paid their last respects and downed a fatal draught — like Socrates fearlessly drinking the hemlock millennia later.

Who had told those Sumerians about the afterlife so convincingly that they were prepared to follow their king into that unknown realm as casually as they would have followed him to a new summer palace by the sea?

You didn't have to be a Sumerian courtier from five millennia in the past to go that way. Cult leader Jim Jones murdered United States Congressman Leo Ryan and his investigative team in a Guyanan jungle as recently as 1978. On Jones's orders 1,000 of his followers then promptly drank cyanide before the might of the United States government could descend to avenge their lost congressman. Who or what had convinced Jones that he was some sort of charismatic guru, prophet, or messiah? How had he impressed that fatal delusion on his followers?

Although we, ourselves, believe that such evidence as we have examined over the years points to survival rather than to annihilation, it is vital to keep that belief safely balanced and moderated. An obsessive religious fanaticism like that exhibited in the mass tragedies of ancient Sumer and modern Guyana is the dynamism of disaster.

Any religion that lacks an essential core of hedonism, rationality, a love of life, and a broad-minded toleration of others is a potential danger to its adherents as well as to their neighbours.

Religious belief is fine in its place, but its place is definitely not at the front of our lives. When all is said and done, the firmest faith is only a *belief*, not a *fact*. We must always accept the possibility that our own cherished ideas could be hopelessly *wrong*.

A rational, loving, creative, caring, and sustaining God does not demand irrational thought or behaviour from his creation. Real love — whether human or divine — seeks the happiness, the independence, and the *freely given* companionship of those who are loved. Real love does nothing and commands nothing except what will bring happiness to those whom are loved. Love and the desire to give and receive happiness are inseparable, just as love and freedom are inseparable.

Any alleged "revelation" from God, from a pantheon of gods, from angels, or sublime spirits, is open to serious questioning if it advocates unnecessary self-denial, irrational taboos and prohibitions, celibacy, chastity, poverty, or any other form of avoidable misery.

A "revelation" that advocates the pursuit of goodness, reason, freedom, joy, love, mercy, creativity, kindness, generosity, humour, and tolerance would seem *infinitely* more likely to have had a *genuine* divine origin.

The belief in some sort of afterlife is ubiquitous. Apart from the well-known survival ideas of the ancient Egyptians and Sumerians, Greeks and Romans hoped to go to the Elysian Fields or to the Garden of the Hesperides. Norsemen longed for Valhalla with its glorious fighting all day and its feasting, drinking, and love-making all night: an afterlife that has an irresistible appeal for co-author Lionel, provided there are big, black Harley-Davidsons there as well!

The early Jews believed in Sheol, a rather indistinct and gloomy half-life among insubstantial shadows. The Pharisees of Christ's era

RELIGIOUS TEACHINGS AND BELIEFS
ABOUT THE AFTERLIFE

believed in a joyful resurrection of the righteous, who would certainly have earned it ten times over if they'd managed to keep all the Pharisaical rules on Earth! Christian teachings about the afterlife differ significantly from denomination to denomination. Some believe in survival and perfect continuity of existence. Others believe in a period of waiting in the grave until a great day of resurrection and judgement arrives. Some believe in two distinct destinations: Heaven and Hell. Others think there may be some sort of halfway house variously alluded to as limbo or purgatory. Some believe in a judgement that can mean permanent and painful separation from God and from all that once gave them pleasure. Others, like the brilliant, deep-thinking, Victorian Scots minister George MacDonald, are Universalists, who prefer to think that all of creation will eventually be brought back to enjoy the delights of Heaven for ever more.

For some Hindus and Buddhists there is the concept of Nirvana: a state of inexpressible joy, but one in which the believer is somehow *absorbed* into God, or becomes *part* of God, while still retaining some kind of shared, communal *awareness*.

If we accept, for the sake of pursuing the religious argument, that Jesus really was who he said he was, and whom his disciples believed him to be, then his teachings about the afterlife must be uniquely significant.

What exactly did Jesus say about it? It was customary during the first century A.D. for a man to marry his brother's wife — if his brother had died — so that he could sire children by her on his dead brother's behalf. The Sadducees, unlike the Pharisees, did not believe in the Resurrection. They posed what they considered to be an unanswerable question to Jesus. They related the case of a hypothetical woman who had been married to each of seven brothers in turn. The men had died one after the other, having done their fraternal, husbandly, conjugal duty faithfully for the much-married widow. The woman herself finally died as well: it is tempting to suggest that she may well have welcomed death as a happy release! Christ regarded their question as stupidly trivial and irrelevant. "In Heaven," he told them, "they neither marry nor are given in marriage, but are as the angels in Heaven."

Advocates of celibacy have frequently seized on this text and misused it as a reinforcement of their own quaintly repressive and unfulfilled lifestyles. Jesus may well have meant exactly the opposite: that all loving relationships were totally open and shared in Heaven, not restricted to monogamous marriage contracts as they

The Christian concept of the Risen Christ reigning in glory in Heaven.

were on Earth. He may equally well have meant that the joys of Heaven differed so vastly from those of Earth that even the exquisite delights of human sexuality would be transcended, replaced perhaps by some type of interpersonal relationship that will be even better — although it is impossible for us to imagine such an experience from our present human perspective.

On the cross, Jesus told the dying thief, "This day thou shalt be with me in paradise." This seems an unequivocal argument for survival and immediate continuity of life, rather than for a long period of non-existence, waiting in the grave, prior to eventual resurrection on some great future Judgement Day.

Where was Christ himself between his death on the cross on Good Friday and his physical resurrection very early on the first Easter Sunday morning?

This raises massive, controversial, and thought-provoking theological questions as to the nature of God, and the concept of the Trinity. For Athanasius, or any other self-appointed early Christian religious "expert," to presume to create a creed involving the Trinity that "all must accept or be damned" is breathtakingly arrogant, even by our standards! We simply do not know — and cannot possibly know this side of Heaven — what God is really like, what his supra-personal character consists of, or how the mystery of the Trinity can be resolved by human thought. It is simply beyond us to comprehend that enigma. If Christ is God — and we, ourselves, believe that he is — and the Son of God, the pre-existent Logos, or Word, of God — as we also believe him to be, then how can God die? If Jesus is God, and if the God-in-human-form who is Jesus, is dead, then where is the omnipotent, omniscient, omnipresent Being who controls and sustains our universe and all life within it? Where, also, is the Holy Spirit, the third person of the Trinity? If God is Trinity in Unity and Unity in Trinity, if the Father, the Son, and the Holy Spirit are all separate supra-personalities — yet one and the same great and eternal Being — what happens if Jesus, the Son-of-God-in-human-form — dies?

If his divine, immortal power transcends mere death by a factor of infinity then, of course, he does not die when his human body dies, any more than any other human being dies when his, or her, body ceases to function. Just suppose, for the sake of following the argument, that Jesus is truly and uniquely God in a very special and particular sense. He takes human form via the Virgin Mary at his incarnation. If we follow this scenario, then, by taking human form he also accepts the inevitability of human death in order to be thoroughly and completely human. The incarnation is not a charade, nor is it a masquerade. It is totally real and completely genuine: in Jesus Christ, God has become truly human.

When the body of Jesus dies, his immortal soul, spirit, or non-physical essence, survives. Not for the most fleeting fraction of a microsecond does the immortal part of him cease to be. The Christ-who-is-God goes on, and this provides yet another argument for the continuation of human existence after physical death and the eventual decay of the mortal body.

This argument seems important enough to be re-phrased from a slightly different perspective. As God, following the Jesus-is-God line of argument, Jesus cannot logically be segregated from the other essential elements of the divine, triune, supra-personal God. He cannot, therefore, cease to exist when his human body dies. As the incarnation made him genuinely human, it must already have been an essential part of human nature to survive physical death.

But where was the living soul of Jesus from Friday night until his resurrected body was seen in the garden early on Sunday morning? It is, perhaps, meaningless to speak of *where* in connection with a non-physical entity such as a soul, or spirit. If a thing is immaterial, it does not exactly "occupy" physical space. It has *existence* but no *dimensions*.

Evidence of out-of-body experiences suggests that astral travel is under the control of the traveller's mind and will. The astral voyager is able to reach his or her destination simply by thinking of it. There is no reason why the spirit of Christ could not have moved in this way as well, prior to his full, physical resurrection on the Sunday morning.

Where did that valiant, loving spirit go? There is a strong, early, Christian tradition that he "preached to the spirits in darkness." *Who were they?* Is it logical and reasonable to speculate that they were the spirits of those who had died before Christ's incarnation, before God himself broke into history?

Again, purely for the sake of pursuing the argument, and allowing for that purpose that Jesus of Nazareth was the Christ, the Messiah, and the unique Son of God, what *really* happened in the garden near his empty tomb first thing on that amazing Sunday morning?

His immortal spirit seemed to have been re-clothed in a physical body, yet one that closely resembled the body that had died on the cross. The scars of crucifixion were still visible and tangible. Thomas was able to touch them. There appeared to have been a solid, tactile element to it because when Mary Magdalene first saw him, he asked her not to touch him. *Why?* Was the process of physical resurrection not yet complete?

The new body was able to eat in the normal way, as shown by the "fish and honeycomb" episode. It was indistinguishable from a normal human body as far as Cleopas and his companion were concerned when Jesus walked with them to Emmaus, yet there must have been some differences in its appearance because they did not recognise him until he broke bread in his characteristic way.

What of the evidence for his Ascension? It has become fashionable among some "liberal" and "modernist" Christian theologians to dismiss the whole idea of the physical resurrection and the Ascension. Some of them do not seem terribly sure about whether they believe in life after death at all, for Christ or for anyone else. Others don't think that he experienced any kind of *physical* resurrection, while admitting that his *spirit* might have survived.

But what if the evidence for the Ascension is reliable? What if the disciples actually saw him physically ascending among the clouds?

RELIGIOUS TEACHINGS AND BELIEFS
ABOUT THE AFTERLIFE

What did it *mean?* Where was he going, and *why?* During his other post-Resurrection appearances, he had demonstrated that his new body was able to enter or leave a room at will, regardless of whether its doors were closed or open. *If* the narrative is true, and *if* the evidence for the Resurrection, the post-Resurrection appearances, and the Ascension is reliable and accurate, then the case for human survival is as close to being finally proved as anything can be.

The problem is that there is also a substantial and widely known body of arguments *against* the Resurrection evidence. Some of this is in the form of Gospel dating, Gospel authorship, and a few of the curious old Nag Hammadi documents. Theories have been advanced that Jesus was not dead when he was taken down from the cross, and that the mysterious figures in white raiment in the tomb were not angels but Essene healers.

These objections to the historicity of the Resurrection have to be faced fairly and squarely, and given the open-minded, balanced, and objective assessment and evaluation that they deserve. In our opinion, having weighed up both sets of arguments for many years, the evidence for the Resurrection and Ascension wins the battle of probabilities, but, as Wellington said of the Battle of Waterloo, "It was a damned close run thing."

CHAPTER ELEVEN
Interviews with Psychics, Mediums, and Investigators

In the course of our recent research work, lecturing, and broadcasting, we have had the pleasure of meeting a number of other expert investigators, impressive psychics, and gifted mediums, whose personal experiences are extremely interesting. They have kindly allowed us to interview them and to include their responses in this chapter. We must emphasise that this chapter is a collection of pieces of up-to-date, first-hand evidence from helpful, interesting people who are involved in various ways with the paranormal. Their views — like their experiences — are their own, and we are very grateful to them all for allowing us to share their evidence with our readers.

The following is the basic questionnaire that we used, although where it was not strictly relevant to the interviewee's work we have included his or her evidence in a freer format:

Questionnaire

1   *At what stage of your life — childhood, adolescence, or maturity — were you first aware of your psychic gifts and talent?*

2   *We've seen and heard you in action and you're very gifted. Which of your psychic powers do you consider to be the best developed, or the most important?*

3 When you are actually using your powers would you compare them to seeing, hearing, or tactile sensations? In other words, how do psychic powers manifest themselves to one who has such knowledge?

4 What do you consider as the most mysterious or inexplicable psychic adventure you've ever had?

5 Powerful and perceptive sensitives like you are excellent judges of character. What is the psychic mechanism that makes it possible? For example, would you say that you can see auras, or do you feel positive or negative vibrations? Do "good" people give off a "warm" feeling and "bad" people a "cold" feeling?

6 What are your views on astral projection and OOB experiences? How well does it work? What's your experience of it?

7 What do you think about hypno-regression and reincarnation?

8 Do you also have psychometric powers? How would you describe their mechanism? What does an object absorb, and how does it radiate what it has absorbed to a sensitive, powerful psychic?

9 Are psychic powers born into a psychic, almost like something genetic, or can they be trained and developed by almost anyone who is sincere and keenly interested?

10 What are your teachings about the survival of the human personality after death? What's the spirit world like? What will we do when we get there? What sort of experiences can we look forward to in the next life? How can we contact loved ones who've gone ahead of us — and how can they contact us?

The first interviewee is Derek Acorah, who is a particularly gifted, active, and impressive psychic. He was a professional footballer at one time, and is now an author and radio and television broadcaster on the paranormal. He and co-author Lionel have worked together on several occasions on Granada Breeze TV in Manchester, England. Derek is a very kindly and helpful man, whom it is always a pleasure to be with. Here are his responses to our questions:

INTERVIEWS WITH PSYCHICS, MEDIUMS, AND INVESTIGATORS

1   *At what stage of your life — childhood, adolescence, or maturity — were you first aware of your psychic gifts and talent?*

I had my first psychic experience when I was seven years of age, when I saw my deceased grandfather on the stairs of my grandmother's home. From that age onwards I had many psychic experiences and this continued on through my adolescence and into maturity, until I became a professional medium approximately twenty-five years ago.

2   *We've seen and heard you in action and you're very gifted. Which of your psychic powers do you consider to be the best developed, or the most important?*

Although I am both clairvoyant and clairaudient, I consider clairaudience to be more important as this is a direct link with my spirit guide (and also other spirit people). Clairvoyance is largely a matter of dealing with symbols that can be open to misinterpretation. Consequently, for me, clairaudience is more important. From approximately 1994 I became aware of an extra dimension of my work. When in general conversation with people, I could both subjectively and objectively see symbols that I could immediately interpret, and give answers to unspoken questions regarding problems that were affecting the person with whom I was speaking. (This part of my gift has nothing to do with my connection with spirit guides and my clairaudience.) It is working with people's "voice vibrations": this is very exciting to me, and most satisfying.

3   *When you are actually using your powers would you compare them to seeing, hearing, or tactile sensations? In other words, how do psychic powers manifest themselves to one who has such knowledge?*

I use both subjective and objective clairvoyance. I also use clairaudience. Although I am also clairsentient (as most people are to some degree) it is not actually a tactile experience, although I will sometimes feel my hair being ruffled or the pressure of a consoling hand on my shoulder at times when I am feeling low. At times, I can also smell fragrances that are brought in memory of loved ones in spirit. I find also as I go forward in time that I have become aware that my higher consciousness never stands still and at certain periods of time, it has been very noticeable to me that shifts and changes of sensitivity take place. This I find to be linked to progressive development.

4   *What do you consider as the most mysterious or inexplicable psychic adventure you've ever had?*

In January 1999 I was taking part in an investigation of The Comedy Store, in Hollywood. This was a club once known as Ciro's, and was frequented years ago by many (if not all) of the Hollywood "greats." This was filmed by "E! Entertainment" and was actually aired two weeks ago across America. Whilst I was there, a young man showed himself to me. He was dressed in an American army uniform, but said that he had not been in the army. He said his name was Sean and told me to expect his father (who turned out to be Errol Flynn) to be named in the top fifty of all time greats of Hollywood stars within the next twenty-four hours. He was smiling and told me to tell people that there was going to be a very large earthquake in July of this year in California. My psychic feelings didn't feel comfortable with this part of the communication and I told him that I didn't believe he was telling me the truth on this matter, whereas the information he had given up to that point, I felt quite comfortable with. He then laughed and said, "Oh, you're good! Haven't you got a sense of humour?" The next day a photograph and story were faxed to me by "E! Entertainment" that showed Errol Flynn's son, Sean, who had been a photographer in Vietnam and who had disappeared. It was later established that he had been shot dead by the Viet Cong. Also, it gave a short character and personality analysis of this man — it was stated that he was known as a prankster and practical joker, and would always "buck the system." Shortly afterwards, the media in Hollywood read out the fifty nominees for awards for all time greats, and Errol Flynn was on that list, as his son had told me he would be twenty-four hours before. On checking records, this communicating soul was never known to frequent Ciro's, which to me was strange because up to that time, in my experience, spirits only **ever** frequent places that they had actually visited in or resided in during life.

Whilst doing an investigation at Belgrave Hall in April of this year [1999], following the capture of what appeared to be two ghostly images on CCTV film, I was communicating with the Ellis family, who had lived in Belgrave and had owned the property up to the time when Leicester Council bought it and turned it into a museum. There were many members of the Ellis family making their presence known to me. What was different on this occasion was the fact that they used one family member [John Ellis] as a spokesperson. Also, I had never come across a group of spirit people before who collectively encouraged our investigation and were such a happy family unit, with the exception of one [Edward Ellis] who seemed to be very much against the investigation taking place, and in fact told me so. John and Margaret Ellis were both very apologetic for Edward's attitude and stated clearly, "As in life, so we shall be in the kingdom of Heaven." Until he consciously wished to progress and change his thoughts, Edward would retain his earthly characteristics.

5   *Powerful and perceptive sensitives like you are excellent judges of character. What is the psychic mechanism that makes it possible? For example, would you say that you can see auras, or do you feel positive or negative vibrations? Do "good" people give off a "warm" feeling and "bad" people a "cold" feeling?*

Yes, I certainly do see auras and am most aware of the vibrations of positivity or negativity given off by different people. I do not necessarily consider it a fact that good people are warm, and cold people bad. Nervousness can sometimes make people appear cold and withdrawn, and sometimes bad people can be very warm, hearty, and jovial in their approach. I have noticed that when I shake someone's hand in greeting, feelings that seem to surround me give me strong indications of that individual's personality and character. [Authors' note: In George MacDonald's book *The Princess and Curdie*, there is an interesting reference to a similar psychic gift that the young hero, Curdie, is given by the princess's mysterious, magical great-great-grandmother. When Curdie shakes a person's hand, he can feel an animal paw, claw, or talon, which gives him a clue to that person's real nature and character. Derek's gift seems to have something in common with Curdie's. Did George MacDonald — a deeply perceptive and spiritual man — really know someone who could do this? Or did he have the gift himself, and disguise it as fiction?]

When viewing a person's aura, I generally find that good and positive people have the colours of light orange, turquoise, and blue contained in their auras, whereas people of negativity tend to have dark yellow, grey, and even black. If there are deep red tones close to these dark colours, those people I find will invariably be living their lives in entirely the wrong way.

6   *What are your views on astral projection and OOB experiences? How well does it work? What's your experience of it?*

With regard to astral projection and astral travel, many times I leave my physical body and one of the most simple and fun things that I enjoy doing is to journey to far off places on this planet. I love to fly over areas and look down at the landscape from great heights. I gain wonderful feelings of exhilaration and peace from doing this.

As is well documented all over the world, there is substantial evidence to confirm and validate that out-of-body experiences are a true fact. These experiences give certain individuals the opportunity to understand that there is a life after physical death, and that we can all at certain times and under particular conditions experience what the moment of passing from this life to the next life is like. I believe that people who undergo this experience are not sent back by the God Power, but that certain mechanisms that take place trigger off a way for our spirit to leave the physical body and then, after a short period of time, come back and retain the ability to recall these experiences.

7   *What do you think about hypno-regression and reincarnation?*

My feelings on hypno-regression are that it is an area that has to be treated with great care and only undertaken by people who are emotionally stable. Also, the person conducting the regression should have the highest qualifications.

Regression can be achieved very successfully provided the subject is totally at peace with the idea of allowing their consciousness to be taken down to a past life. I have seen and experienced this on a number of occasions and have found it fascinating.

I am of the opinion that reincarnation is a fact, although I do not agree that a person can be reincarnated as a lesser consciousness, for example, as a dog, cat, or any other animal, and this tends to be borne out by my experiences when involved in hypno-regression. I have never come across an instance when somebody has started barking or miaowing whilst under regression! However, I do wonder why certain subjects while under hypno-regression can only give a certain amount of information regarding their past lives, whereas in other cases great detail is gone into.

8   *Do you also have psychometric powers? How would you describe their mechanism? What does an object absorb, and how does it radiate what it has absorbed to a sensitive, powerful psychic?*

I have found that at times, when asked to use psychometry, certain objects given to me have a more profound feeling than others do. These objects tend to have been solely owned by one person and to have been in his or her possession for a considerable length of time. In cases where an object has been passed down to another person or has been owned by a number of people, the vibrations are diluted and therefore weaker. If the owner of an object has experienced great physical or mental trauma, this tends to be absorbed by the item. When handled by a sensitive, he or she is immediately made aware of these past traumas, by an almost physical feeling of dread or pain. In some ways, even a photograph of an item or site under psychometric study can transmit information — although on a lesser scale than when the actual item itself is held by, or the site visited by, a sensitive person.

An object can absorb information about its creator. This even seems to apply on a large scale — a building, for instance, absorbs information about its architect and builder. It also holds information about the time scales regarding its construction and the feelings and emotions of the people involved with it. What comes to the sensitive are mirror images of experiences that have gone on around the item, building, or site under study.

9   *Are psychic powers born into a psychic, almost like something genetic, or can they be trained and developed by almost anyone who is sincere and keenly interested?*

Psychic powers in many cases are inherited gifts, and yes, I do believe that they can be described as being genetic. However, I also believe that it is possible for a person to develop his or her psychic ability, should he or she sincerely wish to do so. In my opinion, what lies dormant in all of us is the potential ability to develop our psychic side. I would say that a great amount of hard work and dedication is required, and even then the results will not be as great as those of a person who has inherited the gifts.

10 *What are your teachings about the survival of the human personality after death? What's the spirit world like? What will we do when we get there? What sort of experiences can we look forward to in the next life? How can we contact loved ones who've gone ahead of us — and how can they contact us?*

I can say with great certainty that people's personalities and attitudes do not change because they have "crossed the veil." This is a question I am very often asked and I have to say that upon physical death, people do not become instantly angelic or cherubic. I mentioned earlier my experiences when investigating Belgrave Hall, where Edward Ellis was still the gruff and grumpy personality that he had been in physical life. Many times when communicating with a spirit who had used "colourful" language in their life on Earth, I have to delete the expletives when passing the information on to their family, though I do make a point of telling the family members this fact in order that they may identify the person with whom I am communicating.

There are a number of realms in the spirit world. The higher the level, the greater the feeling of love is experienced by the dwellers of that particular realm. The dwellers in the higher realms seem to be of far greater understanding of the traits and personalities of the inhabitants of the lower realms. They are more sympathetic and more benevolent, and seemingly more at peace with themselves. They are the spirits who have progressed up the chain and become teachers and even guides to people in the lower regions of the spirit world and to every single one of us who is incarnated into this physical world. As we come down the scale from the higher regions, the spirit inhabitants do not have the ability to transport themselves to view the higher regions — they have to earn that right through experience in a given physical lifetime, i.e., through reincarnation. We are all here in any given physical lifetime to learn lessons through experiences (good, bad, or indifferent) purely for our soul growth. The dwellers on the lowest regions of the spirit world are people who in their physical life chose through free will to live their lives in a negative way, i.e., tyrants who hurt their fellow beings.

When we immediately arrive in the spirit world, we are surrounded by loved ones who have gone before us and who have come from their realms to greet us. It will be pointed out to us that there is a system to be followed. Not unlike our physical hospitals and convalescent homes here, there are areas of recuperation and restoration there, and for a period after physical death this is where we reside. After a short time spent there, the hurts that we were exposed to, i.e., the reason for our physical death, are taken away and we are then renewed. After that, we are taken to our designated place that has been earned by us in the course of our life's experience. Certain souls who have passed from physical life at a young age are given the opportunity to reincarnate quickly if they wish to do so. Before coming once again into physical life, we choose our parents, our mode of life, what experiences we will undergo within that lifetime, and the method of our passing once again into the spirit world. We all eventually acquire the knowledge that our true habitat is the spirit world, and that this physical life is only a school, a place of learning.

The experiences ahead of us in the spirit life are determined solely by our thoughts and actions in this, our physical life. As you are here, so you will be there. When a person lives a good life, things that have been wished, but not necessarily achieved, are generally afforded us on merit when we arrive back into the spirit realm. In most of the spirit realms, there is peace, harmony, tranquillity, beauty, and great joy. We still find to our fascination that we have a greater sense of free will there, which seems to enable us to do a lot more than what we could do in our physical life on Earth. There are great Halls of Understanding for all inhabitants of the spirit realm, where many people congregate to further their understanding and their spiritual education — which helps each individual to climb the "spirit ladder."

Our second interviewee is our good friend, Bremna Howells, who writes her excellent novels under the pen name of Rosie Malone. We have known Bremna for many years, and worked with her on numerous radio and television shows dealing in depth with various aspects of the paranormal. She has a lively, outgoing personality, a great depth of knowledge and human understanding, and a range of remarkable psychic gifts. She is also a close friend of another of our psychic colleagues, Pamela Willson, and these two gifted exponents often work together.

Here are Bremna's responses to our questions:

DEATH

Psychometrist and expert on the paranormal Bremna Howells, alias novelist Rosie Malone, with Lionel Fanthorpe.

1　*At what stage of your life — childhood, adolescence, or maturity — were you first aware of your psychic gifts and talent?*

I remember as a young child (around four or five), I had "imaginary friends." Two particular friends were Sara and Oas, although there were lots of others, too. I didn't think anything particular about them, they were just friends, and as I was so much younger than my late sister, who was at the age when she would not demean herself to play with her baby sister for too long, I was very glad of their company. As the years passed, Sara seemed to fade in importance, but Oas is with me to this day and is my chief guide and confidant. As to being aware of such talent as I have, I do remember being conscious of abilities that others did not seem to have, although I took things for granted. I had never known anything different, and what other people referred to as "psychic talents" seemed quite natural to me.

2　*We've seen and heard you in action and you're very gifted. Which of your psychic powers do you consider to be the best developed, or the most important?*

I do not consider myself in any way a specialist — for instance, I would consider Pam Willson a specialist tarot reader, although she has many other psychic talents. I'm more a "jack of all trades," in that I have a knowledge of, and to varying degrees a talent for, a wide spectrum of what can be classified as "occult practices." In my own life's pilgrimage I have come across many aspects of these practices, with varying degrees of success. As to my chief talent, I think that would be clairaudience, although psychometry and scrying are very successful for me.

3 *When you are actually using your powers would you compare them to seeing, hearing or tactile sensations? In other words, how do psychic powers manifest themselves to one who has such knowledge?*

This is interesting: for clairaudience, hearing is paramount; for scrying, seeing is paramount; and for psychometry, tactile sensation is paramount. I, myself, therefore, would seem to use whatever sense is the most practical relative to the method being used. The one question you do not ask is, "How do you interpret what you are seeing, hearing, or touching?" and that's just as well, because I really do not know how I get the things that I get. Some of them Oas explains for me, especially if I get in a muddle. I would describe clairaudience as being a giant switchboard to the other side, and my function is that of telephonist. With time, you get to be a better telephonist!

4 *What do you consider as the most mysterious or inexplicable psychic adventure you've ever had?*

Without doubt, astral travel is for me the biggest adventure, although mastering the practice of lucid dreaming ranks fairly high up there. However, these tend to be techniques rather than gifts, and can be learned by anyone with, or without, natural, inborn sensitivity. You have often asked me where I get my ideas from; well, now you know. I either travel or dream, and meet people who can put different slants on the normal, or a small twist on the ordinary. From this have come some good ideas, as you know. Again, this may just be another example of being a good telephonist.

5 *Powerful and perceptive sensitives like you are excellent judges of character. What is the psychic mechanism that makes it possible? For example, would you say that you can see auras, or do you feel*

positive or negative vibrations? Do "good" people give off a "warm" feeling and "bad" people a "cold" feeling?

I don't know if I am that good a judge of character, although I do get a feeling of whom I should be wary. I cannot describe it as any more than "a feeling." It's as if an amber light goes on in my brain if someone is winding me up, or is not on the level.

6   *What are your views on astral projection and OOB experiences? How well does it work? What's your experience of it?*

My only contact with OOBEs and astral projection are in the line of astral travel and lucid dreaming. I find it works well for me personally, but as I have said they are just techniques and rely on being able to alter levels of consciousness, by relaxation and concentration.

7   *What do you think about hypno-regression and reincarnation?*

As you know, this was the most recent project that I studied in depth. I found the results of my research fascinating.

8   *Do you also have psychometric powers? How would you describe their mechanism? What does an object absorb, and how does it radiate what it has absorbed to a sensitive, powerful psychic?*

I do have psychometric powers, as you know. I think that objects soak up vibrations, like a sponge soaks up water. It then depends on where you squeeze the sponge which bit of the water it has soaked up comes flooding out. When you hold an object to be psychometrised it gives out different sensations and pictures in your mind as you hold it. If you notice, when I am working with an object, I tend to move it around in my hand and from one hand to another. This allows me to see different pictures, and home in on what I think looks interesting. Again, I can only liken it to squeezing a sponge. Different pictures appear during the process of handling the object.

9   *Are psychic powers born into a psychic, almost like something genetic, or can they be trained and developed by almost anyone who is sincere and keenly interested?*

INTERVIEWS WITH PSYCHICS, MEDIUMS, AND INVESTIGATORS

I think everyone is born with a certain degree of psychic ability. Children tend to be very psychic. However, the abilities seem to diminish with age — strangely enough, if you think about it, psychic ability tends to diminish at the same rate as curiosity. Kids drive you wild with, "Why? Why? Why?" but adults do not seem to have the same wish to find things out, and tend to be more accepting, without question, of what they are confronted with. All power can be enhanced by training and development, although some really gifted people are just that — gifted. For example, I can play and read music. I was taught as a school kid, and although I play all the right notes, in the right key and in the right order, it doesn't sound the same as someone who has a "feel" or natural talent for music. Again, we come to this interpretation thing. I obviously do not have a feel for the music, but I do have a feel where interpretations of the psychic voices in my head are concerned.

10 *What are your teachings about the survival of the human personality after death? What's the spirit world like? What will we do when we get there? What sort of experiences can we look forward to in the next life? How can we contact loved ones who've gone ahead of us — and how can they contact us?*

My research into hypnotic regression affirmed my belief in life after death, although I was already a believer, having been in contact with the spirit world since I was a child. I think that life, this one or any of our other excursions on to the Earth plane, is for the purpose of learning. Either we must learn a new lesson, or learn better a lesson that spirit has tried to teach us in previous lives, but that we have not quite got the hang of to their satisfaction. As to what the spirit world is like, to be honest, I don't really know. Spirit does not give much away about this, and they tend to go vague if you ask — they tend to say that it is much the same as the Earth plane. I get the feeling that they are all still on a learning curve, on whatever plane they happen to be on. So when we get there, I think that there will be a time for rest and recovery and then a meeting with the powers that be to decide the next stage of our existence: whether that be a return to the Earth plane, or a move to another stage of development, in whatever environment they decide is best for our learning process to continue. I think that on this side of the divide, help from mediums or some other type of psychic contact is necessary to interpret what is going on. Even on the other side they seem to need some kind of intermediary to make good contact, although their ability to make themselves known to us seems to be better than ours. I know that when I make contact by "tuning in," loads of them turn up, and they all start talking at the same time. This is again where my telephonist abilities come into their own — but this improvement only comes with training. Some spirits are not too keen on contacting their loved ones, but then, if they have been returned to the Earth plane for some more learning they are then not in a position to contact us. Those left on the spirit plane, of course, do have the opportunity to contact us, which some take, and some do not. People ask why babies die. I think that, again, the learning process is responsible for this. Perhaps the baby-spirit needs to learn something from the actual birthing process, but does not need to spend years on this plane once the lesson has been learned. Conversely, the parent may need to learn from the death of a baby, something that has not been learned in previous existences. This seems to me a reasonable explanation of what, on the surface, seems an unreasonable loss of a child. I doubt that you will be contactable when you pass over — like me you will be too busy rushing about asking questions, and too fascinated by all the new sights and sounds around! Things to do and places to go will be right up your alley! I, personally, imagine the other side to be like a huge university campus, but a place where you can choose any course you want. And where you know that you are going to get the answers that have always eluded you on the Earth plane.

Another of our highly valued friends is Bremna's friend Pamela Willson, who is a very talented artist and psychic. Again, we have had the pleasure of knowing her for a number of years, and have always been impressed by her total honesty and integrity as well as by her considerable paranormal abilities. These are Pam's answers to our questions:

1   At what stage of your life — childhood, adolescence, or maturity — were you first aware of your psychic gifts and talent?

I became aware of my psychic gifts and talents when I first met a female astrologer and tarot reader who lives in Palmer's Green,

North London. I was about twenty-five years old at the time and she told me that I would do psychic readings myself in the future and that I was an artist and that these two talents would come together. How right she was. When I was thirty-two I met a Greek woman psychic who gave me a reading and asked me, "You see pictures, don't you?" This is what you would call being clairvoyant and is a gift from birth. I have seen pictures all my life, as far back into childhood as I can remember. The Greek lady made me aware of my clairvoyance, although it had always been with me. My next stage of awareness was when I was asked to do a spirit drawing for a medium called Joy in Finchley. This was very new to me then. As I came away from her home, I was aware of a spirit guide around her who was a nun. Two days later, I sat down in my lounge with a blank canvas board, charcoal, and a putty eraser and I thought, right, I will tune in and let spirit take over. This was my first spirit drawing. When I took it back to her, she said this was the guide she saw when she was on the platform at different spiritualist churches and halls, and also in her own home.

I would like to explain the feeling I got. It wasn't so much that I pictured the nun on this occasion, it was as if I was being instructed to shade something in here, or make the mouth smaller, or lower the top lip a bit, and so on — that's how it came through. Spirit makes you aware at the right times in your life of progress on a spiritual path. We must also remember that we have free will and choice. You can go along that path or you can block it and reject it — it's up to the individual. The esoteric, the unknown, has always intrigued me — so, consequently, I have always followed it.

2   *We've seen and heard you in action and you're very gifted. Which of your psychic powers do you consider to be the best developed, or the most important?*

The most important psychic power I have is being able to tune into the spirit realm for guidance to help other people — and to help myself, as well. This is a true gift and I can use it in regard to my other gifts such as healing, psychic artwork, tarot readings, psychometry, palmistry, clairvoyance, and clairaudience. Which do I consider most important? I am truly grateful for all of those gifts that I have been given and that have developed slowly over the years. The most important, I would say, is healing. I think that if you have the gift of healing and are able to help somebody who has gone through all the orthodox system of medicine without success, then that is a very important gift indeed.

3   *When you are actually using your powers would you compare them to seeing, hearing, or tactile sensations? In other words, how do psychic powers manifest themselves to one who has such knowledge?*

Psychic powers — let's call them that — manifest themselves in numerous ways. When I give healing, I get a very strong heat sensation in my hands — like holding them near a fire. I also experience a tingle in my palms. Being clairvoyant and clairaudient, when I get clairvoyance it's like switching on the television, except that spirit switches it off and on for me. Sometimes it comes when you don't expect it; at other times, it will come when I am trying to tune in for different reasons, such as investigating old places of historical interest and tuning back into the past to see what happened in those places.

When I give a reading to a client — albeit psychometry or the tarot or whatever I use as a focus — then it is just tuning in to the other side, and, if spirit is willing, information will come forth for me to give to the client. Clairaudience comes to me like a sound pattern from the ethereal world and this can happen at any time and in any location. You must make sure you are on the right wavelength because in the spirit world — the same as the Earth plane — there are the positive and negative forms, just as there are positive and negative people on the Earth. I have met many in both worlds and if you have anything that is negative and you sense that it's negative, send it back to the plane it belongs to in the spirit world. In the same way, if you meet somebody who is highly negative on Earth, and sense that they are not for your highest good, then you eradicate the situation as soon as you can and end your involvement with that person: that's the same attitude I adopt on a psychic level.

4   *What do you consider as the most mysterious or inexplicable psychic adventure you've ever had?*

One that was really inexplicable occurred when I was living in a flat in Arnos Grove and I woke up at about two o'clock in the morning. I am going back to the end of the 1980s. I woke up and there was this monk-like character sitting by the side of my bed, grinning at me. I was rather startled, to say the least, and I just looked. Then I shut my eyes and mentally said the Lord's Prayer. I also asked the strange visitor to return to the realm from which he came. I found his visit a little disconcerting because I wasn't expecting that kind of thing at that time.

When I was staying up at White Webs, sitting up in bed reading a book on the history of China, I looked up and there was this cavalier-like figure standing in the doorway. I didn't feel uncomfortable with him whereas with the grinning monk I did. The cavalier just looked across and I looked back and thought, "No, I'm not actually seeing this, am I?"

I looked down at my book; when I looked up again he was gone and the door was closed. I was intrigued. Apparently, in that area up in Enfield and around White Webs there is an old pub called "The King and Tinker." It goes back into the sixteenth century and there was a lot of military activity in that area: Roundheads, Cavaliers, and King Charles I, I would presume.

Also, I did learn that Henry VIII used to go hunting over there and the old house of White Webs — which was a retirement home for men in our day — had quite a history going back to Henry's time: hence it did link in from an historical point of view.

There was the dream that I had that was very prophetic. It was a year before my father passed over: my mother had passed twenty years before — and when I woke up the dream was as clear as crystal. I was standing at Cardiff Central Station but it was all beautifully cleaned like creamy marble walls. My father was sort of ascending those station stairs, looking down, grinning and smiling at me. He wasn't a man in his late sixties in this vision — he was a man of about thirty. He was smiling and waving at me, and I was saying to him, "No, Dad, not that way; we've got to go this way."

Then my mother appeared and said to me, "Your father is coming to meet me and it will not be long after that that your Uncle Billy will be here also." My Uncle Billy was my mother's brother and it was only a year later that my father passed over, in April. That's when I came down to Wales, just before he passed over in Landough Hospital, near Cardiff. It was in December that I lost my mother's brother, my Uncle Billy, who lived on the North Road in Cardiff. So that dream was very prophetic. It always stands out in my memory because it was so true, because my father was first and my Uncle Billy did pass over afterwards.

DEATH

Pamela Willson, the gifted psychic artist, near her home in haunted Dinas Powys, in Wales, UK.

Another one I would like to mention is the one involving Dinas Powys Castle, where I used to sit in the centre of the site and try to tune in. It is in ruins; there are just a few of the old stones left and it's rather like a stone circle. One day, I thought, well, I'll sit here and try to tune in to what it used to be in the past. Mentally I was expecting a very peaceful, tranquil situation — but, oh no — it was going back into the fifteenth or sixteenth century. It was an area where there was a lot of commerce, trading, and so forth: very, very busy, full of people and activity.

Just recently I was mentioning this fact to a friend called Tom Clement, who has investigated the history of various local areas. He said to me when I was relating the Dinas Powys tale to him, "You don't know how right you are, and how well you tuned in. This was once a capital, a centre like Cardiff is today."

5   *Powerful and perceptive sensitives like you are excellent judges of character. What is the psychic mechanism that makes it possible? For example, would you say that you can see auras, or do you feel positive or negative vibrations? Do "good" people give off a "warm" feeling and "bad" people a "cold" feeling?*

I don't like to judge anybody. I take them as I find them until I find them different. On a psychic level, I have found personally through the years that when I have first met someone, if that deep, inner, gut feeling says to me, "There is something about him or her that I am picking up that I don't like," if I have gone against that instinct I have always paid the price — whether it be a person, or, maybe, a job situation. Something inside says, "Ah, ah! Not for you!"

I think quite a few people possess that warning mechanism. What we need is to become aware of our ability. Maybe sometimes we do go into certain situations against our better judgement — especially where it concerns the character of people. Possibly it's so that we can learn lessons and grow stronger on the spiritual path — that's my feeling about it. Seeing auras? I have seen something like a hazy mist around certain people — or even animals. I haven't gone along that path, or tuned in, or developed it to any great stage when it comes to auras. For me, it's more a vibration, or a feeling. The question of whether good people give off a "warm" feeling and bad people a "cold" feeling? Well, for me it's a bit deeper than that: it's just that inner sense of the person's character. It can be quite painful sometimes, because he, or she, might present as very clean and tidy, a good person, and all the rest of it but inside you're getting, "I don't think you're quite what you purport to be."

At the end of the day it's what you felt at the first impact that counts. Then, perhaps, later you start to think, "I must have been wrong." Yet it may be that ten years down the road that first gut feeling, that deep inner feeling, was right after all.

6 *What are your views on astral projection and OOB experiences? How well does it work? What's your experience of it?*

Being a medium, obviously I have had experience of it because when you get spirit coming through in picture form — especially if it's in association with somebody's relative who's passed on and things that they want to project or put over to the person — I might get a picture of an object of significance. I had a lady here just recently, on 10 September 1999, and I was in the middle of reading the tarot for her. Suddenly I got this older person with very thick, white, wavy hair. I saw a picture of this coming through the astral, the invisible realm. She was showing me lots and lots of embroidery silks and they were being embroidered on to a piece of material into crinoline ladies. I asked the person who was sitting opposite, "Does this mean anything to you?" She laughed and said,

"Yes, because when I was younger I always used to embroider pictures and especially crinoline ladies." So it definitely meant something to her.

I have found on numerous occasions with different people that spirit will show pictures of places, objects, even musical instruments that they played, or that the sitter plays, things to do with their lives, to identify them. You'll get a name sometimes of the person who has passed over and who is making contact and you will say to the individual, "Does the name Joan Williams [as an illustration] mean something to you?" They sometimes want the person who has passed over to give the time of passing and where they used to live, to show that they're actually around in spirit.

As I have often stated, you can't command spirit. The person sitting with me wants to know this and wants to know that. But it does not happen that way. If those in spirit want to come through, they will — that's just my own, personal experience. Also, you have to be very careful. If, say, you were sitting down on your own tuning in, as I did in my early days, then you have got to distinguish clearly and carefully between what is actually coming through from the spirit realm and what is being created by your own imagination — and this is bringing it into the area of OOB experience.

There are numerous cases that have been documented where people have been on the operating table and have actually described the experience of hovering above their bodies. They have seen the clock on the wall; they can state the time, and the different things that were going on as part of the surgical processes they were undergoing. So we carry this astral body with us. I think that in that comfortable half-asleep, half-awake state, when you get into bed and you are just drifting, I think that if I wanted to indulge in what they classify as astral travelling that's the time to send yourself off. I haven't done this personally, because I know that when you indulge, or you allow that to happen, I probably put a block to it during that half-conscious state.

When a person is in a sleeping state, then, yes, you are off, and can be away astral travelling. Astral travellers have to be careful because in the invisible realm there are numerous entities that are both positive and negative. I think if I was to indulge in this in the future, then I would have to feel one hundred percent secure. If I was in that half-awake, half-asleep state, I would want to be absolutely protected on my astral travels.

I think that I would be, but as for actually undergoing an

operation of some kind and having an OOB experience during it — I haven't had one in that sense. But astral projection, yes, because with my work you have to go into the invisible realm and as far as I am concerned it is one of our two worlds.

It is the world of form that we live in, and then there is the invisible world that is made up of its own rather different atoms. There are many invisible atoms in this chair that I'm sitting on while I'm recording this interview for you. It is easily accepted that speech can be recorded and played back over the radio, for example, when it's needed, but there's a sense in which it's all coming through the airwaves. People switch on the television and its messages are coming to us through the invisible. Our human minds haven't generally been focused for a long while now on the fact that everything that is here has come through a thought pattern from the invisible, but if we sit down and really think deeply about that concept, we realise that it is absolutely true.

Invention is thinking about something in a way that nobody has thought about it before.

7   *What do you think about hypno-regression and reincarnation?*

Reincarnation does provide a lot of answers to questions of the enquiring mind. There is an old song that goes something along the lines of, "It seems we stood and talked like this before. We looked at each other then in the same way but I can't remember where or when." Now that lyric provides a useful link into this question, because a lot of people meet up and they might say, "You are not a stranger to me."

They feel inexplicably at home with that person, and I personally believe that that feeling of familiarity does link in with a previous life. Also you might travel to the other end of the world and arrive, say, in the Caribbean area. You walk through Bridgetown and you think, "Well, I should feel strange here, but I don't — and it's as if I have been here before."

This, I feel, also links in with a previous life and it definitely links in with reincarnation — something in which I personally believe.

I think we come back to this earthly plane (which can well be described as the "Vale of Tears") to learn lessons — until we can reach such a stage of personal, spiritual development that we don't have to come back any more.

DEATH

We go through different phases — whatever they might be — according to the individual's stage of spiritual growth, to learn the lessons and slowly, slowly shed off unnecessary, unwanted things until you are refined to such a state of perfection that you are acceptable in the invisible realm to progress there on a much higher level.

I view the spirit realm as somewhere we are all welcome and have our place, and I believe that we may continue to learn, progress, and grow once we are on the other side.

There are also many cases of apparent reincarnation that have been written about, and the principle is well accepted in Tibet and India. If we go back into the old religions of our own ancient Britain — and I am including *the* Old Religion here — those worshippers definitely believed that we travelled on to another realm, and came back again, and so forth — in association with life on this earthly plane.

There seems to have been some kind of block that's been created that impedes the flow of memory and knowledge in this area.

I have toyed with the idea of being regressed to link in with what was going on with me in past lives. I feel that I have had quite a few previous lives, and, possibly, if I don't get rid of one or two habits, I will have to come back to this Earth plane yet again.

I think reincarnation theory is a good idea, and also that it is helpful. If you are hypersensitive and have been told by various people such as mediums, clairvoyants, or whatever over the years that you've been this, or that, in a previous life, it may be helpful to consider going to see an expert to be regressed. I think it could well provide confirmation of what you have been told.

I also feel that the strong likes and dislikes that you bring with you into this life, together with "natural abilities" — especially those of creative children, such as those who can play the violin like any maestro on the concert platform when they're only three years old — have been brought back from a previous life.

[Authors' note: During our discussion with Pamela about reincarnation in general, and her reference to the particular theory that *instinctive* preferences and dislikes may have come over from an earlier existence, she commented on co-author Lionel's strong dislike of tight, or snug-fitting shirt collars. As a 210-pound weight training and martial arts instructor with a nineteen-inch neck and with roughly the build of a silver-back gorilla, he finds it difficult to get shirts with comfortable collars, anyway. But Pamela felt sure he had been a highwayman in an earlier existence and had finished up on Tyburn Gallows — as most highwaymen did — hence his inherited dislike of anything tight around his neck in this life!]

Also linking reincarnation theory in with psychic abilities, I believe that those who are more advanced than others on certain spiritual levels — like those with normal, human talents such as music — may have brought something back with them through their higher consciousness into this life again.

I would also like to say on this reincarnation theme that there was a young boy in India who said to his parents, "I used to live so and so." He even gave the names of his earlier mother and father, who were still alive, because he had passed over as a very young child and had reincarnated through his current parents. They actually went along and checked it all out and it was absolutely accurate. The other family confirmed that they had lost this child.

It is an interesting thing with children because their minds haven't become bogged down with all of the world of form and what it demands of us — so the mind of a young child is nearer to what it was in a past life. I think that if any deep research was to be directed into this area, the most useful approach would be to see what young children from two up to the age of about six would be saying in connection with their imaginary friends. Are these friends as "imaginary" as we like to think? Or are very young children more in tune with the world of spirit than their parents?

Additionally, there are so many simple illustrations of invisible forces at work: the power of the moon, for example, in association with the ocean tides, the influence of the first phase of the new moon where growth is concerned, or the planting of seeds. The old lore that is still practised by farmers today — planting on that first phase of the new moon. There is some magnetic power, or force, there that is coming through the invisible. On windy days we see the leaves on the trees move: it is an invisible force that moves them. The evidence is there in the movement, but we don't see the wind, do we?

8   *Do you also have psychometric powers? How would you describe their mechanism? What does an object absorb, and how does it radiate what it has absorbed to a sensitive, powerful psychic?*

I do practise psychometry. How would I describe its mechanism? Well, going back to my belief in invisible, psychic energies and unseen forces, everything vibrates. Everything has an energy that has been impregnated into it at some stage through the person who has worn or owned the object. It's all there, and when you hold a piece of jewellery or clothing — or even a photograph — you can pick up all sorts of things because the vibrations are all recorded in the object. It's having the ability and sensitivity to tune into those vibrations that matters, and hence numerous things come through when you are holding an object.

There was a woman who came to me about a year ago, in 1998. Her name was Tess, and she brought a strange bracelet with her. I tuned into a rather unusual psychic call. I was being told by a father, who had passed on, that that bracelet had been meant for his daughter. He had brought it back from abroad but the mother had claimed that the object was hers. This person had had her thoughts about the ownership satisfied and justified in many ways, and really believed that the present had been meant for her: it's still in her possession today. But that curious, conflictual information was all carried through the bracelet to me, and I was picking up what had once existed around the object. I think the daughter must have been a young girl of maybe ten or twelve at the time; she is now a woman in her thirties. Anyway, that is just one of many psychometric illustrations I could give to you. Here's another: Clive McKay came to me with a photograph that he turned upside down on the table so I could not see the picture, and I held my hands over it. I also held the photograph in the reversed position, and I picked up on this new girlfriend he had met in Holland. I also picked up on the circumstances concerning her family. Her mother was a teacher, and numerous other things came through to me relating to the life of the mother and also the girlfriend herself.

How does it happen? It's an energy I feel; a vibration is trapped there and is somehow existing within the object. At times I ask people when they hand me a ring, or a piece of jewellery, if it is an antique — because you can tune in to a person who owned it in the distant past and, of course, relate facts in association with that person, as well as establish links to the person who is the current owner and has been wearing it for the last ten or twenty years. There will, naturally, also be lots of things in association with the current owner that will come out as well. How does it radiate? Yet again, this is where the clairvoyance and clairaudience part comes in for me. When I hold an object, I will get pictures in association with the past that are given to me from the spirit. I could also hear a voice. In the example of Tess's case, it was definitely a voice: it was not so much the clairvoyance as it was the clairaudience. It's all a matter of tuning in to the astral plane and into spirit realm with the proviso, of course, that they *want* to give the information.

9   *Are psychic powers born into a psychic, almost like something genetic, or can they be trained and developed by almost anyone who is sincere and keenly interested?*

I think that people are at various stages of development when they come back to this plane. I think that if a person is keenly and sincerely interested in spiritual matters, then there is something deep down inside him or her that he or she would want to investigate. It is the same for all of us: certain circumstances cross our path and certain people come into our lives who are more advanced spiritually, and then they start making us aware — and I think that if your abilities are there on the psychic level, although hidden deeply, they will be awakened quite vividly.

Is it genetic? I think a hereditary factor does come into the mystic equation somewhere, and I think that it comes in when you get to the idea of group souls.

It will tend to run in a family. If people search back in their family tree, they will perhaps discover that Great Aunt Flo was a medium, or perhaps someone else was — going far enough back in the family.

Significant people come into your life — you could say the fickle finger of fate moves in mysterious ways — and suddenly this sparks off something in the psychic person and he or she starts investigating. I think a lot of people who are deeply interested and want to know why we are all here and what it's all about will find that all sorts of inexplicable things will start happening to help them discover the reasons.

You haven't mentioned the astrological aspect in your interview questions, but I think it's significant. There are twelve houses and the first house deals with the individual human personality and its make-up: the blueprint that you come back with. Certain planets in there would give an indication of psychic ability. I am not an astrologer, although I have an interest in the subject. I think that it would definitely show the characteristics that tie in with the meanings of the planets in certain positions in the whole of the chart. I would say especially that where your moon node is would show any psychic ability present. I would say definitely, "Yes." People are all born with potential psychic powers but on different levels according to past experiences and our experiences in this life — and some have the advantage of having the right teacher appearing at the right time, as has happened in my own case.

10 *What are your teachings about the survival of the human personality after death? What's the spirit world like? What will we do when we get there? What sort of experiences can we look forward to in the next life? How can we contact loved ones who've gone ahead of us — and how can they contact us?*

Definitely there is survival of the human personality, if you consider the human personality to be carried in the higher consciousness. That does not leave us when we pass over and abandon this old overcoat, this material body, on the mortuary slab, or in the ground. It may be sent to the crematorium, or whatever you chose: perhaps a sea burial? That mysterious but vital silver cord is carried through the higher consciousness; the astral body hovers over — and we travel on.

A lot of people in their astral form are really surprised at first. They simply don't realise what's happened or where they are. Some are very, very attached to this Earth plane. One of the biggest lessons I think any of us can learn is non-attachment. Sometimes hauntings by what clearly resemble departed human beings are caused by those who are still too firmly attached to the Earth plane for numerous reasons. It might be an experience they have undergone in passing.

It might be a tremendous feeling of sadness in association with the life they have just left and what they have experienced on Earth. That may well make them into Earth-bound spirits for a time. As we know this is a very deep subject, and my personal feelings about it are that the more unattached you become to everything material, the more it enables you to go into deep, deep spiritual feelings that are carried over into that higher consciousness that goes with us when we pass over.

One of the best authorities I have ever read is the famous healer Harry Edwards. He too has passed on now, but his explanation of the spirit world is exceptionally good.

INTERVIEWS WITH PSYCHICS, MEDIUMS, AND INVESTIGATORS

[Authors' note: Back in the early 1950s, we had a great friend named Alec Talbot who was a Methodist local preacher on the Dereham, Norfolk, circuit. Alec's wife Gina had severe arthritis that was healed by Harry Edwards.]

As Harry Edwards himself put it, and as I have heard it expressed and have read it, colours are brighter in the world of spirit.

A lot of people who have had OOB experiences — including near-death experiences — talk about going down a dark tunnel and seeing a light at the end of it. They also testify that there is someone there in spirit to meet you and to help you travel on. There are also those in spirit that try to help those that are attached to the Earth plane.

Lots of people don't even become aware of anything spiritual. They are so involved in this present world of form that they don't seem to see any shades of the invisible or the mysterious in between the material things — that's how I feel about it.

It is very difficult to become unattached, particularly if you have had extremely tragic experiences. When we get there, I think we definitely go into schools of learning, and I also think we carry with us aspects, say from the musical point of view as an example. Whatever good and worthwhile talents we have enjoyed and developed here on Earth, I think they still go on with us into the spirit realm.

I also think there are areas, possibly, where you may have to come back a bit quicker than you thought, to go through something again until you have learned that particular lesson. There is the wise teaching of the Cabbala in the Jewish religion, for example: the tree of life, the levels of souls. Those levels include the lower ones, which they have classified as shell-like. Empty vessels make the most noise, and I think that is so evident in the society we live in today.

From the level of the shell-like soul you go into the baby soul; yes, there are people who are baby souls. What happens with a baby? It doesn't have any appreciation, does it? It just goes through a room indiscriminately: it will break, crash, destroy, and so forth — until it is trained and taught otherwise. There are baby souls and they go through life like that: just breaking, destroying, and smashing people and things. From the baby soul you eventually develop into the mature soul, then from that level to the old soul. You will get a wise and discriminating person who will look at some newborn babies and say, "They are old souls: they have been here before." From that stage of an old soul, on passing over maybe they won't have to come back again.

DEATH

I would like to give an illustration concerning passing over to the other side. I was with my mother when she passed over. Among the last words she said as she turned on her side were, "Mama, Mama," which I think is the Welsh for "mother." [Authors' note: *mamaeth* is Welsh for "nurse"; *mam-gu* means "grandmother"; *mam* is "mother."] I didn't have the knowledge then that I have now, and I feel that it was my grandmother near my mother in spirit helping her over to the other side. There are many authorities on the subject who believe that people on the other side help the dying person over into the spirit realm when they are passing.

How can we contact loved ones who have gone ahead of us, and how can they contact us? Generally, people would go along to a spiritualist hall or church and find contact in that way through a medium. I think the spiritualist organisations on this level have helped a lot of people who are bereaved and they have found that contact through a good, honest medium on the platform has comforted them. They have also found a lot of evidence of survival after death and have been able to make contact with loved ones who are in spirit. A person can go along to a spiritualist hall and not get a contact for a long while; it might not come through that avenue. It can come in numerous other ways. Spirit can undoubtedly make itself known to us.

I had the experience of actually seeing my grandfather, whom I had never seen in real life. I was living in a house in Palmer's Green, on the North Circular Road. It was a Sunday afternoon and I was pruning the roses in the front garden. I looked up and there was this person grinning at me. He looked very much like my father, only shorter. My father was still alive.

As I looked down to start pruning again, I thought, "Why am I experiencing this warm and happy feeling on seeing this person? I don't really know him. I looked up again and he was gone. I looked up the road, down the road, and across the road. I looked up the lane by the side of the house: the figure was completely gone. When I went indoors, I thought, "That was my grandfather!" I had always wanted to meet him. It was a strange experience. I wasn't shocked. I wasn't afraid. I had a warm, happy glow. Thinking about it, I realised that what I had always wished to have done was to meet him, which my father didn't allow for family reasons going back to his childhood.

Grandfather had come through and made himself visible to me in a very positive and friendly way. It was not a figment of my imagination. I am certain that it actually happened.

INTERVIEWS WITH PSYCHICS, MEDIUMS, AND INVESTIGATORS

[Authors' note: While doing some harvest work for a relative, Stanley Shickell, at Church Farm, North Tuddenham, Norfolk, in the 1950s, co-author Lionel heard a similar tale of a vanishing spectral figure from one of the other farm workers. His informant told him how he had seen an elderly vagrant woman, known in Norfolk dialect as "an old roadster," coming towards him down a narrow lane between two fields. There were high, impenetrable hedges on both sides of this lane. The man who told the story said that he had ducked into the cover of a gateway in order to try to avoid the old vagrant, mainly because he did not want to be asked for money as she passed! She didn't pass. He peeped out from his place of concealment to see where she'd gone. There was no sign of her, and there was nowhere at all to which she could have gone. One minute she had been in that lane walking steadily towards him, and the next moment she had vanished completely — just as Pamela's grandfather did when she got on with her pruning.]

Spirit can make itself manifest and contact can be made. That meeting with my grandfather was one experience illustrating how loved ones who have passed over can contact us. Another similar experience was when my mother came through in a dream, and I have also had evidence through other good and reliable mediums with messages for me in association with loved ones who have passed on.

Our friend Kevin Carlyon enjoys a worldwide reputation both as a researcher into the paranormal and as a white magician. He is currently recognised as the high priest of the British white witches, and has some remarkable material to share. Here are Kevin's responses to our questions:

1   *At what stage of your life — childhood, adolescence, or maturity — were you first aware of your psychic gifts and talent?*

I am forty-one years old this year [1999]. At the age of five I started to be able to tell school friends about things that would happen in their life: ranging from silly things like what they would have in their lunch boxes to what they would do that night. It culminated in my telling a school friend that he would fall out of a tree the following day, which he did. I was hauled in front of the school priest and the headmistress and told that I had the Devil

Sandie and Kevin Carlyon with Lionel Fanthorpe during a recent television production.

inside me and that they wanted to pray over me. I walked out. The following day my mother went ballistic in front of the whole school assembly and I thought, "This is good — I have a gift!" Rather than be scared of it, I decided to follow my instinct.

I was a skinny little boy at secondary school and was constantly picked on, until one day I had had enough. I started body-building and through using my paranormal gift as an aid retaliated on all the bullies. I soon earned their respect and was the talk of the school. My doctrine now is to never use the gifts within for selfish reasons — for need, not for greed — and to use them only as a last resort.

2   *We've seen and heard you in action and you're very gifted. Which of your psychic powers do you consider to be the best developed, or the most important?*

I feel that I have developed my powers throughout my life and that a person is born a healer, not instructed. The gift is inside everyone at birth, but soon fades if not recognised. I think my most powerful gift is using the power of positive thought to help people, including problems with love, luck, health, and fertility. Even large companies enlist my help when they have problems and I am regularly consulted by police forces around the country.

3 *When you are actually using your powers would you compare them
   to seeing, hearing, or tactile sensations? In other words, how do
   psychic powers manifest themselves to one who has such knowledge?*

I feel that my senses detect things and that I can attune to what
is going on around me. When I do tarot readings for people, I
already know all about them the moment I meet them through
vibes and instinct. I don't need the cards, but it wouldn't be quite
the same if I sat them down at a clear table, so in a way I have to
give them what they expect!

4 *What do you consider as the most mysterious or inexplicable psychic
   adventure you've ever had?*

Every day of my life is mysterious and a new experience and I
never know who will be on the phone next. I can't really pinpoint
one particular experience as to me it's normal life, while to others it
would scare the living daylights out of them.

5 *Powerful and perceptive sensitives like you are excellent judges of
   character. What is the psychic mechanism that makes it possible? For
   example, would you say that you can see auras, or do you feel
   positive or negative vibrations? Do "good" people give off a "warm"
   feeling and "bad" people a "cold" feeling?*

I am an excellent judge of character and can tell whether a
person is good or bad. If I get bad vibes I politely tell them to go
away, as my wife, Sandie, and I, and our ten black cats, who are
also excellent judges of character, don't want negative vibes in
our home.

6 *What are your views on astral projection and OOB experiences?
   How well does it work? What's your experience of it?*

I have experienced astral projection and out-of-body
experiences. I can focus on a certain place and person and whether
in their mind, or in their dreams, they see me materialise like
something out of "Star Trek." Through the power of positive
thought I believe that you can "beam" your spirit anywhere.

DEATH

7 *What do you think about hypno-regression and reincarnation?*

I feel that reincarnation is, perhaps, for those who think that they may have messed up this life and so claim they are someone from the past. How can everybody be Jesus, Hitler, Joan of Arc, King Arthur, or President Lincoln — what about the normal people like a butcher or farmer? Reincarnation is possible for the strong-willed in this life, if they have a purpose to fulfil.

8 *Do you also have psychometric powers? How would you describe their mechanism? What does an object absorb, and how does it radiate what it has absorbed to a sensitive, powerful psychic?*

Psychometry I can achieve again through "animal instinct." I believe that a person leaves his or her "trace" on an item. A person who can attune to the other person's frequency, or pick up wide-band coverage, is able to absorb thoughts placed within the item, particularly when the person who left the traces was highly emotional, or even facing death or murder.

9 *Are psychic powers born into a psychic, almost like something genetic, or can they be trained and developed by almost anyone who is sincere and keenly interested?*

Psychic powers are not, in my opinion, passed on genetically; they are instilled into certain chosen people — chosen by whom I don't know. My wife, Sandie, was brought up in a Christian family — but since we met and married her abilities have increased. I stress that everyone has the power inside himself or herself, if they choose to acknowledge their own instincts: a neutral force, just like the "Star Wars" idea — you can cook with it or kill with it. Everything depends on the user. However, those who use the "dark side of the force" eventually have their fingers burned. It has to be used for need, not for greed or selfish gain.

10 *What are your teachings about the survival of the human personality after death? What's the spirit world like? What will we do when we get there? What sort of experiences can we look forward to in the next life? How can we contact loved ones who've gone ahead of us — and how can they contact us?*

INTERVIEWS WITH PSYCHICS, MEDIUMS, AND INVESTIGATORS

I feel that when a person passes on, his or her soul is free and part of the universe, never to return in the same form as their human incarnation. That person's spirit becomes electricity and links with the very essence of nature, earth, air, fire, and water. Once their spirit is added, they link with the whole make-up of the universe — call it a universal soul or god-and-goddess-head. To use a cliché, "they link with the force."

I feel that too many people look to the next life as an escape route when they should live in this incarnation and live for now. It's part of human nature. If a person makes a mistake in this life, he or she looks to the afterlife for an answer. If they can't be strong now they won't survive again. As in all animal species, only the strong survive — but if they can't cope with now they certainly stand no hope for a future resurrection, unless, of course, they are vampires!

Another good friend of ours, Ray Ronson, is a first-class professional stage hypnotist, whose act is both entertaining and intriguing. We ourselves believe that the latent powers available through hypnosis are still largely unexplored, and would well repay careful and rigorous scientific study at the highest levels. The ability of the human mind to control its own body via hypnosis — and, perhaps, to influence many other things in its physical environment — could possibly be the gateway to a utopian future.

Professional hypnotist and hypno-regression expert Ray Ronson of Barry in Wales, whose haunted house was exorcised by Lionel Fanthorpe.

DEATH

Ray also specialises in hypno-regression, and his work in this field is especially interesting. Here are his comments on the subject:

One of my most memorable past-life regression sessions took place in early summer 1998. Silke Scheideriter is a young lady in her twenties and was at that time employed in the German department of AOL.

Her request was quite straightforward. Her father had passed away when she was only nine years old. Her memories of him were not clear at all, and she was anxious that over the coming years the little memories she did have of him would eventually fade away.

Silke lived in Dublin. My wife Maureen and I live in Barry, a town just outside Cardiff, the capital city of Wales. A one-hour appointment with me was out of the question. I overcame that problem by suggesting to Silke that, as she was due some leave from AOL, she could, if she wished, come over to Barry and stay with us as our guest. Silke accepted this invitation with great enthusiasm.

The arranged date, 29 May, soon arrived. Maureen drove to Cardiff International Airport, picked up Silke, and came straight back to our home, a small terraced house in the Dockland area of Barry.

During my first interview with Silke, I discovered that she had only recently come across hypnotism, after seeing a stage hypnotist at an AOL social function. She even took part in the performance. After that experience Silke told us that she had become totally fascinated by the subject of hypnotism. This is how she had heard of regression and through regression she hoped to access the lost memories that she had of her father. We agreed to start the sessions the following morning.

In the evening that followed, Silke was completely engrossed in the books on hypnotism that fill our bookshelves. One book, in particular, that captivated her was *Hypnotism* by Sidney Flowers, published by the American Psychic Society near the beginning of the twentieth century. In my opinion, it's essential reading if a person wants to study hypnotism properly. When she came to a piece in the book on rapid inductions, Silke asked me if it was possible to put a person into deep trance so quickly. I explained that this was possible in only a small percentage of the population, or if the person has been hypnotised on a previous occasion.

"Try it on me," Silke asked.

Now the events that followed I can only describe as incredible. Demonstrating to Silke a rapid induction, I discovered that she could enter into a very deep trance fast: in fact, very fast! Later in the week I found that Silke's sense of taste and her perception of reality could be altered by suggestion alone, without any hypnotic induction whatsoever.

Knowing this made my work with Silke much easier, so the following morning it took just fifteen minutes to restore Silke's dim and distant memories of her deceased father into glorious Technicolor! I also gave her a post-hypnotic suggestion in that whenever she thought of a certain code word she could access even further memories of her father, a technique that Silke still uses.

Our hypnotic work over in such a short time, Silke explored the shelves of our bookcase even further during her stay with us and chose a book entitled *The Power of the Mind*, written by the acclaimed hypnotherapist Joe Keeton. After reading it for awhile, Silke scoffed at the idea of people claiming to have had a previous existence on Earth, and the concept of reincarnation. This is when I disclosed to Silke that past-life regression is an interest of mine. I suggested that she might like to have a try sometime during her stay with us, and I could even have the session videotaped by a friend of mine so she could keep it as a souvenir: this she agreed to with some zest!

Silke's past-life regression was a unique experience for me. For a person who had scoffed at the whole idea of past lives and reincarnation, the events were more colourful than Finnian's Rainbow! But one episode in her regression session has left me with much food for thought. Let me explain. A person may regress to one or more characters from the past. The memories of that character cease at the point of his or her death. The person regressed may become another character in a time after the death of the previous character. In my experience in conducting past-life regressions there are no memories at the point in between each character. Maybe other hypnotherapists can tell me differently.

In total, Silke regressed to five characters: four females, and one male! As I have mentioned previously there was one episode in Silke's regression that left me with much food for thought. Silke had memories of an existence of one of her characters after death, without going into much detail of the character's living memories, and this is what she recalled.

The first character was a young girl called Marie. We joined Marie at the age of seventeen, walking through a wood on her way into town to fetch some milk; it was in the early 1800s. Marie gave me accounts of her life up until she reached the age of thirty-seven. At that age Marie was taken ill with a severe fever, from which she never recovered. The following is an account of an existence Marie experienced after the death of her physical body. First of all Marie fears the oncoming of death and the thought of leaving her family. By now Marie is married with two young sons. These are the words of Marie in death, "Everything is blurred; I can't see anything." When asked were she was Marie replied, "I'm looking down on a room; it has a bed in it; there are two people sitting by the bed; a women is sleeping in it; it's very bright! I'm not myself! I'm somewhere else! I'm not myself any more! It feels so nice!" At this point I questioned Marie on her family. "I miss them all; I feel as if I'm floating, going up to the stars; it's a wonderful feeling." When asked to describe what she was seeing Marie gave an answer that I still ponder to this day: "I don't see, I just feel. I'm complete happiness! I'm calm." Then, quite unexpectedly, Marie exclaims, "It's all changing! It's getting darker! I feel as if I'm being pulled down! I have to leave this place! I have to go back! I've let my family down! I have to go back! I don't know how!" Marie suddenly finds herself in her former home. "I see them now; they can't see me! I'm trying to speak; they can't hear me! I can't reach them; I'm not in their lives anymore!" Marie decides to go back and says very calmly, "My family don't need me anymore." I asked Marie where she was going. "It's like fog," she replied. "I'm in a big dark room; there is a light coming in from the ceiling." When questioned once more on her family whom she had left behind, the answer I received was from a rather puzzled voice telling me, "I've not left anyone behind."

"Who are you?" I asked. A very calm and relaxed sounding voice gently replied, "I'm no one."

Silke's stay with us and her experience with hypnotherapy and past-life regression changed the direction of her life completely. Shortly afterwards she returned to her home in Germany to raise funds so that she could make a serious study of hypnotism and psychology. I feel I must add, after Maureen and I had come to know Silke better, I can honestly say she does not do things by halves! Up until the time of this interview, Silke has completed a study of neurolinguistic programming, tutored by the co-author of the best-selling book entitled *Frogs into Princes*, and has been coached in hypnotic techniques by the internationally renowned hypnotist, Paul McKenna. Well done, Silke!

INTERVIEWS WITH PSYCHICS, MEDIUMS, AND INVESTIGATORS

If Silke's, or should I say Marie's, account of what happens to us all after physical death has occurred is one day proven to be true, when the good Lord above decides to shine His light down on to me, I shall be there with a large smile across my face and my arms widely outstretched.

Margaret Challenger and her husband Paul are well known spiritual leaders and teachers. They run a college for psychic studies in South Wales. Here are Margaret's comments in response to our questions:

1 At what stage of your life — childhood, adolescence, or maturity — were you first aware of your psychic gifts and talent?

I was aware of them from two years of age. Born into a mediumistic family, I found that my mother would encourage me to talk to the people I could see. I would tell her that there was someone in the corner, or just in the room; she would reply by saying, "Well, ask them their name and talk to them." So I did!

2 We've seen and heard you in action and you're very gifted. Which of your psychic powers do you consider to be the best developed, or the most important?

I am daily striving to improve my mediumistic ability, this being the most important to me. Everyone is a psychic in some degree or other but not everyone is mediumistic. Mediumship has to be worked at to attain the right vibration to work with the people who come to talk with us from the realms of the spirit world. We need to work at making the contact between the two vibrations easier for both physical and spiritual contact to take place and more accurate information to be obtained proving the continuation of life.

3 When you are actually using your powers would you compare them to seeing, hearing, or tactile sensations? In other words, how do psychic powers manifest themselves to one who has such knowledge?

Psychic powers are quite different from mediumistic powers. A psychic will obtain information from a living person who is with him or her. A medium obtains information from someone in the spirit world and relates the information to you. This can usually be upheld by the evidence behind the message. A psychic will tap into your aura/energy. Each of us from birth builds up this energy, which can be related to something like that of an onion, layers upon layers of vibration. It can be in the form of colour or just vibration; how it is read will depend upon the development of the psychic. Fortunately, I have developed all three of the mediumistic senses: clairaudience, clairvoyance, and clairsentience — the words themselves are taken from the French and mean clear hearing, clear seeing, and clear sensing or feeling. I can see people who come to us from the spirit world and I'm able to describe them. I hear what they have to say, the tone of their voices. I feel their emotions. All this enables the medium to give accurate descriptions of the person with whom they are communicating to the recipient.

4   *What do you consider as the most mysterious or inexplicable psychic adventure you've ever had?*

I suppose there are two that are quite amusing. In the first, a girl telephoned me to say that she had been aware that there was a spirit person living in their house for some time and hadn't been too concerned about it as nothing untoward had happened until recently. Her daughter had burst into the living room, as children do, had run across to the corner to use the telephone, and was "pushed over" by no one. The girl was upset. I was asked if I could help. I told her I would telephone her back and spent a moment or two "linking in" with my spirit helpers (some people call these guides). I asked them if it was possible for me to help and they said it was. I always send them first (they are closer than me). I telephoned back and made arrangements to visit that night.

As soon as I entered the room I walked through the vibration of this spirit person. I had never been in the house before. I walked to where the telephone was and I could see her sitting in what would have been her chair in her corner. Now, of course, there was just the telephone. She was very frightened herself and it transpired that the little girl had startled her, and so she defended herself. We talked for a while and she told me that she had a room upstairs with furniture. I asked the couple if they could take me to a room where there was a piece of furniture that had been left at the house when they bought it. They were amazed that I knew about this furniture and so they took me to their bedroom and there it was — quite an old dressing table. The room was icy cold. I asked the couple if they were aware of the coldness in the room and they said that it was the coldest room in the house despite having had a new window put in. The other point they made me aware of was that they always argued in this room. Almost every night! I sat on the bed and asked the spirit why she was here and why she was bringing these bad "vibes" to this room. She answered quite sensibly, "It is my room." The spirit person and I had a good talk; she had been sent away as a young girl when she became pregnant. The baby had been adopted or something like that and she was looking for her. I asked her then to describe to me what she could see other than this house. There was a pause, and the vibration began to change: she became calmer and very emotional. She was beginning to see relatives who had been trying to "rescue" her for some time. She had shut her mind to anything and everything other than that house. She began to realise where she was and the feeling of release and peace was overwhelming. She apologised for her behaviour and asked the mother to forgive her. No harm was done and she went on her way.

A very similar request was asked of me from a family living in Cardiff. The mother had heard someone saying "Shshshsh" when the child of the family was sleeping. I went down and went through the house and the one room again was icy cold. I told them she was in here and after we had chatted and the spirit person understood, the room became warmer straight away. The husband kept saying, "I can feel it; I can feel it; this room is warm for the first time."

A doctor from the Heath Hospital telephoned me to say that his wife had gone. For a moment I thought he meant she was dead, but he said, no, she had gone away. Could I help? The same thing happened: I asked my spirit friends and they said that I could help, and that the family should bring to my house the last item of clothing that she had worn before leaving. They did so: they brought her nightgown and bed socks.

This is where my psychic ability comes in. Using my psychic ability, I felt the garments and was able to pick up the person's last mood and state of mind, and was able to relate this to the husband and the girl's mother, who came also. Now by rising my vibration and linking with the spirit world — raising above the psychic — I asked them what should I do next. They wanted me to make a drawing. I had a piece of A4 plain paper and drew, very crudely, just like a child's drawing, a main street, with a turning off to the left. On the right hand side there was a café where they sold beer and coffee. There would be a couple of houses up this street and she would be in the third house on the right. He would not find her in the first time but he should go to the café, take a photograph with him, and ask in there if she was known. He should then go back to the house and he would find her in. He would go to this place but would not be able to get to the house for three days. They told him that she was fine and that she was with someone she knew. The doctor then asked, "Should I go to her?" and quite categorically I said, "Oh, yes, you will find her: you must go."

They left the house and as they were going the husband turned to me and said, "I shall go to her then."

I smiled as he walked down the path.

"Where do you think she is?" I asked.

He said, "In India!"

I nearly died on the spot. Here I am telling this man to take a trip half way across the world with a piece of paper with scribbles on it.

I spent the worst week of my life during the days that followed. He got to the place; he rang me to say that he could not go to see her for three days as had been said because of transport problems or something similar. The day came when he arrived at the town; he took the "map" I had drawn and there was the main street. He took the left turn where it was suggested: there was the café. He went to the house and knocked on the door — no reply. He went back to the café and showed the picture: she was recognised. He went back to the house — she was there. She was not on her own but with someone she knew — her cousin.

I was so relieved, I can tell you. The responsibility I felt was horrendous.

Of course, the doctor told his parents, who lived in India, all about this and so they wanted to meet me. They came over from India and sat in my lounge, not being able to speak a word of English. As the doctor's mother sat there, the spirit of a lady built up beside her and we spoke (through mind-to-mind communication). The lady told me to say the word "Poppy," but it was not the flower. At this point I thought these people were going to think I'm crazy. They came all the way from India to see what I was like and I was going to say a thing like "poppy" to her. Well, I thought, have courage in what you believe and, of course, I always teach "say what you see." So I told her, and they jumped up and down for joy.

When they were able to speak, the son told me that when the mother was born she was a different colour from her brothers and sisters and so her family gave her a nickname, "Poppy." Now that's what I call evidence!

5   *Powerful and perceptive sensitives like you are excellent judges of character. What is the psychic mechanism that makes it possible? For example, would you say that you can see auras, or do you feel positive or negative vibrations? Do "good" people give off a "warm" feeling and "bad" people a "cold" feeling?*

When you open up your psychic ability and develop your mediumistic ability you are hypersensitive. You can feel vibrations far more strongly than those who have not. Therefore, when you meet someone you meet their vibration. You may either like the vibration or it may offend you. You are entering into the pathway of another person's aura/energy field. We all carry with us our personal identity and to a psychic/medium this is easily accessible and can be "read." This is why you hear someone say, "I took a dislike to him/her the moment I set eyes on him/her." They have experienced the vibrations from this person and "read" them as negative or positive.

If people live their lives using the bad to influence them daily, then obviously this is reflected in their aura/vibration and we are going to take a dislike to this. If, on the other hand, you meet someone who tries to live his or her life as well as he or she can, then you will accept this aura/vibration more easily. This can help you with your judgement of the character of another person — but then who is capable of judging? Perhaps we are reading the opposite of whom and what we are and this displeases us. But who is right?

6   *What are your views on astral projection and OOB experiences? How well does it work? What's your experience of it?*

I have not had any personal experience of either — in the dream state I sometimes remember being somewhere and doing something. This usually follows when — before I go to sleep — I ask the spirit world if I can visit the Halls of Learning to increase my ability as a medium. Occasionally I can remember being with hundreds of others and listening intently to what was being said.

DEATH

7   *What do you think about hypno-regression and reincarnation?*

Wonderful topics for conversation — I would like to be able to prove both but as I am a "seeing is believing" kind of person I reserve my judgement. However, my own opinion is — *regression*. When I was a child, I was always Maid Marion from the "Robin Hood" series and spent hours upon hours acting out the part in the woods. If I was to be regressed would it perhaps open up a dream, a remembering, with, perhaps, precise details? I don't know. They say we only use a fraction of our brain — why? What lies in the bits we don't use? *Reincarnation* — again I have seen documentaries alleging small children to be the former husband of so and so, etc. Could this be that the person with the memory is a very good link with the spirit world, having this information direct from the person they are purporting to be? Some religions believe that as soon as people die they have to reincarnate — I don't know. I would like to have categorical evidence myself.

8   *Do you also have psychometric powers? How would you describe their mechanism? What does an object absorb, and how does it radiate what it has absorbed to a sensitive, powerful psychic?*

This was partly answered in question 4, with the night garments of the doctor's wife who disappeared. The mechanism surrounding this is that the vibration of the person is left with the garment/item that they wear. You may buy a second-hand item of jewellery and if you were to ask someone to "read" that piece of jewellery, they may come up with all kinds of things that you could not relate to — because those items related to the previous energy/vibration/owner. A sensitive will "feel" the aura/vibration that has been left — there is a particularly good exercise you can take part in yourself. Sit in a chair after someone else has just left it. Absorb the energy of the absent person and you should be able to tell them lots of things about themselves: they will be amazed.

9   *Are psychic powers born into a psychic, almost like something genetic, or can they be trained and developed by almost anyone who is sincere and keenly interested?*

I truly believe that everyone is psychic to a greater or lesser degree, and most certainly everyone can develop his or her psychic ability. Mediumship, however, is also easily developed but only by people who will dedicate themselves to their own development. I believe spirits are no respecters of persons — like attracts like. The quality of the result will depend upon the spirit communicator/guide, who will work with the medium. I know that spirits are much wiser than we are and they certainly do not waste time pursing a channel that's no use to them. They will move quickly on until they have found someone to whom they can relate and will make the best of the knowledge that they bring.

10 *What are your teachings about the survival of the human personality after death? What's the spirit world like? What will we do when we get there? What sort of experiences can we look forward to in the next life? How can we contact loved ones who've gone ahead of us — and how can they contact us?*

To survive death we first have to be aware of why we live. Physical life is merely a kindergarten in readiness for the university of life to come. We are born imperfect beings in an imperfect world. Our search for the truth through physical experiences earns us the right to return to the perfection of the summerland of love and light.

Proving survival time and time again, people who are "dead" return to us and show themselves. My own father was seen on the driveway of his house the day after he died, taking the little dog he once loved (which had died the December before) for a walk. The lady who "saw" him was not a spiritualist or believer in anything like that — just a neighbour who bade him "goodnight" as she passed and was amazed to hear the next day that he had died two days before! Our loved ones return with free will to say to us, "Do not grieve for me. I am alive and well, free from all physical restraints."

If you are fortunate enough to find a good physical circle and are honoured by being invited in, you will find a medium who probably has dedicated most of her life to developing her powers to the extent where a substance called "ectoplasm" is formed. This is done by using the energy of the medium and sitters alike, to allow the discarnate spirit to take on a physical form, and you will witness a "dead" person's hand, face, or full body materialise. You might be invited to touch, when you will find that they have a pulse; their hands are warm; they have fingernails and hair on the hands. The full manifestation can even speak to you and kiss you. This kind of phenomena must be the ultimate proof that life is eternal and that we, on physical death, merely discard the overcoat of physical life and return as a true spirit to the spirit world. When, through a physical medium, spirits are able to take on board this ectoplasm and "show" themselves as physical again reveals to us that it is just the state of vibrations that have changed — not us. The personality remains the same: the fun and sense of humour is there and, of course, the love. Anything physical we leave behind. The brain is physical, so we leave that behind — but the mind travels with us forever.

Apart from the physical manifestations, there are good mediums who dedicate themselves to proving survival by means of clairvoyance, clairaudience, and clairsentience — mental mediumship. Usually this is done by giving evidence of their survival by using one or all of these faculties and producing evidence personal to the sitter that the sitter can agree with categorically. Sometimes the discarnate spirit will tell the sitter when they died, the time, how many people were at the funeral, what kind of sandwiches they had, and any problems that may have occurred after their passing. It is known that some people have attended their own funeral in spirit form. The evidence can be phenomenal through a good and truly developed medium.

What is the spirit world like? I don't know first hand! However, I have been told by people who live there that if you had any affliction whilst in the physical body you are completely restored to full bountiful health. You are met by family, friends, and even pets when you pass from this physical world and your surroundings can be as familiar as you need them to be until you realise that your vibration is merely thought and you are what you think.

There are gardens that are tended; there are workshops for children; there are lectures to attend. There are theatres to attend, pubs, and sex if you so desire. There are libraries and hospitals. Why? Because perhaps they would all be bored to "death" if there was nothing to do. Why hospitals in a perfect world? To be able to help the spirit — the person passing from this vibration to the spirit vibration. Depending upon their physical illness on Earth, or other personal difficulties and problems, a period of convalescence may be required and an adjustment period.

This takes us on to "What will we do when we get there?" It is entirely up to you. If you are a lazy person in this physical world you may desire to keep on being lazy and do nothing, alternatively you will be given the "offer" to help where you feel you want to.

Whichever way you chose, your own personal development is your own making.

Experiences? Whatever you want! The one great experience we can all look forward to is the total and unconditional experience of peace and love. The ultimate goal is to become such an evolved spirit that our only desire is to serve the Great Universal Energy-God in the fashion that is comfortable to our evolved soul and in accordance with the laws of the spirit realms.

Contact — this being the last question makes me smile — contact is now, is always, and will be forever. Some people say they think they believe in intuition. Some people say they think they believe in the psychic. A lot of people say they think they believe in God. Mediums don't have to think, they believe, they know. Contact is as natural as I am typing on this keyboard — I only had to switch it on and it worked for me. If I raise my vibration just a fraction, I can contact that vibration and those who dwell in that sphere. If I raise my vibration a lot I can contact a higher sphere and those who dwell there.

Spirits are no respecters of persons — you don't have to be absolutely pure for them to make contact with you, but it will depend upon the way that you use your mediumship what kind of information you will receive. Mediums are the receivers of privileged information from the spirit world and mutual respect must prevail.

Our loved ones contact us. They want us to know that they are well and occasionally they will tell us where we are going wrong in our lives, quite naturally wanting to help us as they did when they were in the physical world. Why should they change? It is we who remain in the physical who change — not the ones who are in the spirit world. We speak of them as if they are "gone" when in fact they are listening to the conversation! They come with us shopping and to weddings and christenings. They will even tell you that they are buying a blue hat for the occasion! No, they are not with us in the bathroom! We are all spirit with the spirit world but no part of it until we sever the umbilical cord of physical life.

Margaret's husband, Paul Challenger, makes an equally fascinating independent contribution to this collection of first-hand evidence:

1   At what stage of your life — childhood, adolescence, or maturity — were you first aware of your psychic gifts and talent?

DEATH

What an incredible feeling! There I was thirty-five years of age talking to a medium — and this awesome feeling can only be described as pure love pervading my body from the heart area and making me become very emotional. The medium advised me that this feeling was caused by the nearness of my grandfather's spirit to us in the room and, as the closeness was causing me some discomfort, she said she would ask him to stand back a little. And then, as if on cue, the feelings subsided and left me.

I had studied Aikido, which is a Japanese martial arts system reliant on coordination of mind and body to release latent intrinsic energy, and had experienced powerful movements of energy in and around me over the long years of study, but nothing as powerful as the feeling of closeness of spirit on that occasion. If I never experience another spirit contact, that experience would be enough to convince me that life is eternal.

Prior to the visit to the medium, I had abandoned religion. As I couldn't accept the Genesis explanation, I ended up not accepting anything. I had no real spiritual thoughts and I had only visited the medium out of curiosity. I didn't think that I myself had any "psychic powers" and was not aware of any psychic talents except for some knowledge of the healing system adopted by Aikido, which is taught as being a natural extension of normal abilities.

It came as a surprise when the medium then said, "You've got a rather large Native American as a guide, who wears a full head-dress of feathers, and he's sitting there just behind you." During this first encounter with the medium she told me that I had a foot in either camp and could work immediately as a "spiritual healer." Also, she gave profound evidence in the form of details supplied by relatives in spirit that could only be verified by referral to my parents for confirmation.

You can imagine the effect this first encounter had on my thoughts and I immediately looked for confirmation by testing her statements about talents I may or may not possess.

2 *I know something of your reputation and you're very gifted. Which of your psychic powers do you consider to be the best developed, or the most important?*

Healing gifts became apparent almost immediately thereafter but the healing effects were not dramatic, initially, although spirit healers are now achieving good results through their work with me. Initially, I conducted healing work as an extension of the healing used in Aikido but, with greater experience, this has taken on a different direction. Training, study, and experience in linking with the spirit world have shown me that I have the ability to make this link and I would rate this ability as the highest use of my psychic faculties.

3   *When you are actually using your powers, would you compare them to seeing, hearing, or tactile sensations? In other words, how do psychic powers manifest themselves to one who has such knowledge?*

I manifest "psychic powers" through linking with the spirit world and the link is made so naturally that it would be difficult for one who does not make such a link to tell any difference. The naturalness takes the form of "guided meditations" in healing sessions or in "reading" auras in the form of an auragraph drawing (which is a symbolic representation of a person's life where symbols and colours are drawn and an interpretation applied to it) or in delivering philosophy or a prayer in public. I feel "inspired" when I undertake all these activities: with the inspiration, in my opinion, coming directly from great minds in the spirit world. This inspiration is difficult to prove and where there is real quality to the work, I am sure some others could believe that I myself was responsible for the quality and give me all the credit! I wish!

I believe that the greater intellect comes from spirit minds. I don't believe that I am manifesting true psychic phenomena (derived from the actual working of my own mind) but rather that I open my mind to allow others, whom I trust, to use it.

In my opinion, psychic activity is the use of the mind — by the mind — when it is aware of heightened states of natural mental activity. For example, a "Gypsy-" style "fortune teller" can read a person's electromagnetic field (aura) and give details about the person's past, present, and future (including his or her future wishes) because the sitter impresses the reader's aura with his or her own thoughts. This same fortune teller need have no personal belief in life beyond physical death at all. Such "psychics" can also "read" the impression left in the magnetic field around objects and can demonstrate countless other related phenomena. I am able to do this myself to a minor extent but I wouldn't dream of trusting to such abilities when I could link with spirit and achieve a better result. (Because of the wonder of spirit, it is easy to see why a medium would skip the "psychic" level and leave this aspect of the work relatively undeveloped.)

In linking with spirit I use a mixture of clairvoyance (seeing) and clairsentience (feeling/tactile sensations) and am still struggling with clairaudience (hearing) although I feel that "inspiration" uses the full range with an ease that becomes effortless and cannot be said to be any one particular "clair."

In clairvoyance I see images as if I was "daydreaming." In a public demonstration this may be like seeing a spirit person standing by their contactee, together with any animal or object that they may bring with them. Or the daydream could take the form of a symbol, or series of symbols, which run through my mind like watching a film. In clairsentience, I get the physical impression of an illness, or pain, to a part of the body. The sensation disappears as soon as I acknowledge to the spirit who has brought it that I am aware that that spirit had the condition itself. In clairaudience I have heard my name called and have heard the occasional brief message from an unknown source in my ear. But I struggle in this area because sound from spirit is much more commonly "heard" in the form of "sensing" — a difficult concept to grasp (a bit like the way LSD transmutes sound into colour, and vice versa).

This is the difficult part of psychic activity or much of "mental" mediumship (where you communicate "subjectively" — mind-to-mind — as opposed to "objectively" — as if seen by the physical senses). You just seem to "know" that you're getting it "right."

[Authors' note: After answering question three, as per our interview questionnaire, Paul drew his own theme together and followed his own distinctive line of argument. Where the particular points he made still relate specifically to the questionnaire, the question numbers appear in brackets.]

Such development does, indeed, make one more sensitive but this does not necessarily make you a better judge of character! [5] Recently I was driving to mid-Wales and knew a straightforward route to get me where I wanted to go. On the way I saw a hitchhiker and, although I usually try to do a "good turn" for someone when I can, I didn't like the look of him, so I didn't stop. But not much further on, I stopped in a lay by and made a cup of coffee from my flask. Lo and behold! The hitchhiker rounded the corner, walking fast. He approached rapidly. Should I jump in the car and leave? No.

When he reached me, I asked him where he was going and, finding that I could take him part way to his destination, I offered him a lift. I found him to be a likeable person and when we came to the junction where I should have dropped him off and changed direction, found myself agreeing to drive a "little" further north to use a much more level and less dangerous road than the one I had originally proposed to take. I ended up going miles out of my way, costing me a lot of time. When I opened the back door later, my flask fell out of the car and smashed! Yes, I had had a psychic feeling but overrode the sensation with logic and ended up losing out — but then who is to say whether or not this had been meant to take place?

The question of "destiny" crops up again and again in the life I am leading. There have been so many occasions in my life since that first encounter with the medium that I have come to feel that a plan is in place for my life and those close to me. I am a firm believer in "free will" but am also glad that I have followed the plan as it fits very neatly with my own personal happiness. The plan seems to involve the idea that I have agreed to comply with it. This suggests to me that it was made before I, myself, and the other key players in my life were born and this then implies that our different circumstances were planned — including our dates of birth.

I had heard of various arguments for and against reincarnation and, in particular, how hypno-regression "proves" reincarnation. I don't believe it does. [7] The late Arnold Bloxham was a pioneer in this field and one of his subjects was a lady living in Cardiff who was regressed under hypnosis and who described half a dozen previous lives that she believed she had lived. These sessions were taped and became known as "The Bloxham Tapes." In one previous life the subject had been a Jew during the York riots in medieval times; this Jew had hidden in an underground chamber in a Christian church. This chamber was not known about at the time of the tape recording, but was discovered later when building work was being undertaken on the church. This particular tape seems to "prove" the fact of reincarnation. Or does it?

Could it not be possible for a spirit person to give the information and sound as if it was a previous life of the subject? Another of the tapes described an ordinary life in Roman times in a Roman villa in Britain with the household preparing for the arrival of an emperor.

One particular researcher did not believe that the York Jew's tape proved reincarnation. He kept the subject in his mind for some length of time and one day read in a second-hand book an almost word-for-word account of the regressed life at the Roman villa. The book he read the transcript from, however, was taken from a novel written about twelve years before the Cardiff lady had been born! If it does nothing else, this part of the Bloxham Tapes shows a glimpse of how incredible the human mind is. The woman could well have read the novel in her childhood and completely forgotten about it — only for a page from it to be brought out of her memory by the hypnotic trigger. Does this mean that everything we read, hear, see, etc., is stored in our memories and can be retrieved on cue if we know how to trigger the recall?

I'm just not experienced enough in hypno-regression to use it. I think that "false memory syndrome" could be very real and for this reason have some distrust of regression. The times I have used it, however, I have seen trends appearing over a number of supposed previous lives, and the patient can be directed to examine the cause of these trends and to re-evaluate his or her responses to the cause. The causes of emotional problems are real but they relate to the person's existing physical life not, in my opinion, to a previous life.

Having said that I discount hypno-regression as proof of reincarnation, and that I believe that a spirit mind can supply the details of a previous life (which I think may also account for children's "memories" of previous lives), I do, in fact, believe that reincarnation is possible. The form this takes, or the rules attached to it, are presently beyond me. But I like the Native American philosophy that life is a circle and that we are born on Earth, live our lives, "die," and return to spirit to live on. Then we enter another Earth life to bring the circle to a full conclusion. This gives scope for the planning stage in spirit for the Earth life to come. My partner is a number of years older than I am on Earth, but I feel older as a spirit than she is. And, as she has experienced traumatic events in her life, sometimes twice over, I feel that we must have made an agreement before we got here for her to go ahead of me (she is a little impetuous!) so that I could benefit from her experiences and, if I had to go through them, only had to do so once.

Being born with a mind is to be born with psychic abilities [9] but how these abilities are recognised and developed differs from one person to another, just as sporting, artistic, literary, or scientific abilities differ in individuals. Not all of us achieve greatness in a particular field — or even in any field — but the learning and trying can be fun! To be "mediumistic" (i.e., to be sensitive to the spirit world), if it is not something you're born into, does appear to be more pronounced in certain families than others, as if genetically linked. The parent who is a medium will, of course, develop their children differently from non-mediumistic families, in respect to knowledge of spirit communication, as would any other parent with a particular talent. But I have developed mediumship despite being in a non-mediumistic family, therefore, anyone can.

Of course, developing mediumship can be a lengthy process. The development can be very rewarding in terms of personal growth as a human being and because of the interesting people you meet and make friends with, but it does not usually come without a price — even if the only "cost" is time and effort!

The price you pay should never be beyond what I think of as what God knows you are able to bear. I look at it in terms of a bank account with debits and credits. There is nothing new in this, as the Venetians made God part of their commerce. By making Him (or, more accurately, His representatives, the Church) a shareholder in every sea-going trading activity, they were hedging their bets against nature or an act of God. They argued that God wouldn't sink a ship in which He was taking a share of the profits, would He?

Debits in such a bank account arise from any "wrong doings," while credits come from those activities that are "good" — so that when we eventually return home and meet our Maker our spiritual bank account should stand well in credit!

In the credit column of my life, one experience of working for spirit I have had occurred when my partner, Margaret, met a soldier in spirit who gave her the experience of his death. [4] Initially, Margaret could see the soldier on a ship that was on fire. She allowed the soldier to "overshadow" her own personality and he gave her the horrendous experience of being burned alive! I, naturally, was not very comfortable with the situation, and Margaret seemed to be taking on the soldier's distress. I began talking her out of the difficulty and said to her that she did not need to experience the situation further and that she should control it.

The situation came under control very quickly but not quite as I expected — I found myself talking to the soldier through Margaret, who was moving into a deeper trance state. The soldier found my voice intriguing and wondered who or where I was. In turn he was suspicious about my questions about his name or parents or their address — probably he was considering security implications! "Why do you want to know my mother's name?" he asked. I found that he was in a NAAFI type of place, drinking beer with about two hundred other servicemen. I asked if he noticed whether or not anyone got drunk. "Funny you should ask ... no one gets drunk." I asked whether or not anyone ever left the room. "A friend's mother came for him and he left."

"Hasn't your grandmother come to fetch you?" I asked.

"Don't be silly, she's dead," he replied. All very logical and simplistic replies.

I closed the encounter by saying to the soldier that I had news for him and said that his orders had come through. He was ordered to leave the room by the double doors and cross a field where he would meet old friends and relatives. He must then return and take every other serviceman in the room across the field with him. Margaret came out of the trance-like state of control and said she could see the soldier return to the NAAFI and that all the servicemen were picking up their belongings and were leaving. This is typical of "rescue work," where people who have died suddenly, or in confusion, haven't realised they have died. They seem only to traverse the astral planes or, as in this case, create an environment collectively and reside within it. These servicemen felt to me as if they had died in the Falklands War and had, therefore, created their astral environment for some ten Earth years before Margaret and I came into contact with them.

Such rescue work is very mysterious in that it seems so incredibly real to the mediums experiencing it, but it comes into the category of anecdotal evidence only — and is difficult to prove.

Occasionally, some feedback comes from spirit via "messages" from other mediums. One message I received via a trainee medium in Hungary came from a murder victim who said I knew her. I said that I didn't know anyone who had been murdered but I was reminded that I had helped her "into the light," for which she thanked me.

Spirit helpers tell us that such people who have passed suddenly or in confusion remain close to the Earth and relate more readily with those still alive in the physical body rather than with the more evolved people who pass into higher vibrations of spirit — i.e., they see physical people more easily than they see other spirit people.

Perhaps we are capable of travelling on the astral planes in our dreams or in meditations. [6] I'm sure those taking drugs make such visits, but where is their control over where they go? Everyone born is sentenced to die in the physical at some time and not every person who has lived has lived a God-aware life, as I understand it. Some people are exceptionally evil in their characters, having committed heinous crimes against humanity. These people do not become "saintly" just by dying! Where do you think they go? Obviously to the lowest level of spirit: as far away from the light and power of God — as I believe him to be — as they can go. Surely, such people would create a place for themselves to exist, which would be a Hell for anyone remotely "good."

In healing sessions, I have been taken by spirit doctors to visit patients during absent healing sessions. These visits operate telepathically in the form of a mediation and are again only anecdotal in that no attested feedback exists. Maybe one day we will have the opportunity to gather proof of some kind, but this is a part of science where proof has yet to be accepted. I read recently that the existence of ESP is being refuted.

So it is with much of the paranormal, including psychometry. [8] I have witnessed Margaret and others "read" objects psychically and the owners of the objects have agreed with the accuracy of the readings. I don't consider myself to be adept at this and, if I had a measure of success in reading any object, I would probably give the credit to a spirit person helping me — why settle for the psychic when you can so easily rise above it?

The mechanism of psychometry presumably rests in the psychic's ability to raise his or her own personal vibration to "tune into" the mental thoughts of the person who left the imprint on the object being read. To understand this we need to understand "vibration." How did Moses lead the animals into the Ark? Two by two? Moses didn't, of course. Noah built the Ark. But if you ask this question to a group of people you will see how many of them are actually listening carefully. This demonstrates that the sense of hearing can fool your mind, and there are countless other such examples. Optical illusions abound also and countless examples of these are easily obtained. Magicians and illusionists have been making a living deceiving the senses in this way for millennia.

I first heard in yoga nearly twenty years ago — but which I only understood when I came into spiritualism — that all life is "Maya." Maya means "illusion," and the ancient Indians were passing on the knowledge that the physical world is not what it appears to be.

Modern science has now proven this by descriptions of atoms, molecules, etc., where there is much microcosmic space inside atoms. Starting with the most basic atom, which is the hydrogen atom, the nucleus is made up of one proton positively charged, which gives the atom its "weight." The negatively charged electron spins around the nucleus, defining the shape of the atom. There are many other particles contained within the atom such as neutrinos, quarks, and anti-quarks — as theorised by atomic scientists. The hydrogen atom has only one proton in its nucleus, whereas all other atoms detailed in the periodic table contain more protons (together with corresponding electrons) building up to the heavy uranium atom, which has well over two hundred protons in its nucleus. The atoms link together to form molecules, which give us all the matter contained in the physical universe. For example, all the things around us — wood, metal, plastic, flesh, and so on — are made from these atoms.

The electrons defining the shape of atoms vibrate at particular rates for each kind of atom. Molecules also appear to vibrate at particular rates and seem to have different "weights" due to the number of neutrons and protons in the nuclei of the distinct atoms.

The vibration of the atoms explains why the ancient Indians believed all matter to be an illusion — but it is only an illusion because our physical senses give us their idea of what surrounds us.

Physical sight works by focusing images through a lens onto the retina at the back of the eye. This image stimulates the cells in the retina, which transmit a message to the brain via the optic nerve. But it is then the "mind" that interprets the message and creates an understanding of what the image is. Mind means that part of consciousness that produces thought, understanding, and is not physical (as the brain is).

What we refer to as "white light" is made up of the spectrum of colours as seen in the rainbow or split with a prism. (You can use a white feather and a lit candle to produce the spectrum by looking through the feather at the candle.) A red car is red because the pigments in the molecules of paint on the car absorb all the colours of the spectrum except, in this case, red. Every colour we see is a reflection of the one colour that is not absorbed by the object — what colour is the red car if you found it inside a completely darkened garage where there is no light whatsoever?

Light, sound waves, the feel of physical objects, the smell of scent, etc., are interpretations of vibrations perceived by our physical senses. These senses only respond to vibrations between two fixed rates. These rates are not exact and our senses register matter broadly between 34,000 and 64,000 waves to an inch or 400-750 billion waves to a second. Anything vibrating between these limits is capable of being appreciated by our senses. Clearly, there are numerous examples of vibrations in existence beyond the range appreciated by our senses — such as sound heard by an animal when we cannot hear it, microwaves, infrared and ultraviolet waves, radio and television waves, gamma and X-rays. Just because our senses cannot normally appreciate them doesn't mean that the vibrations do not exist.

A psychic is able to perceive vibrations above the normal range of physical senses while a medium attuned to the "spirit world" is able to raise his or her sensitivity to become aware of even finer vibrations. Using this faculty, the medium makes contact with the "mind" of another human being living in a discarnate world, which — such "spirit people" tell us — is at a higher vibration than our own. Not only one level of vibration higher, but many.

Look at it like a ladder: halfway up is a section painted a different colour. This section, sitting between two rungs, represents the physical world perceived by our everyday senses. Immediately above it comes the astral plane, where the vibration of its infinitely small particles works at higher frequencies than the physical and cannot normally be sensed unless the mind (or consciousness) of the individual is altered. Just as our minds need a physical body to traverse the physical world, an astral or electromagnetical body (part of the aura) is needed to traverse the astral plane.

The next rung above the astral is a yet finer vibration, and so forth. [10] In the lower levels of spirit, "bodies" appear necessary for the mind to use as a vehicle to traverse the new environment — as evidenced by the various spirit people who visit the Earth plane to talk through mediums to loved ones. If Uncle Joe had lost his leg in the physical world, he would probably show the medium this for recognition purposes — but would regain the leg as soon as the loss was recognised. It's the same with age. Why have the infirm body of an old man, if you can recreate the body of your youth? The older body is required only for recognition.

Walls in the physical are no impediment to someone alive in spirit. Because of the frequency of vibration, the wall simply does not exist in the interpenetrating spirit realms. Should a wall be built in the spirit world at the same frequency as that level of spirit, then the wall would exist — but from the physical perspective, you wouldn't know it was there. I've been taken to many fine landscapes, gardens, and buildings in the spirit world during meditations that look as "real" as the familiar "natural" ones on Earth. Several people can make the same journey together, and it is interesting to note that others will see the same thing as the guide — often before a description is given — or the medium may describe a particular relative or friend jointly seen.

Such meditations suggest that the next environment we find ourselves in beyond physical death is very similar to our present environment — but every facet has the potential to be manipulated to conform to our highest ideals.

[Authors' note: Paul's excellent argument at this point is reminiscent of Plato and Socrates, and their exciting ideas of a realm of ideals. It would be interesting to speculate whether those wise, contemplative old Greeks received some of their highest thoughts as inspirations from the realm of spirit.]

Just as on Earth we manipulate our environment (a house is first designed, then materials are accumulated before building commences) so it would be in spirit except that the process would be much faster. As our minds become much more used to manipulating the energy in the new environment, further progress can be made.

In evolution, matter seems to rise from denser to finer, always seeking perfection. As progress is open to every soul, evolution tells us that "mind" also evolves from denser to finer. So it is to be expected that progress up the ladder of vibration is refinement of mind and, in the more refined levels of spirit, the need for a body, or vehicle, becomes less. I have been aware of a number of evolved spirit people who only show a face or hint of a body. In spirit worlds, minds communicate directly with other minds by telepathy (which is also how they communicate to people on the Earth).

The existence of the spirit world proves the continuation of the human mind beyond physical death and, as spirit people demonstrate a degree of evolutionary progress of mind, it can be assumed that at the peak of evolutionary progress is an exceptionally highly developed mind. As one philosopher has said, "That which nothing can be conceived to be greater than represents this peak of evolutionary development of mind — otherwise known — by some — as God." Whether this supposed God created life —

or was created by life — I know not. But people in the spirit world tell me that they abide by this God's laws and work with his permission only. The purpose of life is, therefore, simple — to follow the pathway of progress that leads from imperfection to perfection, heading always in the direction that takes you nearer to the peak of perfection and that which is at the peak — what we call God.

My discourse has not conclusively answered your questionnaire, and much more can be said on the subject, but if every question that could be conceived could be answered conclusively, how would we occupy our minds in a life everlasting? Infinity is a very long time.

Our close friend Robert Snow is the secretary of the Ghost Club, and a very experienced psychical researcher and investigator. He has access to a vast store of reports and records of intriguing psychic events. These are Robert's responses to our questions:

1   *At what stage of your life — childhood, adolescence, or maturity — were you first aware of your psychic gifts and talent?*

I think that I first became aware of the fact of my gift or talent for seeing ghosts when I was about fifteen years of age, that is if one could call it a gift or talent.

Lionel Fanthorpe and fellow psychic investigator Robert Snow, secretary of the Ghost Club.

DEATH

2 *We've seen and heard you in action and you're very gifted. Which of your psychic powers do you consider to be the best developed, or the most important?*

I suppose that my ability to dowse is probably the most developed of my psychic powers, that is if you could call it a psychic gift or power. I do sometimes have feelings about certain people, either good or bad, that I either like or take a distinct dislike to and often — not always — they are correct; a sort of instinct.

3 *When you are actually using your powers would you compare them to seeing, hearing, or tactile sensations? In other words, how do psychic powers manifest themselves to one who has such knowledge?*

When I am actually using my psychic powers or gifts they seem to manifest themselves quite unexpectedly; out of the blue, so to speak.

4 *What do you consider as the most mysterious or inexplicable psychic adventure you've ever had?*

The following incident is probably one of the most mysterious experiences that I have ever had. I have never considered that I have psychic powers, although I have had some interesting supernatural experiences in my life. When I say psychic, I mean telepathic, or in communication with someone else who is some distance away from me by thought transference.

I will get to the point. I have friends who live in America, in the state of Vermont to be precise. The spouse, Jeff R....., was at the beginning of the year diagnosed as having terminal cancer. The disease was untreatable, but he did have a couple of surgical operations to slow down the advance of the disease and prolong his life.

Jeff's cousin, Sylvia T....., lives in Cheshire, England, and used to telephone me from time to time and keep me informed about his condition, as also did Jeff's wife Elma, who she contacted me by fax.

I had not heard from either Elma or Sylvia for some time and assumed that Jeff's condition was very much the same, or if there was a deterioration there was no immediate cause for concern.

On the morning of Friday, 14 August 1998, I awoke at seven a.m. from a vivid dream. It is unusual for me to wake up so late; I usually get up anytime between five and six in the morning. Anyway, for some reason I woke up late on this particular morning from an extremely vivid and realistic dream. In the dream someone told me that Jeff had just died, but I do not know who it was who told me. I remember that I kept on asking the person who told me why Sylvia had not told me that Jeff had died. "Why did Sylvia not tell me that Jeff has just died?" I asked repeatedly.

When I woke up from that dream I felt very disturbed and unsettled, feeling that something was wrong, but what I did not know. As the day passed I became easier in my mind, dismissing it as just a dream. The next day passed and by the fourth day I had almost completely forgotten the dream.

On the evening of the fourth day Sylvia left a message on my telephone answering machine telling me that Jeff had died. When I was able to do so, I phoned Sylvia to get more details and she told me that Jeff had died at two a.m. on the morning of Friday, 14 August. In Vermont they are exactly five hours behind us here in the United Kingdom. So when I woke from my dream at seven a.m. here in England, it was two a.m. in Vermont; the same time that Jeff had died. The story does not end there. Sylvia did not tell me earlier because she was away from her home on holiday, so she did not know until four days after Jeff had actually passed away. I can only think that as he was passing away, Jeff was either thinking of me or perhaps trying to communicate with me telepathically. Surely this must be a genuine case of telepathy. Elma and Jeff have been close friends of mine for many years and I firmly believe that Jeff really was thinking of me as he was passing away. Not that I have ever doubted that telepathic communication can take place, but this particular incident, did, for me, confirm beyond any reasonable doubt that under certain circumstances telepathic communication can take place. This is the only time that I have ever had such an experience in my life, but who knows what might happen in the future?

5   *Powerful and perceptive sensitives like you are excellent judges of character. What is the psychic mechanism that makes it possible? For example, would you say that you can see auras, or do you feel positive or negative vibrations? Do "good" people give off a "warm" feeling and "bad" people a "cold" feeling?*

DEATH

When I meet people I do sometimes, not always, get feelings about them either good or bad; they seem to give off vibrations of a positive or negative nature, depending how I feel about them. In other words I either take a distinct liking to them or I feel that they are not nice to know. Having said this, I do not always have these feelings and I guess that this depends on how strong the vibrations or feelings are that I receive.

6   *What are your views on astral projection and OOB experiences? How well does it work? What's your experience of it?*

As regards astral projection or OOB experiences I do not really know what to think as I do not really know enough about the subject, but I am certainly very interested in it. I have myself not had any experience of this. I certainly don't dismiss it and I am always interested to know more.

7   *What do you think about hypno-regression and reincarnation?*

Hypno-regression interests me also but again I don't know enough about it to form any clear-cut opinions, and I must admit that I certainly do, as a Christian, believe in life after death — but I do not believe that we are reincarnated as someone else on this Earth. In other words, I have doubts that our spirits come back to inhabit another body. However, I am always, as with anything connected with the paranormal, prepared to listen with interest to other people's opinions and experiences.

8   *Do you also have psychometric powers? How would you describe their mechanism? What does an object absorb, and how does it radiate what it has absorbed to a sensitive, powerful psychic?*

As far as I know, I do not personally possess any psychometric powers. I am quite prepared to believe that objects do absorb some sort of energy or aura. This is, I think, the case with such items that have been used as murder weapons, such as axes, guns, and knives where they were associated with strong emotional deeds. It is probably a kind of atmospheric absorption of the type that one associates with the fabric of certain buildings where strong emotional experiences and dramatic deeds have taken place. In a church one gets a marvellous feeling of peace and tranquillity, but in places such as the Tower of London there is rather an unpleasant feeling, as terrible deeds have been committed in the confines of the building.

9   *Are psychic powers born into a psychic, almost like something genetic, or can they be trained and developed by almost anyone who is sincere and keenly interested?*

I think most people, if not all, posses psychic powers but only some are able to use them. Probably most people could develop these powers with practice.

10   *What are your teachings about the survival of the human personality after death? What's the spirit world like? What will we do when we get there? What sort of experiences can we look forward to in the next life? How can we contact loved ones who've gone ahead of us — and how can they contact us?*

Regarding life after death and the survival of the human spirit and personality after death, I am certain that when we die our spirit does survive and if we have been good on Earth we will be bound to have eternal peace and happiness in the after-life. If a person is evil on Earth, he or she will be doomed to an existence of damnation, torture, and misery in the next life after death. Having said this, I believe that God does eventually forgive sinners and when the wicked people have served their penance they will eventually be given leave to go to Heaven after they have learned the errors of their ways.

The late Michael Bentine was the president of the Association for the Scientific Study of Anomalous Phenomena (ASSAP) until his death. The authors were tremendously honoured when the ASSAP invited us to become their president and first lady as successors to Michael. Philip Walton, the ASSAP secretary, has kindly supplied us with a very helpful contribution for this chapter, describing the work of the Association and its relevance to the whole question of psychical research and human survival of bodily death. These are Phil's comments:

The Association for the Scientific Study of Anomalous Phenomena (ASSAP) does not have a corporate view or policy with regard to the use of mediums in its investigations. It is left to the investigator in charge to decide when or if a medium will be brought into a case. Before taking into consideration the accuracy of the mediums involved, the investigator should be aware of the problem of introducing another opinion into a case. Setting aside whether or not the medium is accurate in his or her descriptions, the mere fact that he or she suggested a certain area of a house or building, or that a particular part of a person's past or character should be investigated, may prejudice the opinion of those involved in the case. It is often better to go into a case with the clean sheet of paper and no pre-conceived ideas. This is why in many investigations we would recommend that the researcher in charge studies the case as much as possible, and that secondary investigators are told nothing until after the initial investigation. This means that anything seen or heard will be free from interference or suggestion.

One problem with relying on feelings in a case is that when they conflict with hard evidence the person is often reluctant to give up their initial idea. One case in particular springs to mind. While the vigil was taking place, all those in the room noticed an interesting smell. The smell of toast or bread being baked. The two mediums whom we had called in told us all about the ghost of a baker and for the next ten minutes I watched and heard the mediums bounce various ideas from one to the other, building up more and more of an elaborate picture of the baker, the bakery, and the life and tragedy that had befallen him. All of a sudden a member of the house staff jumped up and ran downstairs, coming back a few minutes later to apologise to everyone. The vigil break that was supposed to have started in a few minutes would be delayed ten minutes. Instead of switching on the tea urn, she had in fact plugged in a toaster oven. The curious thing is that when the source of the smell was revealed, the two mediums continued to talk of the baker yet they had not sensed him before the toaster had been plugged in. They refused to believe that what they had conjectured was not in fact the truth, despite the now clear and unequivocal evidence that the smell was not in any way psychic.

One of the most surprising cases that I have been involved in centres around a young child who lived in a house that had seen a lot of poltergeist activity. The child had described a friend whom we would describe as an imaginary friend, whom he played with. Finally fed up with all the problems, the family called in some experts to help rid the house of the unwanted guests. The children had been kept away from most of the problems and on the day in question, when many experts came to visit the premises, the children were on holiday. When they arrived back from their holiday the next day, the young lad announced during breakfast that his friend was no longer present in the house.

To this day the case involving the child has been one of the most perplexing I have come across, and to my mind is the best reason to study the subject.

The final piece of survival evidence comes from Graham Dack, author of *The Out-of-Body Experience* (1999). This is an outstanding book that deserves to become the definitive standard work on the subject. Graham has that priceless gift of being able to explain the mystery of psychic experience in terms that are clearly comprehensible to those who have *not* shared it, as well as to those who have. This is Graham's first-hand, personal description of how his out-of-body experiences work:

> I decrease my pulse rate slightly, gently exhale, and with a final sigh those gentle vibrations that innocently played over the surface of my body suddenly explode into a blasting electrical rush that blanks all my thoughts and feelings and ends any control I have over my body. I feel as though my very "self," my very "soul," is being ripped out of my insides with the tearing of a thousand stitches that hold me together. It pulls at the inside of my ears and at the back of my nose in a frantic haste to escape my physical shell. I wish that it was over quickly and cleanly, and most times it is.
>
> As quickly as this internal volcano erupts, it also subsides and with it goes all my earthly aches, pains, and problems. Once again I find myself free, perfectly free, to dwell in a place that could easily be mistaken for "paradise." My conscious mind is as clear and as "normal" as yours is at the very moment you are reading this. My mental clarity is such that I am perfectly aware that my physical body resides at home in bed. I have the use of all my usual memory facilities and all my normal reasoning ability. In fact, I retain all that I regard as

the essential "me" but minus that dragging, anchoring material body.

This must surely be the greatest, the most ultimate, experience that can possibly be achieved while still being alive on this Earth of ours. My conscious mind has the ability to truly exist outside of my physical body and travel this Earth, and other planes, in a way that has been rarely understood.

The rest of Graham's book presents the amazing facts about his out-of-body experiences in a thoroughly effective, convincing, and challenging way. It provides some of the most telling and positive evidence yet for human survival — and very joyful survival at that.

EPILOGUE

This book has been an attempt to bring together the vast questions of the true nature of our human personality and individual consciousness and the evidence that it survives death. We have tried to analyse what a ghost — or spectre — really is. We have provided just a few random examples from the millions of hauntings that have been reported for many centuries from all over the world. If only one percent of such cases are genuine, survival seems highly likely.

We have studied near-death experiences and out-of-body experiences. They, too, seem to provide strong evidence of survival. Hypno-regression has been evaluated as well, and it seems to point in the same direction. So do automatic writing, a spectacular range of séance phenomena, and the first-hand experiences of contemporary mediums, psychics, and investigators who gave us their up-to-date personal evidence.

Religious teachings about the afterlife vary widely, but prophets and saints alike have made massive contributions to faith in the hereafter. The teachings of Christ, Mohammed, and the other great holy men and women about the life to come also make an immense contribution to the evidence as far as their faithful followers are concerned.

Each individual psychic clue may seem only a grain of sand in the balance of the survival argument, but taken together they present a formidable case for life going on after physical death. The ultimate proof, of course, consists of arriving in that glorious Eternal Land and saying with delighted surprise, "So we were right!"

BIBLIOGRAPHY

Arscott, David. *Curiosities of East Sussex*. Seaford, East Sussex: S. B. Publications, 1995.

Attard, Joseph. *The Ghosts of Malta*. San Gwann, Malta: Publishers Enterprises Group, 1990.

Bernstein, Morey. *The Search for Bridey Murphy*. Garden City, N. Y.: Doubleday, 1965.

Bezzina, Joseph. *The Ggantija Temples*. Malta, 1995.

Blashford-Snell, John. *Mysteries: Encounters with the Unexplained*. London: Bodley Head, 1983.

Blouet, Brian. *The Story of Malta*. Rev. ed. Malta: Progress Press, 1993.

Blundell, Nigel, and Roger Boar. *The World's Greatest Ghosts*. London: Octopus Books, 1984.

Bonanno, Anthony. *Malta: An Archaeological Paradise*. Valetta, Malta: M. J. Publications, 1993.

Bord, Janet, and Colin Bord. *Mysterious Britain*. London: Paladin, 1974.

Boudet, Henri. *La Vraie Langue Celtique et le Cromleck de Rennes-les-Bains*. Nice, France: Belisane, 1984 reprint.

Bradbury, Will, ed. *Into the Unknown*. Pleasantville, N. Y.: Reader's Digest Association, 1988.

Briggs, Katharine M. *British Folk Tales and Legends: A Sampler*. London: Granada Publishing in Paladin, 1977.

Brookesmith, Peter, ed. *Open Files*. London: Orbis, 1984.

Brown, Theo. *Devon Ghosts*. Norwich: Jarrold & Sons, 1982.

Budge, E.A. Wallis. *The Book of the Dead*. Secaucus, N. J.: Citadel Press, 1984 reprint.

DEATH

Camilleri, George. *Realms of Fantasy: Folk Tales from Gozo.* Victoria, Gozo [Malta]: G. Camilleri, 1992.

Cavendish, Richard, ed. *Encyclopaedia of the Unexplained.* London: Routledge & Kegan Paul, 1974.

Chambers, Aidan. *Aidan Chambers' Book of Ghosts and Hauntings.* [Harmondsworth, England]: Puffin Books, 1973.

Clark, Jerome. *Unexplained USA.* Detroit: Gale Research, 1993.

Cohen, Daniel. *Encyclopaedia of Ghosts.* London: Guild Publishing, 1989.

Dack, Graham. *The Out-of-Body Experience.* Braunston, Northamptonshire, England: Oobex Publishing, 1999.

Dixon, G. M. *Folktales and Legends of Norfolk.* Minimax, 1983.

Dunford, Barry. *The Holy Land of Scotland.* Scotland, Brigadoon Books, 1996.

Dyall, Valentine. *Unsolved Mysteries: A Collection of Weird Problems from the Past.* London:Hutchinson, 1954.

Encyclopaedia Britannica Online. http://www.eb.com

Eysenck, Hans J., and Carl Sargent. *Explaining the Unexplained.* London: BCA, 1993.

Fanthorpe, Lionel, and Patricia Fanthorpe. *Mysteries of the Bible.* Toronto: Hounslow Press, 1999.

____. *The Oak Island Mystery: The Secret of the World's Greatest Treasure Hunt.* Toronto: Hounslow Press, 1995.

____. *Secrets of Rennes-le-Château.* York Beach, Me.: Samuel Weiser, 1992.

____. *The World's Greatest Unsolved Mysteries.* Toronto: Hounslow Press, 1997.

____. *The World's Most Mysterious People.* Toronto: Hounslow Press, 1998.

____. *The World's Most Mysterious Places.* Toronto: Hounslow Press, 1999.

Fanthorpe, Patricia, and Lionel Fanthorpe. *The Holy Grail Revealed: The Real Secret of Rennes-le-Château.* North Hollywood, Ca.: Newcastle Publishing, 1982.

Folklore, Myths and Legends of Britain. London: Reader's Digest Association, 1973.

Forman, Joan. *Haunted East Anglia.* London: Fontana, 1976.

____. *Royal Hauntings.* London: Fontana, 1987.

Fowke, Edith. *Canadian Folklore.* Toronto: Oxford University Press, 1988.

Godwin, John. *This Baffling World.* New York: Hart Publishing, 1968.

Graves, Robert, introd. *Larousse Encyclopedia of Mythology.* London: Paul Hamlyn, 1959.

Green, Andrew. *Haunted Sussex Today.* Seaford, East Sussex: S. B. Publications, 1997.

Gribble, Leonard. *Famous Historical Mysteries.* London: Target Books, 1974.

Guerber, H. A. *Myths and Legends of the Middle Ages.* London: Studio Editions, 1994.

Guirdham, Arthur. *The Cathars and Reincarnation.* Wheaton, Ill.: Theosophical Publishing House, 1978.

BIBLIOGRAPHY

____. *The Great Heresy*. Beekman Publications, 1993.

____. *The Lake & the Castle*. Cygnus Books, 1992.

____. *We Are One Another: A Record of Group Reincarnation*. Cygnus Books, 1992.

Haining, Peter. *The Restless Bones and Other True Mysteries*. London: Armada Books, 1970.

Hitching, Francis. *The World Atlas of Mysteries*. London: Pan Books, 1979.

Hough, Peter. *Supernatural Britain*. London: BCA, 1994.

Knowlson, T. Sharper. *The Origins of Popular Superstitions and Customs*. London: Studio Editions, 1995.

Lambert, R.S. *Exploring the Supernatural: The Weird in Canadian Folklore*. London. Arthur Barker, 1955.

Lampitt, L. F., ed. *The World's Strangest Stories*. London: Associated Newspapers, 1955.

Mack, Lorrie, et al., eds. *The Unexplained*. London: Orbis, 1984.

Mazière, Francis. *Mysteries of Easter Island*. London: Collins, 1969.

Metcalfe, Leon. *Discovering Ghosts*. Tring, U.K.: Shire Publications, 1974.

Michell, John, and Robert J. M. Rickard. *Phenomena: A Book of Wonders*. London: Thames and Hudson, 1977.

Morton, H. V. *Ghosts of London*. London: Methuen, 1939.

Moss, Peter. *Ghosts over Britain*. London: Sphere Books, 1979.

Owen, George, and Victor Sims. *Science and the Spook: Eight Strange Cases of Haunting*. London: Dennis Dobson, 1971.

Playfair, G. L. *The Unknown Power*. London: Granada Publishing, 1977.

Poole, Keith B. *Ghosts of Wessex*. Newton Abbot, U. K.: David and Charles, 1976.

Porter, Enid. *The Folklore of East Anglia*. London: Batsford, 1974.

Puharich, Andrija. *Beyond Telepathy*. London: Souvenir Press, 1974.

Rawcliffe, D. H. *Illusions and Delusions of the Supernatural and the Occult*. New York, 1959.

Rolleston, T. W. *Celtic Myths and Legends*. London: Studio Editions, 1994.

Russell, Eric Frank. *Great World Mysteries*. London: Mayflower, 1967.

Saltzman, Pauline. *The Strange and the Supernormal*. New York: Paperback Library, 1968.

Sampson, Chas. *Ghosts of the Broads*. Norwich: Jarrold & Sons, 1973.

Scott, Michael. *Irish Ghosts and Hauntings*. London: Warner Books, 1994.

Snow, Edward Rowe. *Strange Tales from Nova Scotia to Cape Hatteras*. New York: Dodd, Mead, 1946.

Spencer, John, and Anne Spencer. *The Encyclopaedia of the World's Greatest Unsolved Mysteries*. London: Headline Book Publishing, 1995.

Strange Stories, Amazing Facts. London: Reader's Digest Association, 1975.

Van Buren, Elizabeth. *The Dragon of Rennes-le-Château*. Vogels, France, 1998.

Watson, Lyall. *Supernature*. London: Coronet Books, 1974.

Welfare, Simon, and John Fairley. *Arthur C. Clarke's Mysterious World*. London: Collins, 1980.

Whitehead, Ruth Holmes. *Stories from the Six Worlds: Micmac Legends.* Halifax, N.S.: Nimbus Publishing, 1988.

Wilson, Colin. *Afterlife: An Investigation of the Evidence for Life after Death.* London: Grafton Books, 1985.

_____. *The Psychic Detectives.* London: Pan Books, 1984.

Wilson, Colin, and Christopher Evans, eds. *The Book of Great Mysteries.* London: Robinson Publishing, 1986.

Wilson, Colin, and Damon Wilson. *Unsolved Mysteries Past and Present.* London: Headline Book Publishing, 1993.

Wilson, Colin, Damon Wilson, and Rowan Wilson. *World Famous True Ghost Stories.* London: Robinson Publishing, 1996.

Wilson, Ian. *The After Death Experience.* London: Corgi, 1989.

_____. *Reincarnation?* London: Penguin Books, 1982.

_____. *Worlds Beyond: From the Files of the Society for Psychical Research.* London: Weidenfeld and Nicolson, 1986.

Young, George. *Ancient Peoples and Modern Ghosts.* Nova Scotia: George Young, 1991.

_____. *Ghosts in Nova Scotia.* Nova Scotia: George Young, 1991.

Zammit, Themistocles. *Prehistoric Malta.* Valletta, Malta, 1994.

_____. *The St. Paul's Catacombs.* Valletta, Malta, 1980.